Städelschule
Lectures 1

Städelschule
Lectures 1
2019—1999

Koenig Books, London

2018	Georgia Sagri
2017	Petra Van Brabandt
2016	Willem de Rooij and Philippe Pirotte
2015	Joshua Oppenheimer and Adi Rukun
2014	Josef Strau
2014	Lucy Raven
2013	Douglas Gordon and Philippe Parreno
2013	Monika Baer
2013	Amy Sillman
2011	Martha Rosler
2011	Mark von Schlegell
2011	Josef Strau
2009	Mark Leckey

Preface
Philippe Pirotte

The lectures came about when I was teaching at the Städelschule in Frankfurt. Teaching was quite confusing, especially in that school because the questions that the students ask, and the question of the school in some sense, is what is art's purpose? What are its functions?[1]
— Mark Leckey on "The Long Tail"

Since the year 1999, around 800 lectures have taken place at the Städelschule in Frankfurt. The following texts are transcripts of thirteen lectures, selected to represent the most recent history, cataloguing ideas that might otherwise be buried and forgotten. This volume is the first of a series and focuses on the diversity of artistic perspectives. It provides an insight into the Städelschule's educational program and documents a variety of artistic and theoretical approaches that the school seeks to support in art and society at large. The ongoing series will continuously reflect the school's anatomy and core protagonists—the professors, the curatorial program at Portikus, and the students.

Founded in 1817, the Städelschule is recognized and respected as an institution of global influence in art education. The Städelschule functions equally as an art institution and as an art school, distinguishing it from other art schools in Germany. Throughout its rich history, Städelschule alumni have made a significant impact on society by challenging the status quo and promoting new perspectives, and envisioning alternative ways of living by continuing to question

1 Mark Leckey, *See, We Assemble*, London 2011, pp. 42-43.

what it means to be an artist. In parallel to the public events of the yearly Rundgang studio exhibition and the graduate exhibition, the remit of the lecture program is to be open to the public, thus enhancing the school's inclusive ethos.

Characterized by their fluidity, the lectures follow an initial premise of "anything goes." This has led to a range of different approaches, from conversations to slideshows, concerts to performances. In this volume, this is addressed through the inclusion of lecture performances by Georgia Sagri speaking about artistic labor, by Lucy Raven discussing similar topics in the animation industry, and by Mark Leckey's generous evaluation of Internet culture. In-depth artist presentations are also included by Monika Baer, Martha Rosler, and Amy Sillman, respectively tracing their extensive careers. Another recurring format has been the artist conversation, and this volume features exchanges between Joshua Oppenheimer and Adi Rukun, Willem de Rooij and myself, as well as Douglas Gordon and Philippe Parreno. Further lectures included in this volume are framed by more theoretical and research-driven concerns, like philosopher Petra Van Brabandt's take on queer porn, science fiction writer Mark von Schlegell's literary criticism, and the hybrid fiction and theory musings of Josef Strau.

As such, there is no linear concept of knowledge transfer—the audience is free to move about, to come in and to walk out. Mostly, dialogues are initiated during the lecture only to be continued afterwards, when food is cooked by the students and shared amongst all those present, utilizing the social construct of sharing a meal as a way to break down inherent hierarchies. In this way, potential barriers between lecturer and audience dissolve as the audience—both students and visitors alike—become partners in a conspiracy of reflection. It is particularly important that the program is assembled by the students, and therefore often reflects timely topics or features specific guests that distinguish the lecture program from courses, class-meetings, and seminars at the school. Over the years, the ever-changing student lecture group has proposed, organized, and hosted several lectures. The new networks that have formed through this activity can be said to be a significant part of the students' experience in Frankfurt. Each semester, a poster accompanied and outlined the lecture program, some of which have been integrated into the graphic design of this volume.

If the lecture program reflects an implicit tenet of the curriculum at the Städelschule, it is the tradition of differentiation. The professors, for example, often express contradictory truths. It is what professor and vice-rector Judith Hopf once called the "corrective potential of the faculty." For Hopf, this is aligned with rejecting conformity across all aspects of society. Her perspective within the faculty encourages art that does not claim aesthetics and meaning for itself, but rather tries to dismantle and alter these categories. This viewpoint is furthered in the lecture programming at the school.

By providing such a discursive space, the art school should claim and defend an increasingly threatened social terrain—a place where arguments and statements can be assessed antagonistically and dissentingly. In the face of current global affairs, validating multiple worldviews and positions is paramount, as any attempt at single-minded indoctrination urgently requires resistance. This is why the Städelschule lecture program is organized with openness and diversity at its core.

This first printed volume was made possible with the generous support of many people and organizations. First and foremost, I would like to thank the students for their substantial contribution to the quality of the program over the years. For their efforts and contributions, I thank all the student lecture groups, the Druckwerkstatt, and the school's Artistic Coordinators for accompanying and organizing the lecture program over the last two decades. I warmly thank the speakers for giving us permission to publish their lectures and for reviewing their transcriptions. I also wish to thank the current core faculty of the program, Johan Bettum, Daniel Birnbaum, Willem de Rooij, Isabelle Graw, Judith Hopf, Hassan Khan, Tobias Rehberger, Amy Sillman, Theodore Spyropoulos, and Haegue Yang, as well as the faculty that were active until very recently, including Peter Fischli, Douglas Gordon, Michael Krebber, and Christa Näher, for their support. I wish to thank my collaborators Jonas Leihener, Marie Egger, Il-Jin Atem Choi, and Paula Kommoss for taking on different coordination and editorial responsibilities in the preparation of this book. Special thanks go to Nina Oeghoede, Adrian Williams, and Theresea Kampmeier for having contributed transcriptions and partly editorial work. Thanks go to Martina Cooper and Christian Zickler for editorial suggestions and reviews. And I wish to express my very special gratitude to Arielle Bier for having accompanied this book on all editorial levels, for writing the introductions, for reviewing and correcting all the texts in collaboration with the lecturers, for her suggestions, her accuracy, and her patience. We would also like to thank *very* for the wonderful concept and graphic design of this book, executed with sensibility and love for an institution they know very well.

This publication was initiated in the context of the celebration of the Städelschule's 200th anniversary. Initial funding was provided through the friends of the Städelschule, who constitute the Städelschule Portikus e.V. In this regard, I would especially like to thank the former president Elisabeth Haindl, and Claudia Orben-Mäckler, her successor. We thank Claudia Scholtz of the Hessische Kulturstiftung for the enthusiastic support of several programs at Städelschule and Portikus over the years, and particularly for financing this publication project. We would also like to express our gratitude to the Dr. Marschner Stiftung, for their substantial funding of our archival research and publication projects, and the Georg und Franziska Speyer'sche Hochschulstiftung for making this publication possible. Additional thanks go to the Friederichs Stiftung, and the Marielies Schleicher Stiftung for their support.

Index of Lectures
2019—1999

07.02.2019	Tala Madani
31.01.2019	Stephanie Comilang
30.01.2019	Paul Clinton
17.01.2019	Carsten Meyer
16.01.2019	Johannes Helberger
15.01.2019	Tim Griffin
11.12.2018	Bojana Kunst
05.12.2018	Bunny Rogers
04.12.2018	Rafael Horzon
27.11.2018	Adam Szymczyk
20.11.2018	Volker Zander
15.11.2018	Wu Tsang

14.11.2018 Kwasi Ohene-Ayeh
07.11.2018 Dan Mitchell
06.11.2018 Daniel Blanga-Gubbay
01.11.2018 Carlos Motta
23.10.2018 Ho Rui An
17.10.2018 Michal Heiman

05.07.2018 Kapwani Kiwanga
28.06.2018 DeeDee Halleck
27.06.2018 Wolf D. Prix
26.07.2018 Arin Rungjang
21.06.2018 Oscar Murillo
20.06.2018 Nikolas Gambaroff
19.06.2018 Stephanie Rosenthal
14.06.2018 Leo Asemota and
Nástio Mosquito
13.06.2018 Daniel Norell
07.06.2018 Kivi Sotamaa
06.06.2018 Melati Suryodarmo
05.06.2018 Julia Bryan-Wilson
30.05.2018 Dagmar Reinhardt
29.05.2018 Georgia Sagri

23.05.2018 Hardeep Pandhal
22.05.2018 Rossella Biscotti
16.05.2018 Ahmet Öğüt
15.05.2018 Cauleen Smith
14.05.2018 Avery Singer
09.05.2018 Lauren Vasey
08.05.2018 Haig Aivazian
03.05.2018 Shajay Bhooshan
02.05.2018 Gabriel Pérez-Barreiro
26.04.2018 Kyle Miller
25.04.2018 Peter Fend
19.04.2018 Davide Quayola
18.04.2018 Minsuk Cho

10.02.2018	Christa Näher, Monika Baer, Daniel Birnbaum, and Philippe Pirotte
01.02.2018	Allison Katz
29.01.2018	Eric Baudelaire
25.01.2018	Peter Testa
24.01.2018	John Smith
23.01.2018	Florencia Portocarrero
18.01.2018	Abraham Cruzvillegas
16.01.2018	Thomas Demand and Udo Kittelmann
12.01.2018	Paul Prudence
11.01.2018	Lucy Stein
08.01.2018	Mark Wigley
14.12.2017	Anne-Mie van Kerckhoven
07.12.2017	Moyra Davey
06.12.2017	A.L. Steiner
05.12.2017	Heman Chong
29.11.2017	Sophie von Hellermann
14.11.2017	Pablo Larios
13.11.2017	Daniel Dewar and Grégory Gicquel
08.11.2017	Elena Filipovic
02.11.2017	Bonaventure Ndikung
01.11.2017	Thomas Meinecke
27.10.2017	Keller Easterling
13.07.2017	Farshid Moussavi
11.07.2017	Susanne Kriemann
06.07.2017	Stephan Dillemuth
05.07.2017	Alex Kitnick
04.07.2017	New Noveta
30.06.2017	Liam Young
28.06.2017	Josephine Pryde
22.06.2017	Michael Dean

16.11.2016	Jonathan Berger
08.11.2016	Elysia Crampton
03.11.2016	Jos de Gruyter and Harald Thys
01.11.2016	Pavel Büchler
06.07.2016	Julia Moritz and Yannic Joray
28.06.2016	Jace Clayton
27.06.2016	Amy Sillman
23.06.2016	Beatrice von Bismarck
22.06.2016	Benjamin Buchloh
21.06.2016	Heba Y. Amin
08.06.2016	Philippe Pirotte
07.06.2016	Jay Chung and Q Takeki Maeda
31.05.2016	Haegue Yang
18.05.2016	V. Vale and Marian Wallace
03.05.2016	Claire Denis
27.04.2016	Antek Walczak
12.04.2016	Lucy McKenzie
07.04.2016	Stefano Corbo
13.02.2016	Willem de Rooij and Philippe Pirotte
12.02.2016	DIS
03.02.2016	Eileen Myles
02.02.2016	Lawrence Abu Hamdan
19.01.2016	Nicolaus Schafhausen
14.01.2016	Mirco Becker
12.01.2016	Dora García
04.12.2015	Antony Hegarty
03.12.2015	Keith Connolly and Tom Thayer
02.12.2015	Raimer Jochims

26.11.2015 Dirk Snauwaert
25.11.2015 Jana Euler
24.11.2015 Jonas Mekas and Douglas Gordon
17.11.2015 Dana Whabira
12.11.2015 Elias Perabo, Ossama Mohammed, and Khaled Barakeh
09.11.2015 Sarah Schulman
21.10.2015 Wolfgang Müller
15.10.2015 Franco “Bifo” Berardi
14.10.2015 Oliver Laric

14.07.2015 Otobong Nkanga
06.07.2015 Justin Lieberman
01.07.2015 Alessandro Nova
30.06.2015 Peter Kubelka
29.06.2015 Benedetta Tagliabue
25.06.2015 Clemens Weisshaar
22.06.2015 Dan Rees
17.06.2015 Kerstin Cmelka
16.06.2015 Sabeth Buchmann
15.06.2015 Joshua Oppenheimer and Adi Rukun

11.06.2015 Jenny Sabin
09.06.2015 Corin Hewitt
08.06.2015 Mai-Thu Perret
04.06.2015 Mario Carpo
02.06.2015 Philipp Demandt
28.05.2015 Louis Becker
27.05.2015 Paul O’Neill
26.05.2015 Bisi Silva
21.05.2015 Bouchra Khalili
15.05.2015 Cara Benedetto
14.05.2015 Jeffrey Kipnis
11.05.2015 Minouk Lim

27.06.2013 Patrik Schumacher
25.06.2013 Dorit Margreiter
20.06.2013 Jürgen Mayer H.
19.06.2013 Pamela Lee
13.06.2013 Johanna Meyer-Grohbrügge
12.06.2013 Heiner Goebbels
10.06.2013 André Rottmann
10.06.2013 John Knight and Michael Krebber
06.06.2013 Simon Critchley
06.06.2013 Tatiana Bilbao
05.06.2013 Niklas Maak
04.06.2013 Brian Mann
14.05.2013 Okwui Enwezor
08.05.2013 Claire Fontaine
30.04.2013 John Knight
24.04.2013 Danh Vo
10.04.2013 Julika Rudelius

05.02.2013 Lutz Bacher
23.01.2013 Juan A. Gaitán
22.01.2013 Dorothea von Hantelmann
15.01.2013 Amy Sillman 275

13.12.2012 Carolyn Christov-Bakargiev
29.11.2012 Michael Stevenson
27.11.2012 Christian Höller
21.11.2012 Jerry Tartaglia
20.11.2012 Charles Esche
14.11.2012 Wolfgang Tillmans
09.11.2012 Georges Didi-Huberman
08.11.2012 Gelitin
01.11.2012 Omer Fast
30.10.2012 Latifa Echakhch
24.10.2012 David Cunningham

12.07.2012 Alejandro Zaera-Polo

10.07.2012 Karl Holmqvist
04.07.2012 Renzo Martens
03.07.2012 Helmut Krausser
28.06.2012 Greg Lynn and
Bill Pearson
27.06.2012 Vera Bourgeois and
Christa Näher
21.06.2012 Peter Cook
20.06.2012 Marc Camille Chaimowicz
12.06.2012 Michael Riedel
05.06.2012 Nairy Baghramian
30.05.2012 Nora Schultz
29.05.2012 Mark Wigley
23.05.2012 Carsten Nicolai
22.05.2012 Suhail Malik
16.05.2012 Gayatri Chakravorty Spivak
08.05.2012 Superflex
25.04.2012 Peter Greenaway
24.04.2012 Etcetera
23.04.2012 Richard Jackson

11.02.2012 Peter Fischli
01.02.2012 Eyal Weizman
31.01.2012 Daniel Wetzel
26.01.2012 Brigitte Weingart
25.01.2012 Emily Wardill
20.01.2012 John Levack Drever
12.01.2012 Daniel Buchholz
10.01.2012 Beatriz Colomina
13.12.2011 Beate Söntgen
07.12.2011 Judith Hopf
28.11.2011 Andrea Fraser
25.11.2011 Martha Rosler

23.11.2011 Monica Bonvicini
16.11.2011 Fergus Henderson
15.11.2011 Ross Birrell and

18.11.2010	Markus Miessen
16.11.2010	Willem de Rooij
12.11.2010	Thomas Keenan
11.11.2010	Eyal Weizman
02.11.2010	Anselm Haverkamp
08.07.2010	Jeffrey Kipnis
07.07.2010	Ewa Lajer-Burcharth
05.07.2010	Bonnie Camplin
29.06.2010	Zak Kyes
24.06.2010	Ben van Berkel
22.06.2010	Joseph Grima
18.06.2010	Jeff Malpas
16.06.2010	Kasper König
10.06.2010	Ei Arakawa
09.06.2010	Achim Menges
08.06.2010	Bassam el Baroni
03.06.2010	Aleksandra Mir
02.06.2010	Adam Caruso
01.06.2010	Jimmie Durham
27.05.2010	Ingo Niermann
25.05.2010	Hal Foster
19.05.2010	Antek Walczak
18.05.2010	Clémentine Deliss
06.05.2010	Marion von Osten
20.04.2010	Florian Pumhösl
31.03.2010	Trisha Donnelly
14.02.2010	Holger Liebs, Tobias Rehberger, and Daniel Birnbaum
13.02.2010	Dave Hullfish Bailey
13.02.2010	Michael Riedel
27.01.2010	Mathias Poledna
26.01.2010	Mike Bouchet
25.01.2010	Jeffrey Kipnis,

	Ben van Berkel, Johan Bettum, and Nikolaus Hirsch	
16.12.2009	Rebecca Bligh	
15.12.2009	Keren Cytter	
09.12.2009	Frances Scholz and Mark von Schlegell	
08.12.2009	Susanne Gaensheimer	
01.12.2009	Isabelle Graw	
30.11.2009	Mark Leckey	411

25.11.2009	Rachel Harrison
05.11.2009	Peter Fend
03.11.2009	Superflex
13.10.2009	Hu Fang
21.07.2009	Att Poomtangon
03.07.2009	Diedrich Diederichsen
02.07.2009	Friedrich Wolfram Heubach
01.07.2009	Boris Groys
25.06.2009	Marie-Ange Brayer
24.06.2009	Daniel Birnbaum
18.06.2009	George L. Legendre
17.06.2009	Christoph Menke
10.06.2009	Nina Möntmann
02.06.2009	Jesko Fezer
28.05.2009	Carolyn Christov-Bakargiev
26.05.2009	Sarah Morris
19.05.2009	Sarah Thornton
14.05.2009	Sylvia Lavin
13.05.2009	Rivane Neuenschwander
07.05.2009	Takaharu Tezuka
30.04.2009	Harun Farocki
28.04.2009	Jürg Halter
24.04.2009	Peaches
23.04.2009	Mark Wigley
22.04.2009	Nina Könnemann

05.02.2009	Nikolaus Hirsch
29.01.2009	Frank Barkow
28.01.2009	Morgan Fisher
27.01.2009	Tirdad Zolghadr
22.01.2009	Charles Walker
21.01.2009	Jan Verwoert
20.01.2009	Sabeth Buchmann
15.01.2009	Beatriz Colomina
14.01.2009	Maria Lind
07.01.2009	Jacques Rancière
18.12.2009	Philippe Rahm
17.12.2008	Judith Hopf
04.12.2008	Tobias Rehberger
27.11.2008	Ben van Berkel
25.11.2008	Will Bradley
24.11.2008	Eyal Weizman
20.11.2008	Tomás Saraceno
19.11.2008	Frances Stark
13.11.2008	Jochen Volz
11.11.2008	Anton Vidokle
06.11.2008	Jürgen Mayer H.
30.10.2008	David Adjaye
21.10.2008	Isabelle Graw
11.10.2008	Anton Vidokle
24.09.2008	Wade Guyton
11.07.2008	Martha Rosler
10.07.2008	Greg Lynn
24.06.2008	Eric D. Clark
18.06.2008	Helmut Draxler
10.–11.06.2008	Thomas Wagner
05.06.2008	Garry Neill Kennedy
04.06.2008	Armin Linke
29.05.2008	Schneider + Schumacher
27.05.2008	Richard Sennett

22.05.2008	Nikolaus Hirsch
15.05.2008	Nahum Tevet and Amy Simon
14.05.2008	Haegue Yang
06.05.2008	Mutsuro Sasaki
24.04.2008	Simon Starling
02.03.2008	Yona Friedman
14.02.2008	Marta Malé-Alemany and José Pedro Sousa
24.01.2008	Paola Pivi
24.01.2008	Elke Genzel and Pamela Voigt
23.01.2008	Wolfgang Tillmans
15.01.2008	Michaela Melián
12.12.2007	Henry VIII's Wives
11.12.2007	Judith Hopf
05.12.2007	Jason Dodge
29.11.2007	Axel Kilian
28.11.2007	Claire Fontaine
27.11.2007	Dietmar Dath
22.11.2007	Achim Menges
21.11.2007	Josephine Pryde
15.11.2007	Frank Sidebottom
13.11.2007	Wolfgang Winkler
12.11.2007	Christa Näher
08.11.2007	Kim Herforth Nielsen
25.10.2007	Mark Fahlbusch
23.10.2007	Michael Beutler
12.07.2007	Mohsen Mostafavi
04.07.2007	Andrea Fraser
18.06.2007	Katja Diefenbach, Kerstin Stakemeier, and Dmitry Vilensky (Chto Delat?)

14.06.2007	Wiel Arets and HG Merz
31.05.2007	Max Hollein
30.05.2007	Thomas Hirschhorn
29.05.2007	Mayo Thompson
23.05.2007	Paulina Olowska and Bonnie Camplin
16.05.2007	Neil Mulholland
10.05.2007	Peter Cachola Schmal
09.05.2007	Christa Näher
05.05.2007	Florian Hecker and Russell Haswell
03.05.2007	Daniel Birnbaum
02.05.2007	Jan Verwoert
10.02.2007	John Baldessari
10.02.2007	Francesco Bonami
01.02.2007	Ignace Verpoest
25.01.2007	Adriaan Beukers
24.01.2007	Mike Nelson
18.01.2007	Petra Blaisse
14.12.2007	Sanford Kwinter
13.12.2006	Michael Krebber, John Kelsey, Josef Strau, and Gareth James
05.12.2006	Jeremy Millar
23.11.2006	Gernot Böhme
20.11.2006	Tal R
15.11.2006	Brigitte Franzen, Kasper König, Klaus Ronneberger, and Clemens von Wedemeyer
09.11.2006	Christian Boltanski
07.11.2006	Steven Claydon
31.10.2006	Willem de Rooij

25.10.2006	Paul Chan
24.10.2006	Hermann Nitsch and Friedhelm Mennekes
06.10.2006	Geeta Kapur
18.09.2006	Raqs Media Collective
30.06.2006	Sabeth Buchmann, Isabelle Graw, W.J.T. Mitchell, and Paolo Virno
23.06.2006	Dan Perjovschi
21.06.2006	Andreas Siekmann
13.06.2006	Karl Holmqvist
12.06.2006	Marjetica Potrc, Tomás Saraceno, and Thomas Bayrle
06.06.2006	Lars Bang Larsen
02.–03.06.2006	Dictionary of War Symposium
31.05.2006	Mike Bouchet
16.05.2006	Chus Martínez
16.02.2006	Michael Speaks
11.02.2006	Simon Starling
10.02.2006	Isabelle Graw
27.01.2006	Sarah Morris
26.01.2006	Werner Sobek
18.01.2006	St. Rose
12.01.2006	Ilka & Andreas Ruby
10.01.2006	Michael Krebber and Kasper König
15.12.2005	Alisa Andrasek
08.12.2005	Luc Merx
01.12.2005	Roemer van Toorn
27.10.2005	Mark Goulthorpe
24.10.2005	Ludger Hovestadt

23.10.2005	William Kentridge
20.10.2005	Richard Jackson
17.10.2005	Charles Walker
10.10.2005	Chung Seoyoung
03.10.2005	Bernhard Franken
12.07.2005	Jeremy Deller
30.06.2005	Carol Bove
24.06.2005	Florian Grond
23.06.2005	Christoph Mäckler
17.06.2005	Regina Römhild
16.06.2005	Sean Snyder
14.06.2005	Stefan Beck
09.06.2005	Brigitta Kuster, Isabell Lorey, Marion von Osten, and Katja Reichard
08.06.2005	Darren Almond
07.06.2005	Aernout Mik
03.06.2005	Tom Holert
30.05.2005	Giorgio Agamben
30.05.2005	Peter Abs and Oliver Tepel
26.05.2005	Jesse Reiser
20.05.2005	Manfred Grohmann
12.05.2005	Wolfgang Tillmans
11.05.2005	Anny De Decker and Bernd Lohaus
02.05.2005	Mehmet Behluli
25.04.2005	Felix Gmelin
19.04.2005	Massimiliano Gioni, Maurizio Cattelan, and Ali Subotnick
11.04.2005	Veton Orana
10.04.2005	Edi Muka

26.01.2005	Barbara Klemm
20.01.2005	Birgit Megerle
14.01.2005	David Medalla
13.01.2004	Mona Hatoum
15.–17.12.2004	Michael Fried
12.12.2004	Renée Green
10.12.2004	Marcel Odenbach
08.12.2004	Dirk von Lowtzow
02.12.2004	André Butzer
19.11.2004	Elaine Sturtevant
17.11.2004	Monika Baer
03.11.2004	Christa Näher
01.11.2004	Akram Zaatari
29.10.2004	Isabelle Graw and Bernhard Stumpfhaus
27.10.2004	Daniel Kothenschulte
29.06.2004	André Butzer
22.06.2002	Marc Cousins
22.06.2004	Matthias Vogel
16.06.2004	Pamela Lee
07.06.2004	Lucy McKenzie and Christoph Keller
03.06.2004	Mark Leckey
27.05.2004	Erhard Schüttpelz
21.05.2004	Peter Cook
20.05.2004	Morgan Fisher
19.05.2004	Johannes Kahrs
14.05.2004	Charles Jencks
06.05.2004	Cerith Wyn Evans
05.05.2004	Scott King
26.04.2004	Louise Neri
22.04.2004	Cecilia Edefalk
20.04.2004	Kasper König
29.01.2004	Yve-Alain Bois

28.01.2004	Karin Sander
21.01.2004	Hinrich Sachs
13.01.2004	Jan Verwoert
12.12.2003	Joachim Krause
11.12.2003	Molly Nesbit
10.12.2003	Lucy McKenzie
05.12.2003	Dagmar Reinhardt
28.11.2003	Ben van Berkel
27.11.2003	Michael Stevenson
26.11.2003	Oswald Wiener
24.11.2003	Manuel DeLanda
19.11.2003	Carl Michael von Hausswolff
18.11.2003	Michaela Eichwald
14.11.2003	Sigurdur Gunnarsson
12.11.2003	Thomas Bayrle
06.11.2003	Daniel Richter
04.11.2003	Spencer Finch
29.10.2003	Liam Gillick
27.10.2003	Sarah Morris
04.07.2003	Tom Holert
03.07.2003	Wolfgang Brauneis
25.06.2003	Wolfgang Tillmans
24.06.2003	Huang Yong Ping
03.06.2003	Johannes Hüppi
28.05.2003	Nils Norman
27.05.2003	Hermann Nitsch
24.05.2003	Felix Kubin
23.05.2003	Benjamin Buchloh
21.05.2003	Ayşe Erkmen
15.05.2003	Joep van Lieshout
13.05.2003	Kasper König
08.05.2003	Willem de Rooij
08.05.2003	William Forsythe
07.05.2003	Marta McClennan
28.04.2003	Isabelle Graw

20.03.2003	Louise Lawler
29.01.2003	Greg Lynn
21.01.2003	Ayşe Erkmen
15.01.2003	Ecke Bonk
16.12.2002	Merlin Carpenter
12.12.2002	Katja Davar
10.12.2002	Marcel Odenbach
29.11.2002	Pawel Althamer
26.11.2002	Monika Schwitte
19.11.2002	Amelie von Wulffen
15.11.2002	Stephan Dillemuth
12.–13.11.2002	Andreas Dorau
30.10.2002	Pascale Marthine Tayou
21.10.2002	Matthieu Laurette
16.10.2002	Isabelle Graw
15.10.2002	Nedko Solakov
14.10.2002	Joseph Kosuth
11.07.2002	Sylvia Lanvin and Sanford Kwinter
03.07.2002	Simon Starling
28.06.2002	Marcelyn Gow
20.06.2002	Philippe Parreno
18.06.2002	Michael Krebber
11.06.2002	William Kentridge
10.06.2002	Isaac Julien
06.06.2002	Tacita Dean
04.06.2002	Donald Baechler
31.05.2002	Jesse Reiser
14.05.2002	Daniel Birnbaum
10.05.2002	Suzana Milevska
03.05.2002	Gianni Romano
30.04.2002	Isabelle Graw
26.04.2002	Dieter Bogner
19.04.2002	Erden Kosova

05.04.2002	João Fernandes
23.03.2002	Gilbert & George
15.03.2002	Kati Deepwek
08.03.2002	Dagmar Demming
22.02.2002	Frank Larcade
15.02.2002	Lionel Bovier
10.02.2002	Charles Esche
09.02.2002	Dan Peterman
30.01.2002	Philippe Parreno
25.01.2002	Hedwig Saxenhuber
18.01.2002	Nasrin Tabatabai
22.01.2002	Janet Cardiff and George Bures Miller
17.01.2002	Peter Halley
15.01.2002	Neo Rauch
08.01.2002	Branislav Dimitrijević
08.01.2002	Maurizio Cattelan
08.01.2002	Massimiliano Gioni
11.12.2001	Marko Lehanka
03.12.2001	Clémentine Deliss
27.11.2001	Anja Niedringhaus
16.11.2001	Njirić + Njirić
06.11.2001	John Bock
30.10.2001	Ernesto Neto
23.10.2001	Lisa Brice
22.10.2001	Tracey Moffatt
10.07.2001	Mark Wigley
09.07.2001	Louisa Hutton and Johan Bettum
28.06.2001	Swetlana Heger and Plamen Dejanov
27.06.2001	Günter Zamp Kelp
26.06.2001	Martin Fritz
20.06.2001	Jens Haaning

12.06.2001	W.A. Hansbauer
04.06.2001	Brian Tolle
21.05.2001	Rosa von der Schulenburg
15.05.2001	Gabriela Seifert, Götz Stöckmann, and formalhaut
11.05.2001	Krystian Woznicki
09.05.2001	Res Ingold
02.05.2001	Ronald Jones and Nicolas Bourriaud
26.04.2001	Isabelle Graw
25.04.2001	Rirkrit Tiravanija
24.04.2001	Monica Bonvicini
22.04.2001	Jörg Heiser and Noemi Smolik
05.02.2001	Sulan Kolatan
31.01.2001	Mike Hentz
24.01.2001	Klaus Klinger
17.01.2001	Steen Hoyer
12.01.2001	Katharina Grosse
11.01.2001	Hans-Peter Feldmann
20.12.2000	b&k+, Arno Brandlhuber, and Berndt Kniess
14.12.2000	Jochen Lempert
11.12.2000	Leni Hoffmann
08.12.2000	Daniel Hunziker
06.12.2000	Carsten Höller
04.12.2000	Ernst Caramelle
22.11.2000	Giovanni Intra
22.11.2000	Frances Stark
16.11.2000	Nathalie Melikian
13.11.2000	Peter Land
06.11.2000	Thomas Wulffen
23.10.2000	Michael Elmgreen and

	Ingar Dragset
19.10.2000	Roberto Ohrt and Raymond Pettibon
05.07.2000	Robert Fleck
26.06.2000	Elke Krystufek
21.06.2000	Laura Cottingham
20.06.2000	Marlene Schnelle-Schneyder
15.06.2000	Helmut Draxler
07.06.2000	Thomas Wagner
05.06.2000	Biljana Tomic
30.05.2000	Thomas Schütte
25.05.2000	Matti Braun
08.05.2000	Mark Wigley
04.05.2000	Roberto Ohrt
04.05.2000	Jim Isermann
03.05.2000	Renate Breufl
01.02.2000	Klaus Klinger
29.–30.01.2000	Charles Esche
26.01.2000	Thomas Wagner
26.01.2000	Kasper König and Stefan Kern
25.01.2000	Richard Leacock
14.01.2000	Marius Babias and Florian Waldvogel
15.12.1999	Hans-Ernst Mittig
10.12.1999	Duncan Lewis
07.12.1999	Klaus Englert
03.12.1999	Marius Babias and Claudia Wahjudi
02.12.1999	Thomas Erne
02.12.1999	Luc Tuymans
01.12.1999	Oskar Bätschmann
30.11.1999	Bazon Brock
22.–24.11.1999	Laura Cottingham

11.–12.11.1999	Paula Larkin
09.11.1999	Andreas Siekmann
06.11.1999	Fred Smith
06.11.1999	Peter Cook
05.11.1999	Enric Miralles
02.11.1999	Heimo Zobernig
25.10.1999	Albert Oehlen
21.10.1999	Filmreihe L.A.
20.10.1999	Florian Haas and Martin Schmidl
19.10.1999	Michael Schumacher
09.07.1999	Frank Barth
08.07.1999	René Block
01.07.1999	Hans Ulrich Obrist
24.06.1999	Peter Pfaff
23.06.1999	Sarah Sze
21.06.1999	Thomas Wagner
17.06.1999	Hannes Böhringer
16.06.1999	Mark Wallinger
07.06.1999	Helga Fanderl
01.06.1999	Olaf Zimmermann
31.05.1999	Marius Babias
30.05.1999	Bernd Drücke
26.05.1999	Olafur Eliasson
20.05.1999	Gertrud Koch
15.05.1999	Emily King and Irene Hohenbüchler
10.05.1999	Martin Fritz
04.05.1999	Ayşe Erkmen
30.04.1999	Kemistry & Storm and Stefan Enders
29.04.1999	Marius Babias, Dirk Paschke, and Daniel Milohnić
27.04.1999	Leni Hoffmann

Juni

5. Julia Bryan-Wi
Material Relations
Goethe-Universität, Campus W
Casino, Raum 1.811

6. Melati Suryoda

7. Kivi Sotamaa*
Sensation

13. Daniel Norell*
In Conversation

14. Leo Asemota & Nástio Mosquito

Vorträge u Veranstalt

Die Vorträge finden, wenn nicht ande
Uhr in der Aula der Städelschule statt

SOMMERS

April

18. **Minsuk Cho***
Challenges

19. **Davide Quayola***
Iconography / Geometry
Nature / Synthesis

Gabriel Pérez-Barreiro
Affective Affinities
33rd Bienal de São Paulo
Kooperation mit der Fundação Bienal de São Paulo

Tow

3. **Shajay Bhooshan***
Collaborative, Cumulative,
Disruptive

osenthal**
Museum

nbaroff

lo

26. Arin Rungjang
Now I know I've got a
cause it's breaking…

27. Wolf D. Prix*
Dean's Honorary Lectu

28. DeeDee Halleck

uli

5. Kapwani Kiwanga

10. Absolventenausstellung
Eröffnung, Städel Museum
11. Juli – 5. August

Städel
Dürerstra
60596 Frankfurt am
www.staedelschu

Por
Alte Bri

SEMESTE

20. **Georgia Sagri and I**
Eröffnung, Portikus
21. April – 17. Juni

25. **Peter Fend**

26. **Kyle Miller***
Errant Trajectories

y/

9. **Lauren Vasey***
ards Cyber-Physical
Systems

14. **Avery Singer**
Untitled

5. **Cauleen Smith**
The Loop
Fast and Slow Reads
ns, Processions, and Objects

22. **R**
Ent
Dis

23. **H**

25.–26. **SA**

Virtual Reali

29.

May 29, 2018
Georgia Sagri

Art Without Work and Work Without Art

Greek artist Georgia Sagri deciphers the origin and intentions of her practice in this artwork, developed as a PowerPoint presentation. Sagri begins by depicting her early years working as a life model to afford to take drawing classes. The act of refusing to choose between the two roles—the model or the artist—soon became an interest in the dichotomies that working artists encounter. Sagri then describes her art space 'Υλη[matter]HYLE, *based in an apartment in Athens, and explains how* staged objects, modules, *and* hyper objects *are used in her practice and performances to transcend singular viewpoints and demand shifts in perception.*

1

(1) When I was invited to do this lecture, one of the first things that came to mind was the time when I decided to be an artist. I was quite young, sixteen, and I had been working at a bar for a year, (2) serving, cleaning tables, taking orders. Because of my young age I was paid under the table; I didn't have health insurance, but at least I had some money. My father had died a few years earlier and this was the only way for me to sustain myself without depending on my mother's little income. (3) At the bar, I was changing roles constantly. Sometimes, I was at the door, sometimes I cleaned or just helped the bartender. During that period of my life, paid work meant being independent, but also

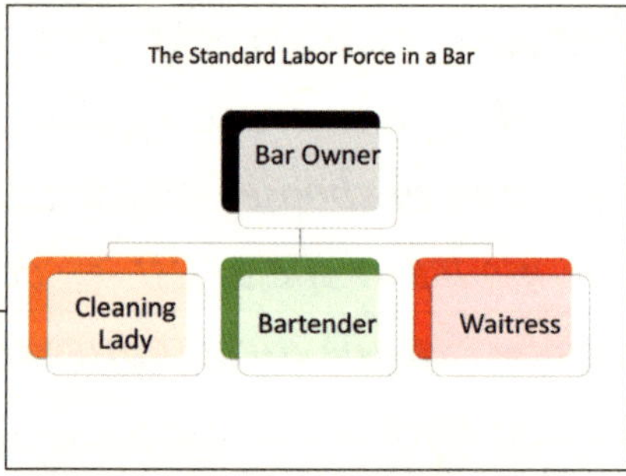

2

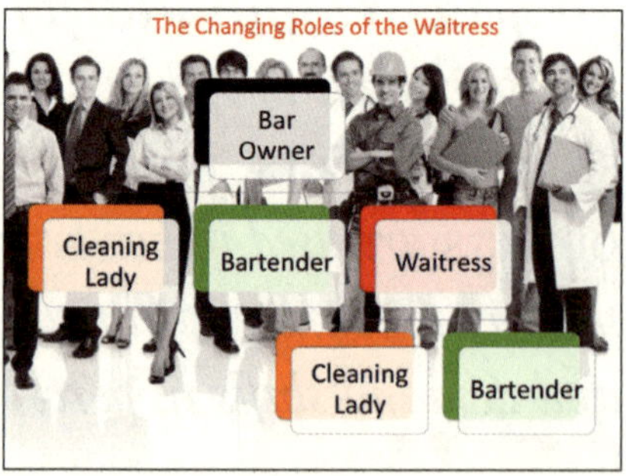

3

entirely giving up any desire to explore who I was; this was something left for my boss to decide, who was using my energy for his own benefit and profit.

During that time, I was sporadically attending preparatory drawing lessons to enter the School of the Arts. When it got too difficult to pay for the classes, I decided (4) that, instead of quitting drawing, I would become the model for my peers. With the modeling work, I was able to continue taking drawing classes. (5) My fellow students, however, were quite vocal about how much they hated the ambiguous position that I was occupying, being both a model and taking drawing classes with them. Although posing for them and drawing with them could seem terribly embarrassing, I was convinced that they were the ones who failed to see the whole picture. (6) For me, the point was that if I was comfortable with posing naked in front of my peers and not offended by their insults, I would continue to model in the best way possible and at the same time continue

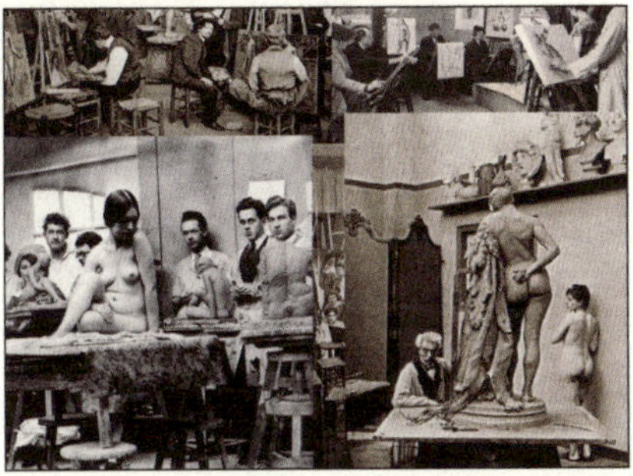

4

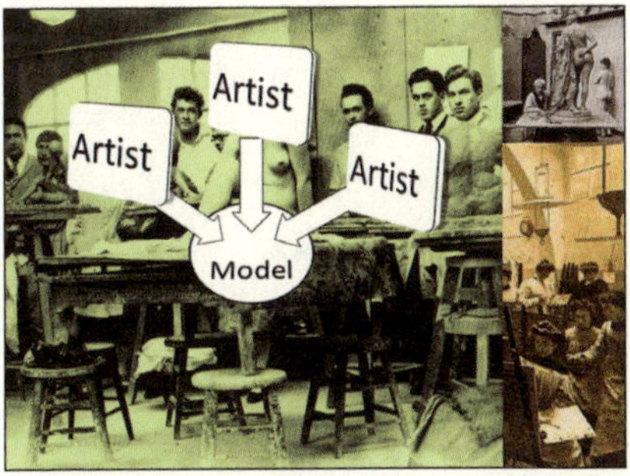

5

6

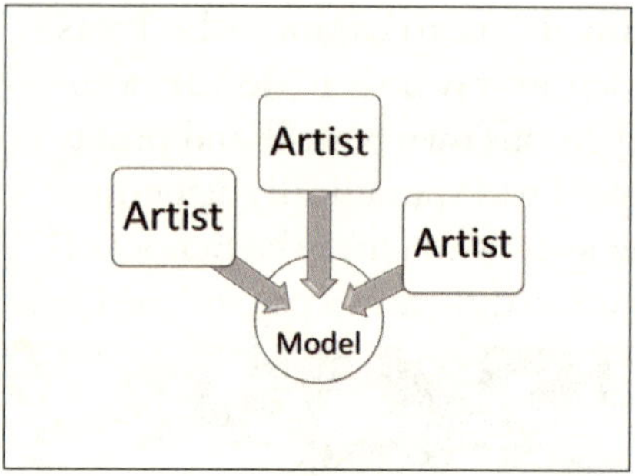

7

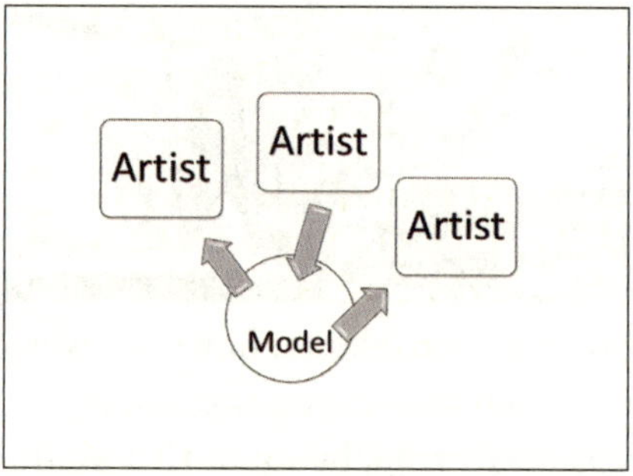

to attend the drawing classes. (7) I refused to see the work of modeling as separate from the act of drawing, neither did I regard it as similar to working at the bar, because, as I saw it, modeling was already part of the act of drawing. I hated having to choose between the roles of model and artist. I simply couldn't participate in this discourse my peers were so desperate to fit into. To me, making a choice was equal to giving up the entire process of drawing. (8) I insisted on my decision not to choose between the two roles and to sustain my drawing process, which involved both activities of posing and drawing. Once I decided not to choose, I became much more enthusiastic about the

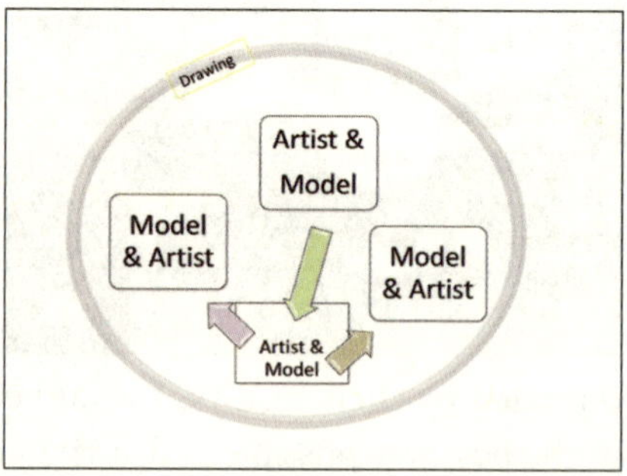

8

drawing than about working at the bar. A few months later I quit the bar job, and for a year and a half, I continued to attend the drawing classes. I insisted on standing still, naked in front of my peers, and drawing with them. Standing motionless meant that I had to develop an altered way of breathing. (9) I invented smaller portions of inhales and exhales from the nose so that my body continued to look the same for thirty, sometimes even forty minutes, in a stable position.

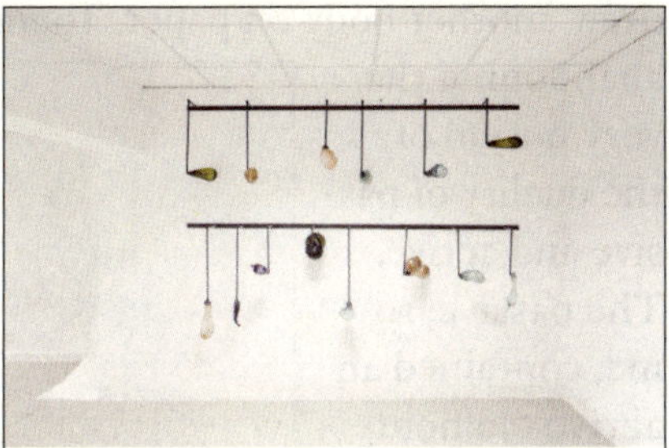

Breathing Score (3_6_3), 2017, hand-blown glass, steel, acrylic paint, 2,00x1,50x30cm
Breathing Score (2_5_2), 2017, hand blown glass, steel, acrylic paint 2,00x1,50x30cm

9

For my peers, the stable image I provided them with when modeling served to improve their sense of observation, form, light, and shadow, while for me, it was a time to do research into my physiology's limits, patience, and breathing—in other words, observation from within. The breathing techniques allowed me to be less anxious about the power shifts involved in alternating between modeling and drawing. I gradually also looked at other bodies in a different way. I wasn't interested in having my drawings

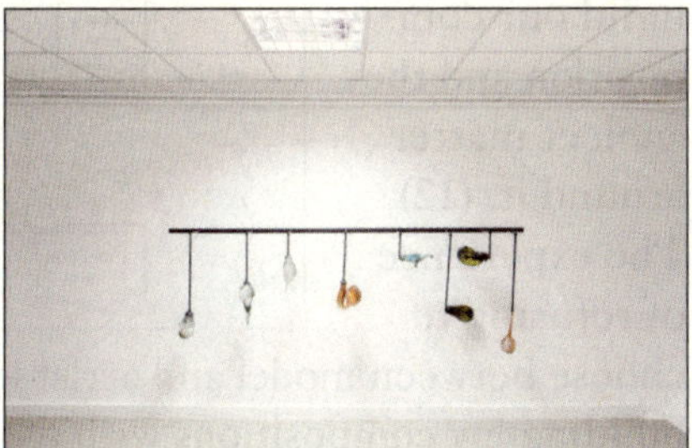

Breathing Score (7_1_7), 2017, hand-blown glass, steel, acrylic paint, 2,00x1,50x30cm;

10

look good. **(10)** I was interested in learning what it's like to stand still for so many hours in front of others' contemplation, being exposed to the gazes of others, and to then take that bodily information and use it to draw another body on paper. To me, drawing meant abandoning the very notion of the duality of passive and active. The passive, to me, contained an active element and the active contained a passive element. The sensitive state of exposing my naked body, my intimate surfaces, already implied the drawing's eventuality, it was a momentum, and this is how I understood representation.

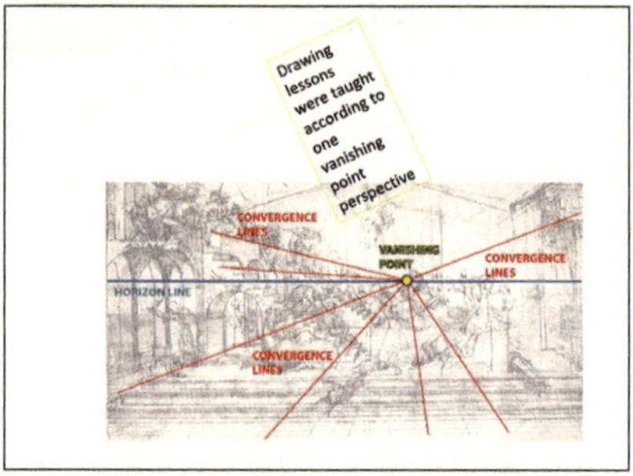

11

(11) The way we were taught drawing was through creating perspective by means of a single focal point on the paper and starting from that point to build our composition and the subject matter around it. **(12)** The experience of refusing to choose between model and artist led me to start building my compositions with pigments of tones and rhythms on the paper without having one starting

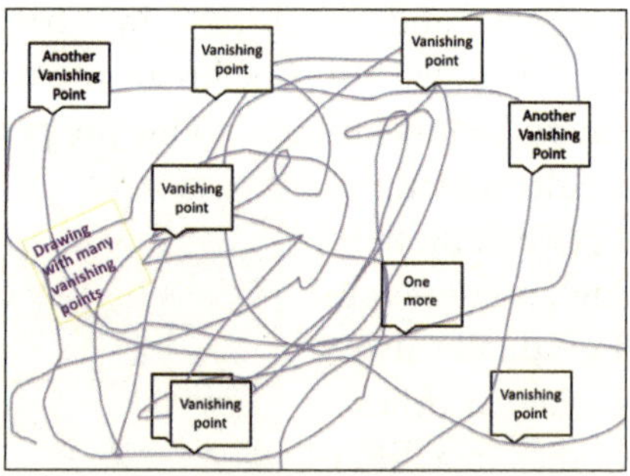

12

point, building up without insisting on having a central perspective. All those bodies on paper, on canvas, photos, and images were only confirmations of the split between object and subject, between the one being depicted and the one depicting. Representation has forever depended on this dichotomy and on building subject matter through a single focal point. So many women artists have shaped the history of art by posing endlessly, and without any argument, for thousands of years in front of another and sacrificed learning how to draw—just as there were many women artists who did learn how to draw by rejecting ever being the models. For me, representation was about continuously shifting between modeling and drawing and the dispersion of the comfortable position of the fixed point on the sheet of paper, as well as the constant return to the act and the training, of breathing in the process of rigidly keeping a pose, while, and through the learning of how to draw.

I was still young, eighteen, when I was accepted to the School of the Arts in Athens, and my idea of how to go about drawing led me to question the approach of the art education system, which suggested that making a choice was the way to build a career as an artist. **(13)** This time, the dichotomy was between material and immaterial production. That

13

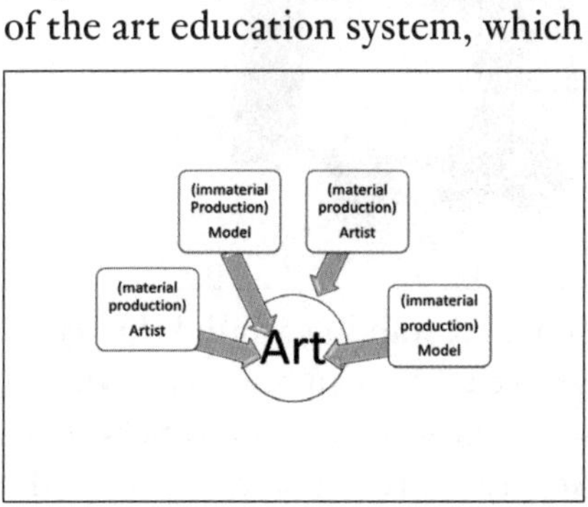

was the main source of anxiety for many art students at that time, and it still is: the constant anxiety of having to choose between material and immaterial production. Our teachers, back then, were split between those who insisted on encouraging us to make something—I called them the artists, the material producers—and those who encouraged us to critique "work" and to reflect more on "language," "research," and "institutional critique"—back then I called them the models, the immaterial producers. Most of the teachers who forced us to make a choice between those two productive modes were male artists.

(14) It was only in working with the artist Rena Papaspyrou, the head of the studio I was part of—and the first woman artist ever to be the head of a studio since the establishment of the Athens School of the Arts in 1836—that I was able to uphold my decision not to choose. The only thing she was adamant about in her studio was daily presence. She insisted that no matter what: She insisted that all students had to be in the studio, otherwise they had to leave. She was there every day from 10 am to 4 pm, taking attendance, walking around the studio, and talking to us. Rena Papaspyrou was—without a doubt—the best educator the Athens School of the Arts ever had. Now that I think of it, she wanted

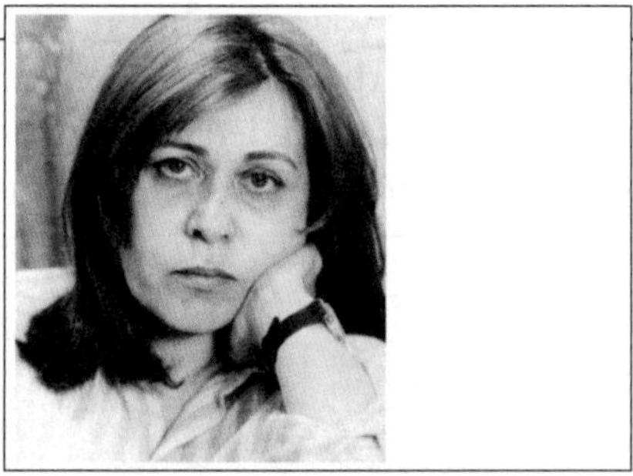

14

us to be in the studio without imposing the need to make any choice. She was simply there to keep up the pace, to encourage us to pursue our artistic practice at our own tempo within the structure of the studio. If she hadn't created this structure by insisting on our presence, then none of us would have been able to actually get anything going and create our own rhythm within it. For the same reason, she required all of us to also be present during bimonthly group meetings. The whole group would tour the studio and critique each student's work, and even when there was no visible, material progress, this activity of touring the studio was important for all of us, as it allowed us to see, hear, and discuss the building process and the routine each of us were establishing. And there were many things going on even in an empty space.

(15) During my first years at the Athens School of the Arts, I did public actions and created drawings and sculptures, some of which I would call *staged objects.* I had no idea that some of what I was doing was called performance. I was enthusiastic about creating space for the active to become passive and the passive to become active. I wanted to focus on the moment of shifting between artist and model and vice versa, and my basic paradigm continued to be the drawing process I had learned in

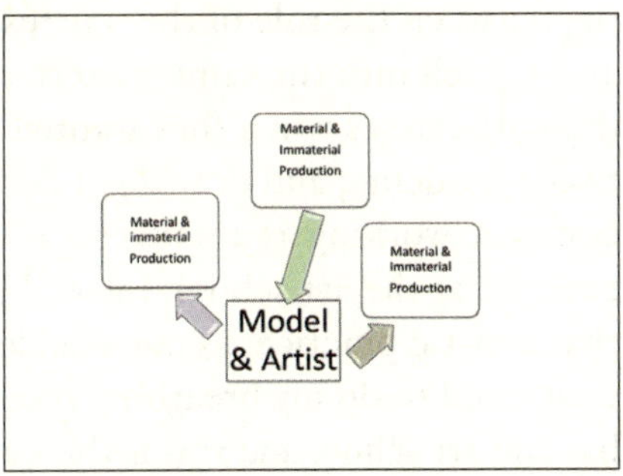

15

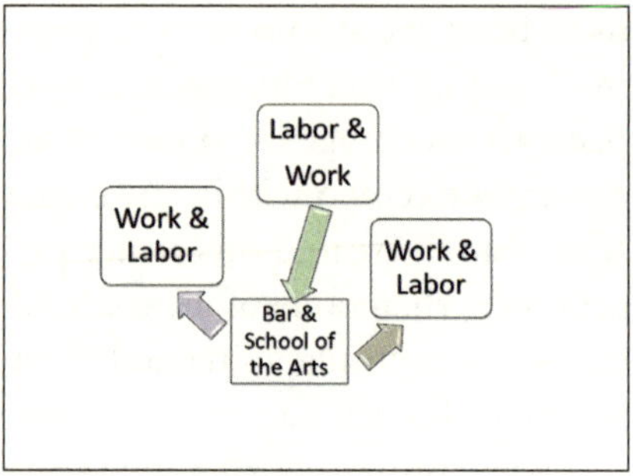

16

my preparatory drawing classes. Performance was the medium that allowed me to sustain the decision to not choose, an empowering tool that perpetuated the limbo state of neither work nor art. **(16)** When I was accepted to the art school, I decided to start working again as a waitress on the weekends. This time, however, the work was no longer about gaining independence but about satisfying everyday needs, so as to be able to continue my studies and keep exploring who I was. The work at the bar seemed much easier—a walk in the park, so to say—compared to the adventures, disappointments, and satisfactions I experienced in exploring my artistic practice. This investigation under the premise of not choosing between modeling and drawing made me realize that there was also no choice between paid work and artistic work. The moment I tried choosing between the role of the waitress and that of the artist, I fell into the same pattern as my peers at the drawing classes when they wanted me to choose between modeling and drawing. I decided that if I could continue working as a waitress, as an extension of my practice at the art school, I would be able to continue that artistic practice, as one enabled the other. **(17)** I continued to do my breathing research between the bar and art school and this is the way I have continued

17

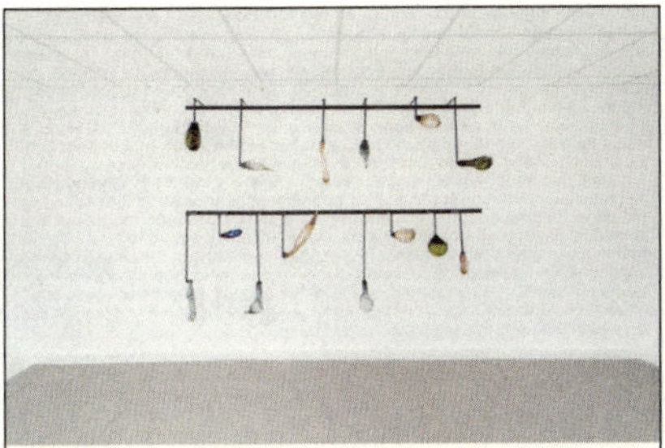

Breathing Score (1_3_1), 2017, hand blown glass, steel, acrylic paint 2,00x1,50x30cm;
Breathing Score (2_7_5), 2017, hand blown glass, steel, acrylic paint 2,00x1,50x30cm;

18

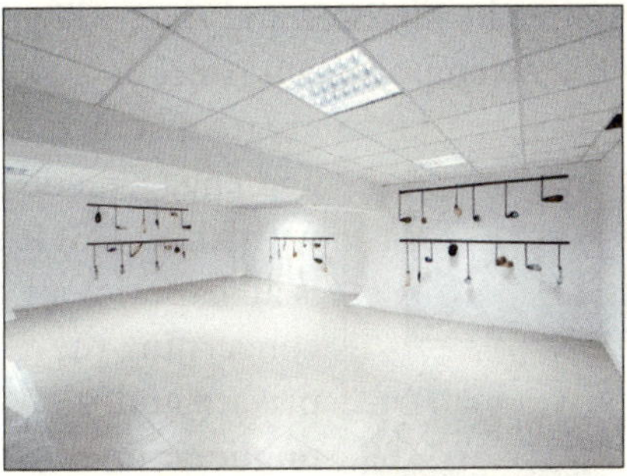

to work since that day. It is a balance between work and art. Doing work without art and doing art without work is the way I have lived ever since. **(18)** This is how I try to organize with others beyond the limits of art and through what I do, which is art. **(19)** In 2014, I decided to initiate ʽΥλη[matter]HYLE with the intention of finding other people who wanted to be involved in a space of no choice with me. **(20)** This process could happen within the caring of an *oikos* (home) in a typical Athenian apartment of a *polikatikia* (apartment block), a building located at a *stoa* (shopping arcade) surrounded by the urban chaos of Omonia Square in the center of Athens. **(21)** The scale of the home can

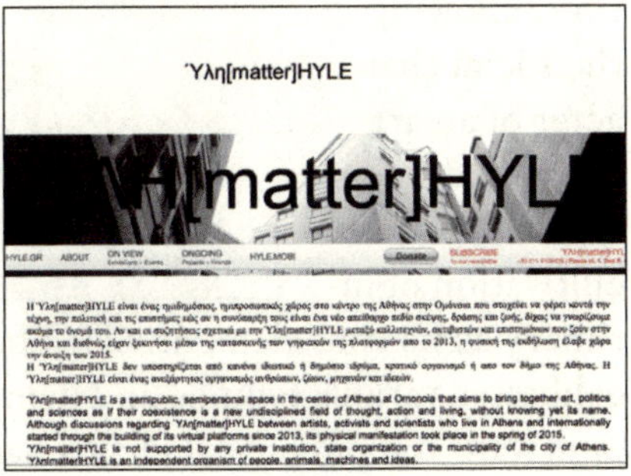

19

give time for intimate, one-on-one meetings and small gatherings. **(22)** It is a small apartment with an entry room, two living rooms and a corridor

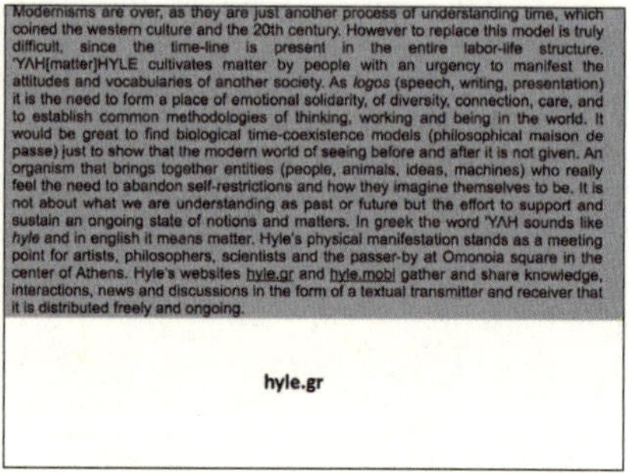

Modernisms are over, as they are just another process of understanding time, which coined the western culture and the 20th century. However to replace this model is truly difficult, since the time-line is present in the entire labor-life structure. 'YΛH[matter]HYLE cultivates matter by people with an urgency to manifest the attitudes and vocabularies of another society. As *logos* (speech, writing, presentation) it is the need to form a place of emotional solidarity, of diversity, connection, care, and to establish common methodologies of thinking, working and being in the world. It would be great to find biological time-coexistence models (philosophical maison de passe) just to show that the modern world of seeing before and after it is not given. An organism that brings together entities (people, animals, ideas, machines) who really feel the need to abandon self-restrictions and how they imagine themselves to be. It is not about what we are understanding as past or future but the effort to support and sustain an ongoing state of notions and matters. In greek the word 'YΛH sounds like *hyle* and in english it means matter. Hyle's physical manifestation stands as a meeting point for artists, philosophers, scientists and the passer-by at Omonoia square in the center of Athens. Hyle's websites hyle.gr and hyle.mobi gather and share knowledge, interactions, news and discussions in the form of a textual transmitter and receiver that it is distributed freely and ongoing.

hyle.gr

20

leading to one bedroom, the kitchen, and the bathroom, and suggests the attempt to gain time, to create distance and engagement with ideas. **(23)** It is an experiment concerning the private and the public, it gives what the overestimated studio

21

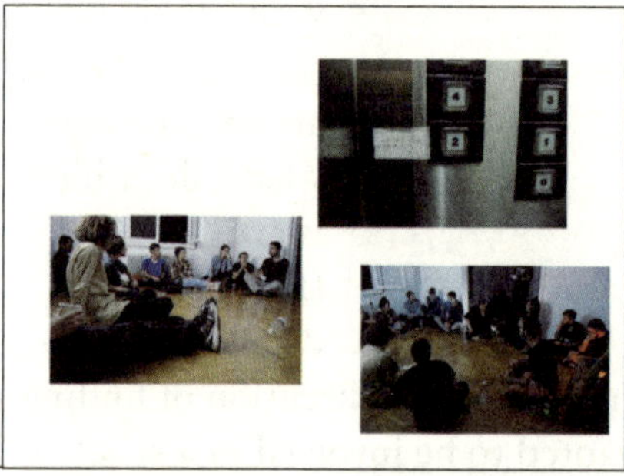

of the singular artist can offer, while at the same time, allowing the social character of an art space to develop and maintain the cultivation of intimacy as its core element. **(24)** The home constantly calibrates various tempos and demands the weaving of private and public. All of this happens in parallel to

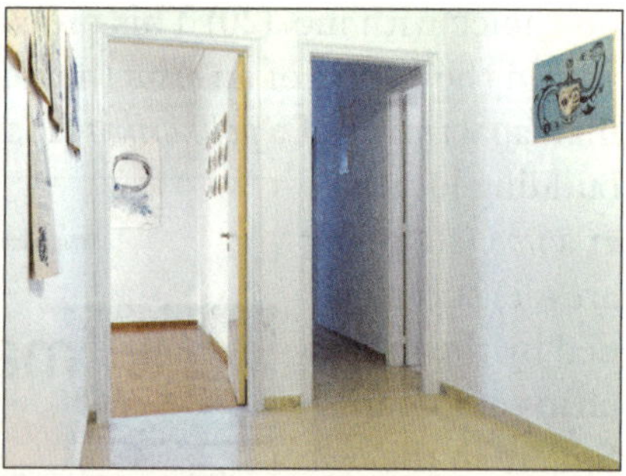

22

the most important element, which is cultivating affinities and budding friendships. The rupture of an individual artist's studio has social implications and this may also happen inside the space of a home. 'Yλη [matter] HYLE aims to call for social activities of all kinds, but often, this work is not seen as work. That is a problem because the space could offer political and artistic programs, but first, there is a need for communities that are able to reproduce their lives, and I don't see those communities existing right now. (25) People seem to be too fragmented in different social bubbles to deal with loneliness as a group activity, while I try to cultivate within this space a sense of care

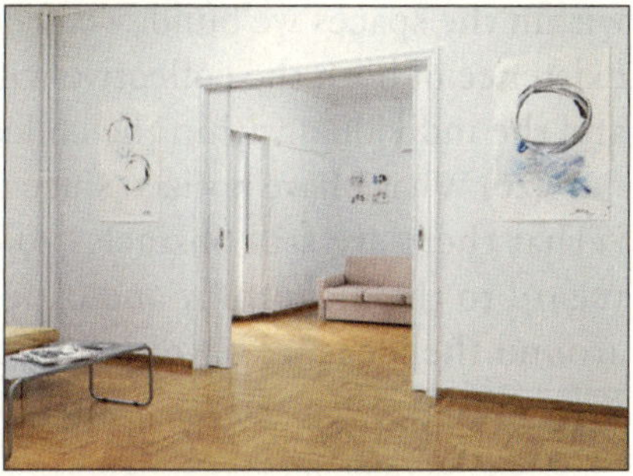

23

24

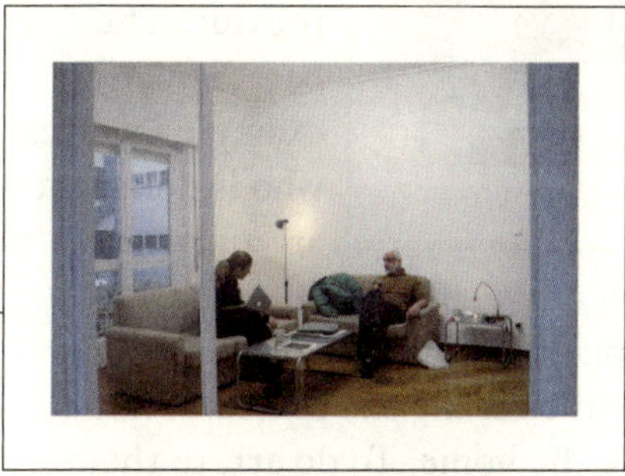

25

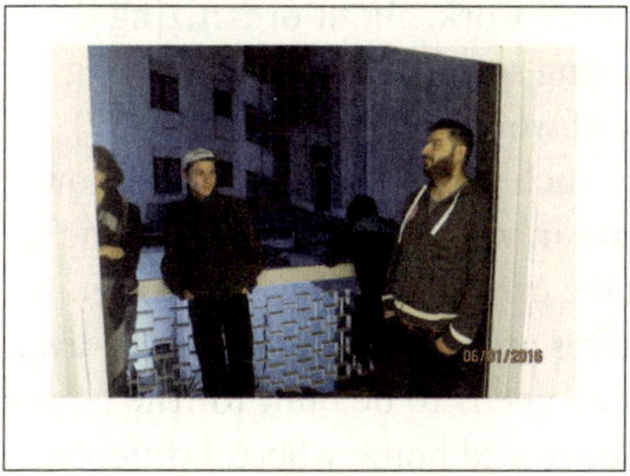

that goes beyond the need for privacy or public address. I insist on not wanting to decide what is more important: the individual or the collective. I feel that within the spaces we build, we need to recognize the existence of both the collective within the individual and the individual within the collective.

(26) What I have noticed since initiating the space is that there are still obstacles to overcome with regard to the dichotomy and expectations built up around the ideas we have about public and private modes of production that an art space and the home may provide. The paradigmatic example involves who is doing the art and who is doing the work. I am often confronted with people who think that simply being at the space and doing nothing, relaxing, and cleaning the dishes, is not part of the art but of the home. To do art, to them, is about exhibiting one's work, about organizing events, about discussing serious matters. Cleaning dishes is either part of work or part of leisure. (27) For me, an art space such as the *oikos* needs to allow for the variety of ways in which individuals assume responsibilities to take care of the space itself. To take care of their selves and others, to be able to live. A breathing technique needs to be built for the power shifts between art space and home where a different

26

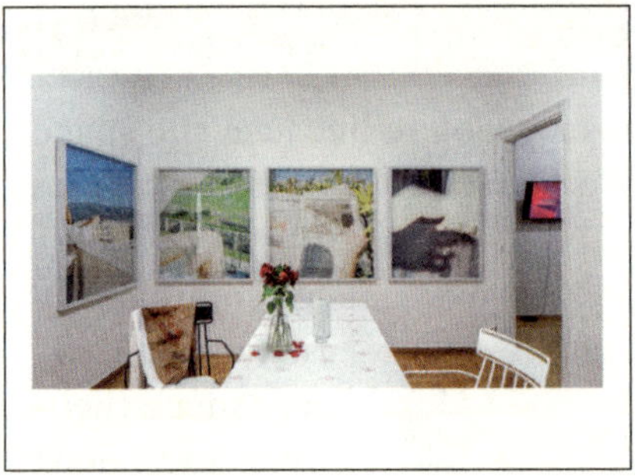

temporality and, as a result, a different understanding of production develops. It is not the maintenance of the modern life and labor-time tempo, which exists only when wage comes into play; it isn't about the duration of a project, which is defined by the start and completion of an objective; and it isn't just about striving for success based on an accounting of profits and expenses. (28) Something else is at stake at the home and the art space. When something begins and ends, it is up to the subjects involved to decide. Taking responsibility comes from caring for the space in order for others to be part of it as well. Maintaining and cleaning are done, not for the purpose of keeping the space to oneself, but rather in order to allow others to be passive and active, without the pressure to choose between the role of the artist and the role of the visitor. To take care of the space is to resist choosing between those who know more than others or between those who are already included and those who want to

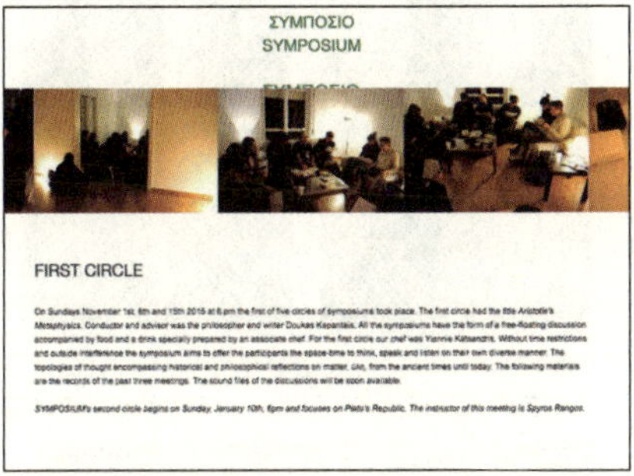

27

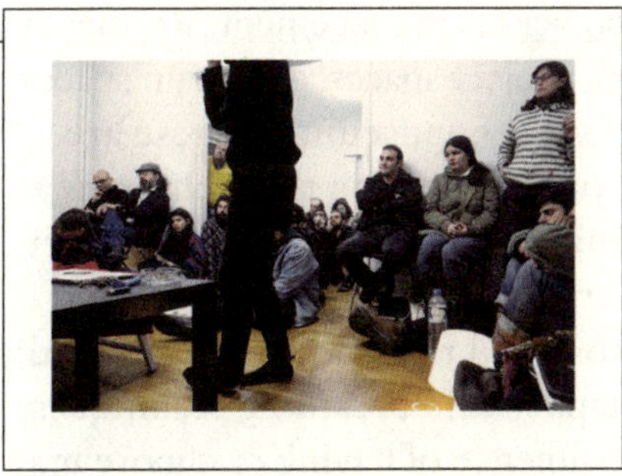

28

29 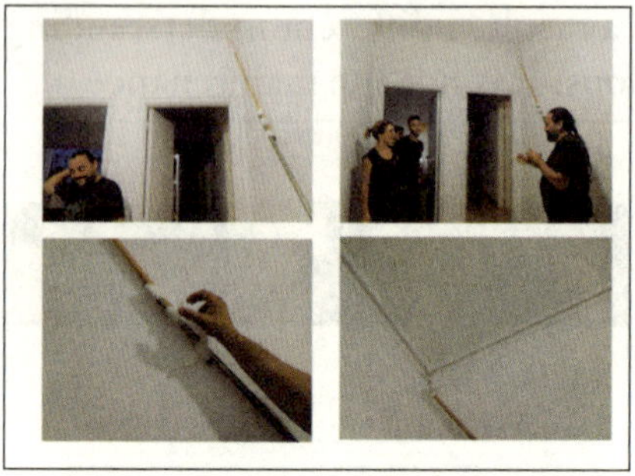

30 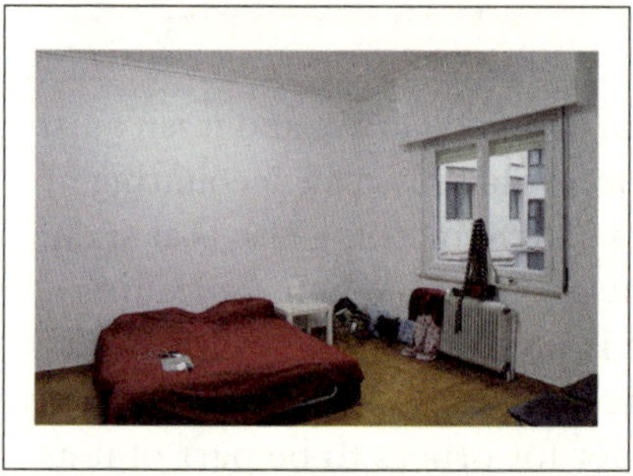

belong—to build respect for the place, which is not just yours but everyone's. And this could create the eventuality, the momentum that would enable skills and interests to emerge, pleasure and joy to appear. **(29)** Many institutions are obviously completely fixated with dichotomy: project versus process, public versus private, exhibition versus event, production versus management. Residency programs, art centers, project spaces, artist-run spaces, art associations, *kunsthalles*, museums—these are all places that insist on maintaining the dichotomy between the model and the artist, object and subject, immaterial and material production, paid work and artistic work, the work and the art, the private and the public. **(30)** Perhaps within breathing techniques, the binaries and the violence of having to choose may go away. We could then decide to spare some time for each other to imagine, to discuss, and to organize structures beyond existing perceptions.

31

(31) Over the past five years, I have been working on inventing tools and words while making my works. For example, the term (32) *module,* which came slowly into the vocabulary of my practice, was created in order to explain the act of **doubling**, (33) and to categorize what happens to the object when it cast its shadow—its similar other in space—and at the same time, to explain what this object proposes.

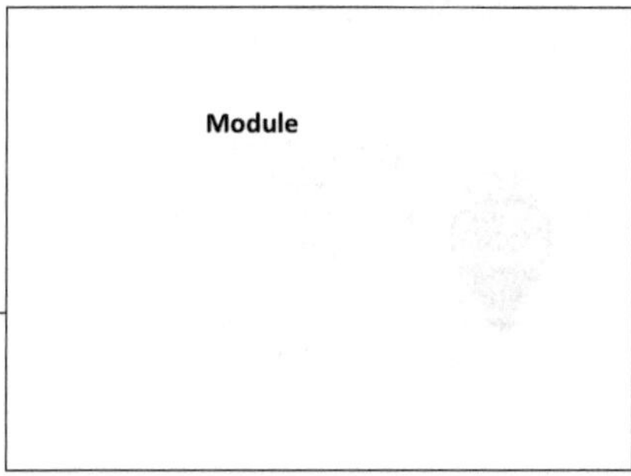

32

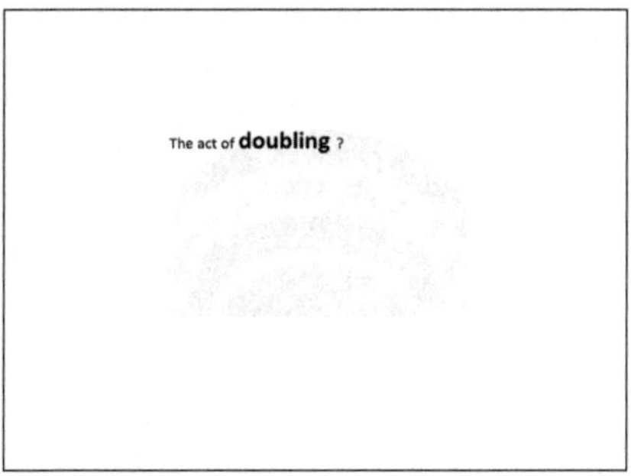

33

(34) Here, we see a flat square on a flat surface. We know that every object has a width, length, and height. Every object also has a length in time, but is this length possible to be represented? Time is a fourth dimension, but how can we present that in a two-dimensional world? And especially, how

can we represent that in visual arts, dominated by two- and three-dimensional perception? (35) In the ancient times, when perception and conviction were dominated by two-dimensionality, a third dimension was introduced by the implication of movement through the circular form of pottery. This third dimension here is the passing of time. (36) When this linear and repetitive perception of time becomes the norm, then the world is not flat anymore, and the movement of front and back is not the only one we can achieve. There is also up and down (37) and the understanding of a force much stronger than the movement of our own bodies on the surface of the earth. This force keeps us, and all

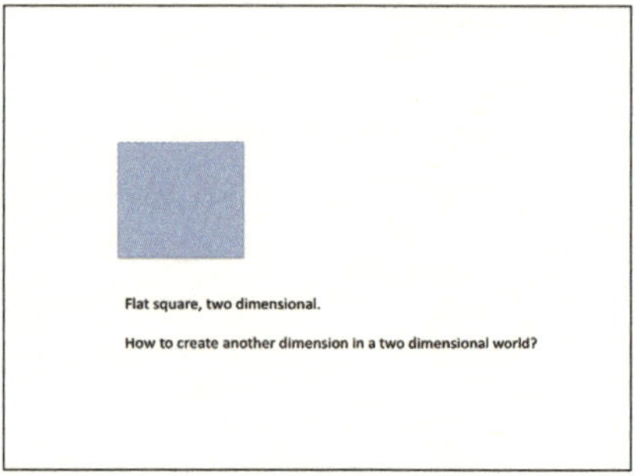

34

35
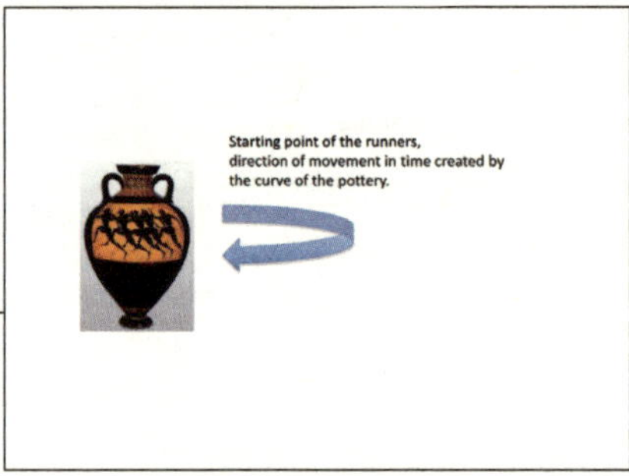

36
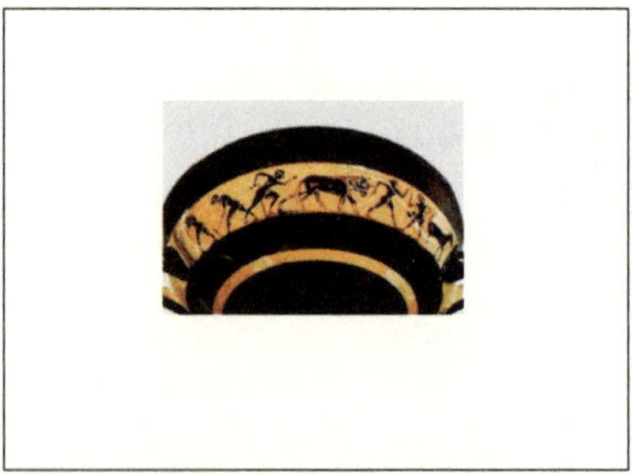

elements stable on the planet, even when we move, we know that it is called gravity, but it took us a while to be convinced that it exists.

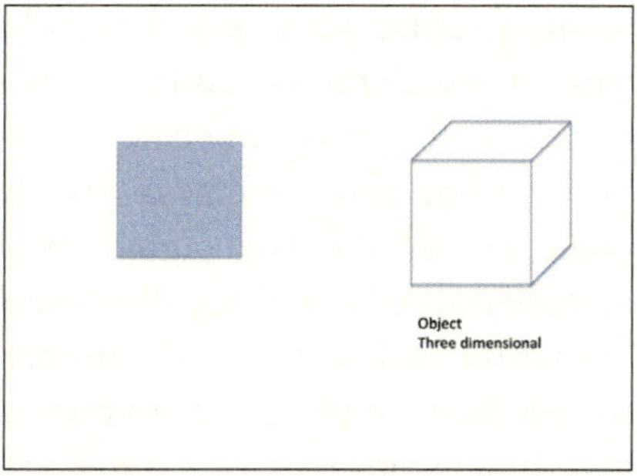

37

38

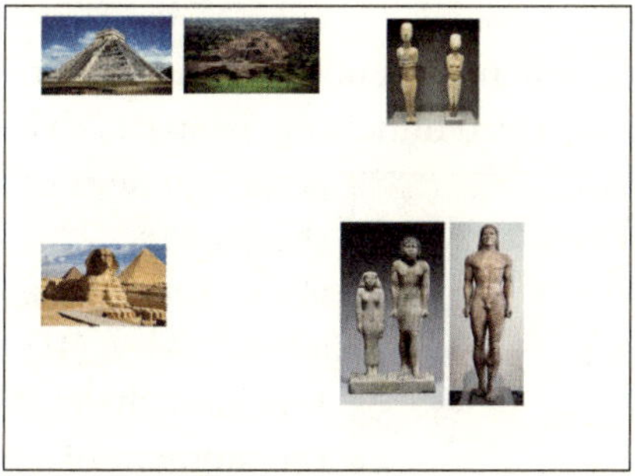

(38) The cube is created when we placed the square in space and there is height and width. There wouldn't be any up and down if we were not able to perceive a square being able to go out of the surface of a flat plane. (39) When we looked around and we tried to represent this third dimension on everything, we used all of our efforts to dominate the planet with height, and when this great invention became the norm, many weapons were created and many wars happened too. For centuries we carried on this conviction, this way of understanding the

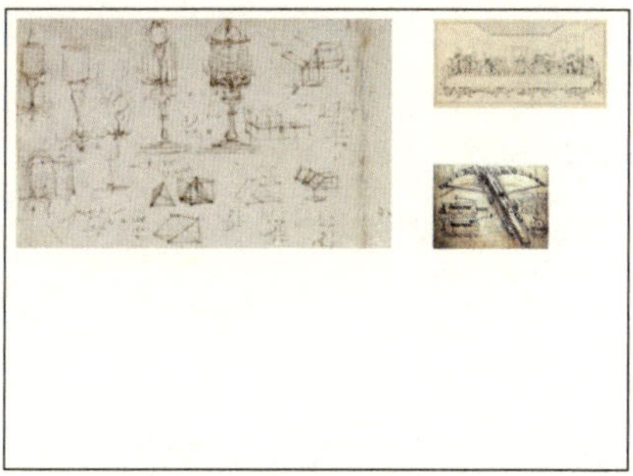

39

world. Conflicts between this and the other, east and west, growing racism and xenophobia, develop from the shift from two-dimensional to three-dimensional perception, and it seems impossible for us to overcome. For all of us to imagine a world that doesn't include only two or three dimensions, but many more, is so difficult because that automatically means that we would need to include in our perception elements and dimensions that we cannot really fully understand measure and control.

(40) For example, when this cube, a three-dimensional object extends its third dimension in space, that is the moment of the *doubling.* That is the *module.* It is a *hyper object.* **(41)** It is how, through the moment of doubling, a three-dimensional object extends its volume in space and creates a fourth dimension. And we know from physics that the fourth dimension is not only *time* but the *projection* of an object in space. But how did this whole idea come to me, how did this happen? Through thinking about

40

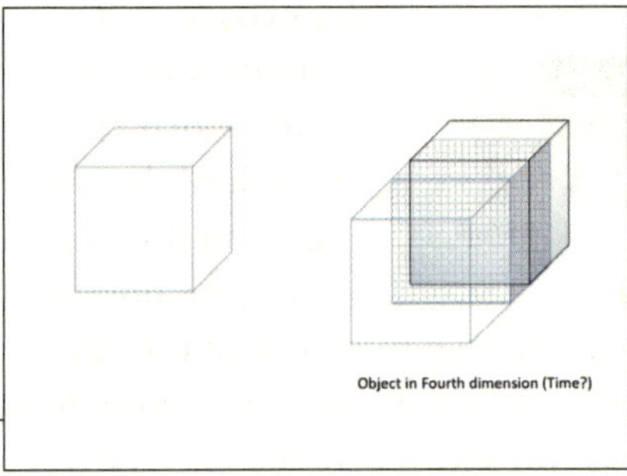

41

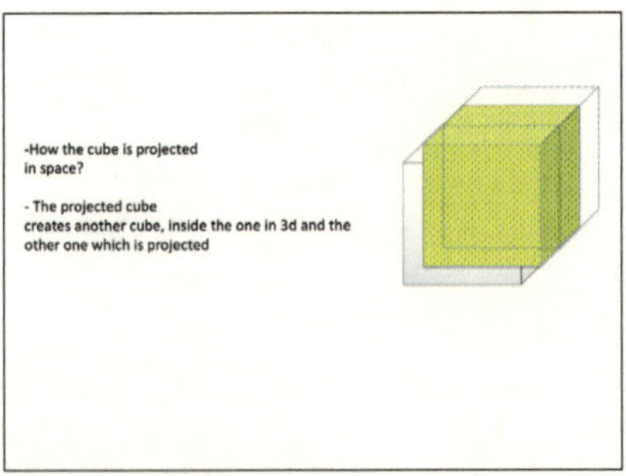

42

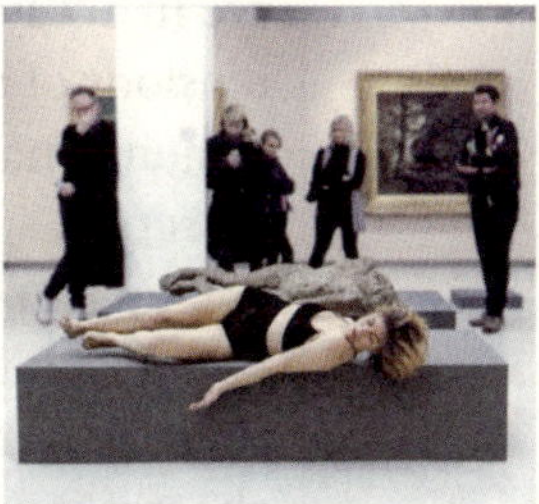

Thank you Rodin (2016) Part of the performance series *Live Portfolio 2011–2016* (2016)
Performance, December 16th 2016, 6–8pm
Installation view National gallery in Prague

performance. **(42)** Many friends and peers were asking me what is the difference of an art object and a performance (object) and I will say that the interesting part of performance is that it brings an extra dimension to visual arts. Performance is

43

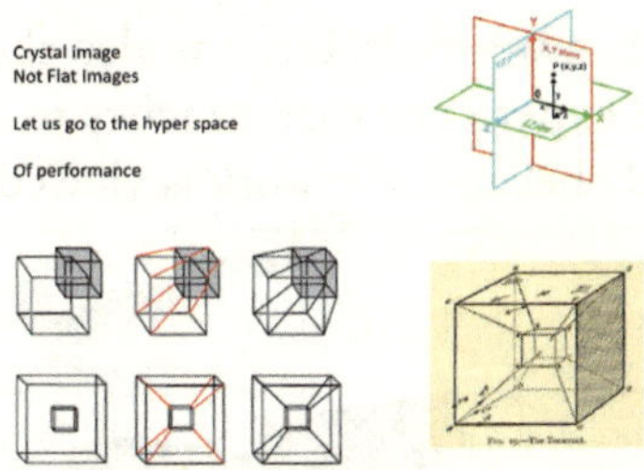

not a time-based medium, but it literally brings an understanding of the fourth dimension to our lives. Exactly because in the moment that an object takes shape, it is also viewed, and it is not only viewed by the one that it is perceiving it but also from the one that it takes its shape from. It is a projection. Performance is the making of a *hyper object*, exactly like what happens when a three-dimensional cube projects and becomes a hyper cube. **(43)** What happens in performance and in the *hyper objects* I have made the past five years, is how a three-dimensional cube extends, projects its three-dimensionality in space and creates a fourth dimension and multiplies. Thus for me, all these works I have been doing since 2014, those *doubled* sculptures, the doubles of doubles,

44

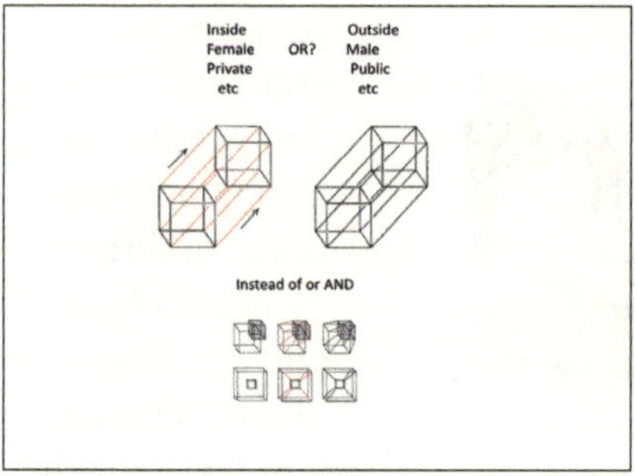

are in a way extensions of three-dimensional objects in space creating an extra dimension by their *modular* character. **(44)** When shifts in perception happen, personal, social, and structural shifts need to happen. **(45)** *Projection* manifests a fourth dimension. When a performance piece takes place, it is not only when we see it, but it is also the shadow, the inscribed experience that attaches to us when we see it. Exactly because the work is viewed at the time that it takes shape, representation happens in our brain (formation in the brain creates its shadow, the projection of the work).

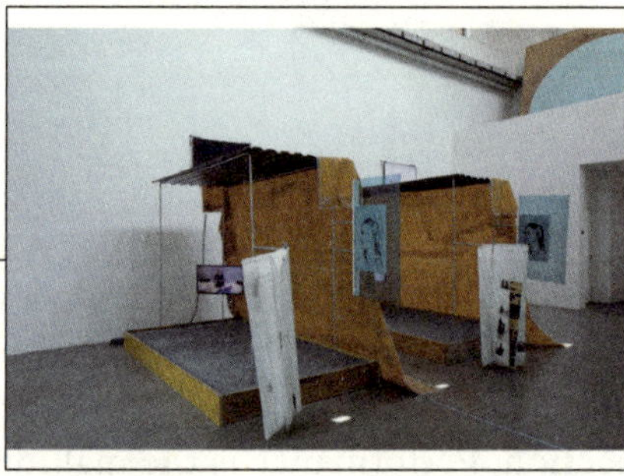

45

(46) We have learned for centuries that there are only three dimensions, but through physics today, we know that there are more than three dimensions. If we apply only two or three dimensions to the way we perceive the world around us, our viewership and making of art today is quite limited. My *hyper objects* demand a shift in perception that cannot stay still, and reject maintaining one focal point and the dichotomy of binary-based structures. (47) The creation of these works autonomously propose their program and technologies (body, emotional and structural attempts, technologies) of how to exist, how to live together in the world, and it is crucial for you to see that the *projection* is not just moving an object from one context to another, it is not a *(ready-made)*, it is not a mirrored object or the bringing of an idea into form *(concept art)*, together in their eventual state. Immediately, the works demand to alter our existing perceptions on how we understand property, to get rid of the conviction that this is the only way we can see things. (48) Each work is not

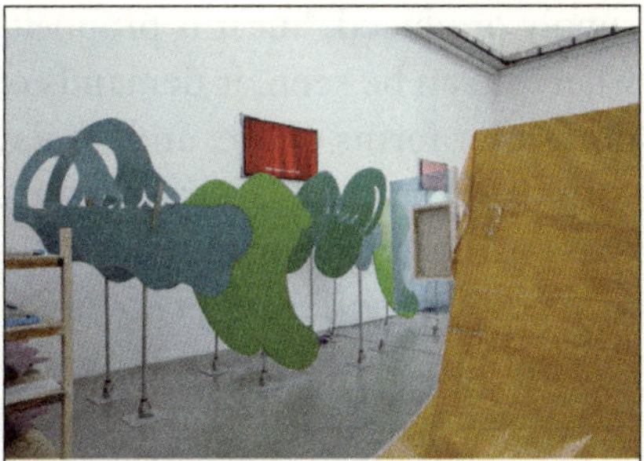

46

47

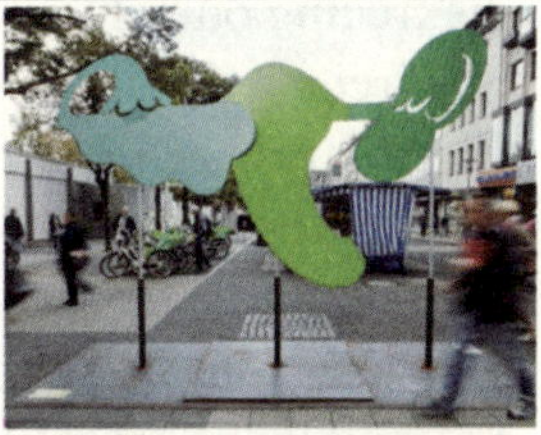

Dynamis (2017) Twenty-eight sculptures and ten breathing scores in Athens and Kassel, aluminum, acrylic paint, glass, rubber, various metallic parts, six days simultaneous performance in Athens and Kassel, *documenta 14*, glass Pavilions Kurt-Schumacher- Straße, Kassel and various public spaces

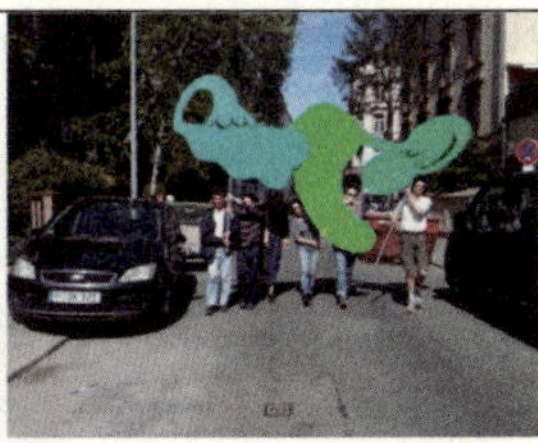

48

Dynamis (2017)
Soma in orgasm as brain, as breast, as ear, as hand, as heart, as leg, as sex
Twenty-eight sculptures, aluminum, acrylic paint, various metallic parts, rubber
max. size 460 × 260 × 30 cm each
Soma in orgasm as sex (2017), demonstration from Portikus to Staedelschule, April 26th 2018

simply produced, but it is proposing its place within where it can be seen, it demands conversation about how other forms of life, and dimensions can coexist with it. My practice is part of a wave of people, entities that spare time to imagine, to discuss and to organize beyond the existing two- and three-dimensional perceptions. In the past fifty years, commercialization has increased, control has grown through technology, and all the ideologies that come either from the left or the right are not relevant anymore. There are two perceptions that are taught about revolution, the one tells us that revolution is freeing ourselves from morals, and the other, that by freeing our morals there is a free market. Both streams are not interesting to me. I am in favor of a history that is not linear, that is not in favor of the grand narrative, of the master; when objects are made from those who are not winning. There is an ongoing underground network of struggles, networks that make things and issues much more complex. (49) There is a wave where struggles are connected and make the issue of revolt much more complex—the connection of the Spanish anarchists of 1936, the revolts of 1848, the Communards of 1871, and what we call today the front line of the demonstration. Historical Materialists, Speculatives, and Accelerationists,

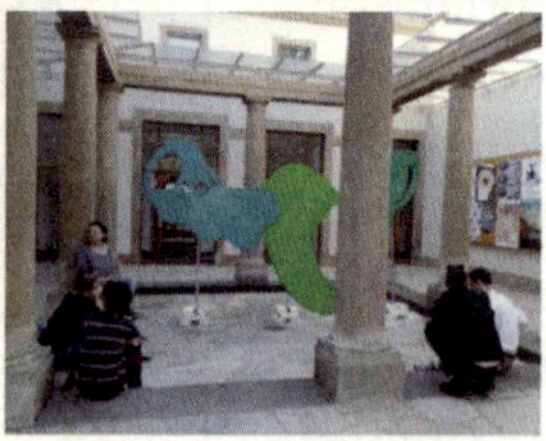

Dynamis (2017)
Soma in orgasm as brain, as breast, as ear, as hand, as heart, as leg, as sex
Twenty-eight sculptures, aluminum, acrylic paint, various metallic parts, rubber
max. size 460 × 260 × 30 cm each
Soma in orgasm as sex (2017), resting at Staedelschule, April 26th 2018

49

left- and right-ideological orthodoxies, oppress us with the metaphysics of an economy that keeps on looking at the world through choice, through dichotomies and binaries. My works are part of a wave that puts life at the front line of the demonstration and a revolutionary animism is cultivated in my practice's discourse and purpose; the distraction of what we call *western* civilization.

Caption: Georgia Sagri, *Art Without Work and Work Without Art*, 2018, PowerPoint presentation, 1–49 slides, dimensions variable.

* **Jonathan Berger**
Archive as Biography: Artist Experiments in Exhibiting Material Culture - Vortrag Curatorial Studies
16 Nov, 19 Uhr, Aula

* **Jochen Volz**
Spiraling Journeys Incerteza Viva - Vortrag Curatorial Studies
22 Nov, 19 Uhr, Aula

* **House of Commons**
Ausstellungseröffnung Portikus
2 Dez, 19 Uhr, Ausstellungsdauer: 3 Dez – 29 Jan

* **Keren Cytter**
Recent Works and More
6 Dez, 19 Uhr, Aula

* **Julia Gelshorn**
Living Networks. Rhizomatic Narration in the Work of

* **Judith Ho**
Up
24 Jan, 19 U

* **Jumana M**
A Magical S
1 Feb, 19 U

* **Helke Ba**
Portikus Ur
2 Feb, 19 U

* **Kerstin S**
Aller Jamai
8 Feb, 19 U

* **Britta Pe**
Skulptur Pr

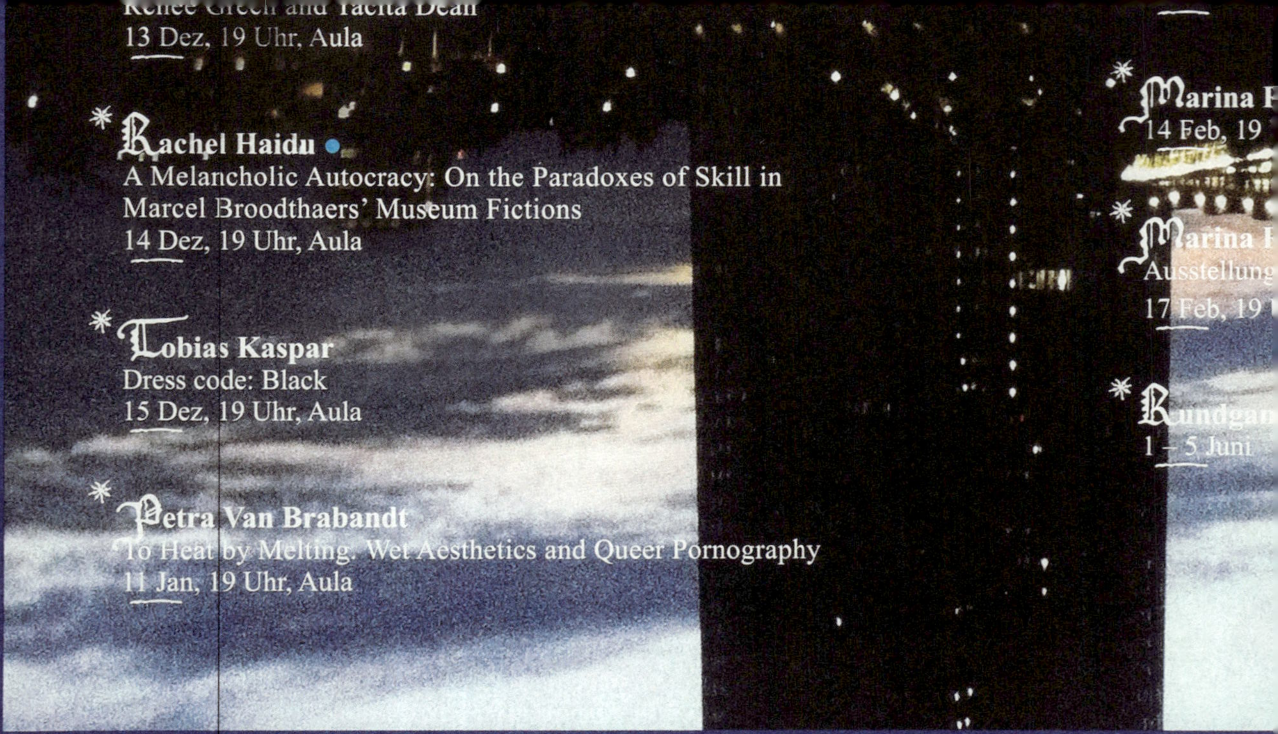

Renee Green and Tacita Dean
13 Dez, 19 Uhr, Aula

* **Rachel Haidu** ●
A Melancholic Autocracy: On the Paradoxes of Skill in Marcel Broodthaers' Museum Fictions
14 Dez, 19 Uhr, Aula

* **Tobias Kaspar**
Dress code: Black
15 Dez, 19 Uhr, Aula

* **Petra Van Brabandt**
To Heat by Melting. Wet Aesthetics and Queer Pornography
11 Jan, 19 Uhr, Aula

* **Marina F**
14 Feb, 19

* **Marina I**
Ausstellung
17 Feb, 19

* **Rundgan**
1 – 5 Juni

January 11, 2017
Petra Van Brabandt

To Heat By Melting. Wet Aesthetics and Queer Pornographic Art

Belgian philosopher Petra Van Brabandt outlines her theories of "wet aesthetics" in this cultural analysis and lecture. Pulling examples from Yves Klein's Anthropometry *paintings, which used women's naked bodies as paintbrushes, to Mona Hatoum's* Corps Étranger, *which took viewers on an endoscopic journey of the artist's body, Van Brabandt describes aesthetic experiences and perceptual interactions with wetness. Topics of objectification are addressed with reference to "gonzo" filming in Internet pornography, while distinctions between queer pornography and queer pornographic art are made, describing the liquefying qualities of queer art and its radical ability to create the feeling of heating by melting.*

What have Cabanel's *The Birth of Venus*, Klein's *Anthropometries*, or Kusama's *Self-Obliteration* in common? What relates Picasso's *Woman Pissing* to Marlene Dumas' watercolors, and Tejal Shah's *Between the Waves*? All these artworks are deploying a wet aesthetics. This refers to an aesthetic experience that is realized by the perceptual interaction with wetness. This wetness can be related to the content, form, medium, or context of the artwork. The countless paintings of naked women bathing in seas, hammams, and ordinary bathtubs, whether or not spied upon by lecherous old men, are the most common examples of how content hints at wet aesthetics. This said, Ed Ruscha's wet word paintings, Carolee Schneemann's *Fuses*, and Joel Cahen's *Wet Sounds* are no less significant form, medium, and context-based examples.

What is remarkable about wet aesthetics is that in many, but not all cases, it affords a strong erotic or sexual resonance. Traditionally, but also in contemporary art, wet aesthetics is not infrequently aiming at an erotic effect on the viewer. This is not surprising; a wet aesthetics produces specific visceral effects in the viewer's body; these are not necessarily sexual stimulation or arousal, but might facilitate these emotions, provided the presence of erotic or sexual signs—think of sexual interactions, nudes, sounds of desire or pleasure …

Wet aesthetics often appears for instance in the context of a carnal aesthetics. Carnal refers here to flesh, of which one of its characteristics is precisely its wetness. Carnal aesthetics, is therefore, a wet aesthetics that plays with the visual, motoric, or tactile characteristics of the (post-)human flesh, and its effects on the viewer. It would be incorrect to state that carnal aesthetics always has an unambiguous erotic dimension; in a lot of cases, it rather produces emotions of terror or disgust. Let's consider for instance Mona Hatoum's *Corps Étranger*, here we are confronted with a radical carnal (and therefore wet) aesthetics resulting in a violent assault on our embodied spectatorship. Whether this assault is void of sexual meaning is difficult to determine; the intimate relation established between the invisible-visible, oneself-other, and outside-inside might have some resonance with Bataille's understanding of eroticism as the affirmation of life up to the point of death. Hatoum takes us on a journey into the wet, red, and beating body of the other, which in normal circumstances is only accessible in the anatomical theater; the latter representing exactly the opposite of what makes this other's body intriguingly alive, and therefore desirable. All things considered, it makes sense to say that a carnal aesthetics is not necessarily sexual in the sense of sexually stimulating or arousing; it can rather drag us into the terror and disgust of life. Paradoxically, this might happen to be the condition of our most violent desires.

Another example of how wet aesthetics establishes an erotic relation with the spectator is Klein's above-mentioned *Anthropometry*. Here, we experience how sexual emotions emerge in the spectator when dry naked bodies meet wet paint. In this sense, Klein's *Anthropometry* is a clear continuation of the tradition of the bathing female nude. The traditional female nude is anything but an instance of wet aesthetics; dryness would definitely be a more appropriate way of qualifying it. The female nude is the representation of the naked female body structured as an object; the image heteronormatively structures the spectator as male. This implies that the erotic effect of the female nude realizes, at most, a possessive desire; the relation between the female nude and the spectator is the relation between a subject that takes an object into its masterful possession. It is the specific visual characteristics of the female nude that account for this relation, Anne Eaton mentions the use of visual metaphor, the positions of surrender and availability, generic beauty, gratuitous nudity … It makes sense to add to this list the dry aesthetics of the female nude, which strengthens its object-like qualities. Imagine one of the many traditional reclining female nudes; notice its shapes and clear contours, distinguished from its surrounding context, contained in a frame, and more often than not, exhibiting sculpture-like qualities, being dry, cold, and firm. The use of oil paint only adds to this quality; as John Berger remarked, oil paint magically turns everything into objects destined to be possessed.

To be perceived as objects of possession, bodies have to be dry; wet bodies slip out of our hands. What is remarkable now is how at the heart of the tradition of the female nude, the bathing female nude sits uncomfortably with its own dry aesthetics. It tests out its limits, significantly confronting itself with a wetness that threatens to flow over the dry objects. Here, the female nude acquires an erotic dimension that goes beyond the desire to possess; it produces the desire to lose oneself in the waves of bodily pleasures. It is exactly this tradition that is echoed in Klein's *Anthropometry*, in which the dry female nudes, the ultimate objects of possession, lose their object-like qualities upon their encounter with the wet paint. At this point, the work evokes desires that are aiming at surrender and gliding. When the wet bodies leave some traces on the wall, we can hardly speak of possession.

The female nude is exemplary of a dry aesthetics, even though the many traditional or more recent artworks of bathing female nudes reveal a tension between dry and wet aesthetics. A more straightforward example of wet aesthetics is Mainstream Internet Pornography (MIP). MIP is characterized by DIY aesthetics. This does not mean that most MIP is amateur pornography; professional producers also adopt these aesthetics because of its popularity. A prominent feature of pornography's DIY aesthetics is "gonzo." Gonzo means that the camera is held by one of the protagonists. In reality, this is rarely the case; there is a shooter who follows the action as closely as possible. Despite the fact that in heterosexual pornography the shooter takes up the male perspective, we can, in gonzo, hardly speak of the construction of the female naked body as an object. This is due to a specific characteristic of gonzo, namely its Breugelian choreography. Most MIP is to the traditional female nude, what a Breugel painting is to traditional landscape painting. In front of a traditional landscape painting, you are invited to overview the land, you are in a steady position of control and mastering the expanse. Now, imagine a typical Breugel painting; you are inclined to zoom in to see the details in the bottom left corner, but seduced to zoom out again to see what happens in the center, then you get impatient to know what happens on the upper right side, so you zoom out, go right, and zoom in again … This is what I call a Breugelian choreography, and it is exactly what happens while watching gonzo pornography. The interesting consequence is that the bodies escape objectification; the viewers are not offered a stable position of overview and control. Any possession is temporary and constantly deconstructed in further movements. Comparing gonzo shooting to more traditional film and video pornography is even more instructive. In traditional pornography, think for instance of the 1970s and 1980s films of Gérard Kikoïne or the more recent work of Marc Dorcel: the camera progresses slowly and retains an outsider-position; the viewer is offered a rather stable overview, regularly interrupted by moments of action and close-ups. In gonzo pornography the viewer is no outsider, she cannot hold the overview, because she is moving on the rhythm of the action. These constant movements that direct the viewer's body are characteristic of a wet aesthetics: what is liquid moves constantly and has no stable position or overview.

A second feature of MIP's wet aesthetics is its use of fluids in the representations of bodies and bodily intercourse. Bodies are wet and oily, irresistible to touch, but impossible to hold. Sweat, sperm, blood, saliva, and milk soften the object's edges and melt down its object-like qualities. The cum-shot is probably the essence of pornography as wet aesthetics. It is a warm, fluid invitation to drown and lose grip. This wetness differs radically from more traditional pornographic film productions, in which signs of sweat, sperm, and juices were avoided. It also breaks with contemporary visual culture and advertising in which the body is disciplined and harnessed as a contained, hygienic, and firm body; a healthy body doesn't leak or overflow. The sweaty, juicy, sperm-covered, bleeding, and blemished pornographic body transgresses these control mechanisms.

And this leads us to the last aspect of mainstream pornography's wet aesthetics, namely its use of taboo fluids. Most of our bodily fluids refer to sexual taboos; they transgress the law that says that our bodies shouldn't show on the outside the dirt of the inside. It is exactly these transgressions that awaken our deepest desires; our bodies react viscerally to the view of taboo fluids, which in a sexual context enhances sexual stimulation and arousal. Using taboo fluids to move the viewer is present in a number of French Extremity films. Claire Denis' *Trouble Every Day*, for instance, is entirely constructed around an aesthetics of blood. She is approving of Bataille's eroticism in her radical interpretation of the love bite: contemporary vampires are reaching for their sexual summits in baths of blood. The soundtrack made by the British band, Tindersticks, supports this blood aesthetics; drums, keyboards, and strings drip and stream blood over the spectator's body. In *Anatomie d'enfer*, Catherine Breillat also explores the sexual potential of blood. She re-appropriates the taboo of woman-as-blood, using the confrontation of a wet aesthetics of blood with a dry aesthetics of the female nude as her dialectical strategy. In *Love*, Gaspar Noé for his part uses 3D technology to explore the arousing potential of sperm. When the sperm flies towards and on the spectator, this realizes a truly un-gendering experience of sexual arousal. And this un-gendering brings us to another genre that extensively plays with wet aesthetics, namely queer pornographic art.

So far, we have said that wet aesthetics has a visceral impact on the spectator's body. In the presence of erotic or sexual signs or contexts, this may lead to sexual stimulation and arousal. More precisely, wet aesthetics plays with fluidity and fluids. Fluidity can refer to wave-like camera movements, dance-like or repetitive body movements, or a sense of gliding that is facilitated by wetness. Such movements are promptly mirrored by the spectator's body, which gives her the physical sensation of moving and gliding herself. Unsurprisingly, these bodily sensations are conducive to sexual stimulation and arousal. A further effect of this fluidity is that it deconstructs our experience of the subject/object divide, and prompts us to experience inter-subjectivity as what Freud called "the oceanic feeling." This experience has further stimulating effects on our bodies. The visceral effect of the perception of (taboo) fluids is a third aspect of how wet aesthetics plays sexual tricks on our bodies. It is in queer pornographic art that these aspects are radically explored, and this in the context of not only a pleasure-positive utopia, but also a queer-normative criticality.

Before we can explore the relation between queer pornographic art and wet aesthetics, there are two issues to straighten out. First, we have to make clear what distinguishes pornographic art from pornography; secondly, we have to consider what this implies for queer pornographic art. The first question is a tough one; it refers to the art philosophical debate on art and pornography. The second one is more of an empirical question. The debate on the compatibility of art and pornography is far from being settled. Those who defend the incompatibility thesis can be divided into two groups: on the one side, you have the "conservatives," who hold that art is beautiful, delicate, and refined, and appeals to our higher aspirations. Since pornography is ugly, repetitive, and vulgar, and involves our base nature, it can never be compatible with art. This position is crude and basic; it starts from a philosophically limited definition of art and pornography. The second defense of the incompatibility thesis is more challenging; it states that art consists of images that aim at a reception that essentially involves attention to form and medium. Pornography, on the other hand, consists of images that aim at a reception that excludes this kind of attention; it invites us to treat images as completely transparent. These two receptions are not compatible, therefore art and pornography are not compatible (Levinson, 2005). This objection to the compatibility of art and pornography raises two problems: firstly, concerning the truthfulness of describing both receptions as above, and secondly, concerning their incompatibility (Maes, 2011). Does art essentially aim at a reception that treats its images as opaque? Does our pornographic attention necessarily exclude appreciation of form, manner, and medium? Even though this position sounds coherent, it seems to be based on a limited experience with art and pornography, and on a suspicion of strong emotions in the experience of art (Prinz and Van Brabandt, 2012). For now, I want to part from this philosophical discussion, and state that a diverse experience with art and pornography, and an appreciation of emotions in the experience of art (Prinz, 2011), call for the compatibility of art and pornography. Pornographic art would then (gradually) differ from pornography in the fact that it integrates a critical and ambitious relation to art history, medium, form, manner, content or context—think for instance of Jean Genet's *A Song of Love* or Alina Reyes' *The Butcher.* Pornographic art, therefore, affords a pornographic reception that is achieved in artistically or aesthetically successful ways.

Now, what does this tell us about queer pornographic art and its distinction from queer pornography? Queer pornography is in itself critical of heteronormative society, and its visual culture and pornography. Its pornographic success is therefore realized as criticality; it deconstructs familiar sexual responses and tries to produce arousal in response to queer images. This condition, however, is not sufficient to recognize something as queer pornographic art. Queer pornography is recognized as art, as far as it is recognized as relevant to the contemporary art world and theory, including art history, medium, form, context, but also artistic and institutional authority. Some queer pornographers purposely limit the distribution of their work to the art world to safeguard their artistic authority and keep control over the viewing conditions. This is all the more relevant when the viewing conditions are an essential part of the work. The viewing conditions can, for instance, be an important feature of the wet aesthetics of an artwork, as is the case in Tejal Shah's *Between the Waves*. *Between the Waves* is a five-screen surround installation consisting of video, animation, and collage. The viewing conditions determine that the viewer is surrounded by images, which realize a fluid, and at times, submerged viewing experience. The spectator has no outsider position; she drowns in images.

To spell out the relation between queer pornographic art and wet aesthetics, it is important to state that not all queer pornographic art is characterized by wet aesthetics. The aesthetic experience that a wet aesthetics afford, however, is compatible with the aims of queer pornographic art. Queer pornography and art envision a queering of mainstream pornography. If sexual identity and orientation, beauty, fetishes, and taboos are socially constructed in performative repetitions, then, according to queer theory, we can also deconstruct them by means of performance and role-play. In this view, desire emerges in the sexual interaction; it is not located in identity or orientation, nor does it precede or predetermine the sexual interaction. Queer pornography and art, therefore, is deconstructive, emancipating, and pleasure-positive. For this, it deploys a radical DIY aesthetics and often also a wet aesthetics.

Queer pornographic art uses wet aesthetics to heat us by melting. The effect on our bodies is melting; we lose stable solidity, and it is exactly this melting that produces sexual stimulation and arousal (heat). This is realized in several ways. First, fluids speak to our hands and skin and awaken a frenzy of the touch. Second, fluids produce fluids: our mouth produces saliva and our vagina gets wet. More, being surrounded by images (of water) makes us gasp for air, which intensifies our bodily sensations. Further, the fluid movements move our body; the spectator's body mirrors the movements on screen. Additionally, we react viscerally to the sight of taboo fluids. Lastly, the fluidity of the subject/object position invites us to leave our stable identity for an oceanic feeling. By means of this wet aesthetics, wet queer pornography conveys that the object (of desire) is slippery and cannot be possessed. More radically, the subject/object distinction is overridden by movement and dance, resulting in the more primitive oceanic position in which the subject doesn't acknowledge where her body ends and the other's starts. The fluids that are culturally structured as taboos are re-appropriated here in a joyful movement, and the fluidity of sexual fetish, identity, orientation, beauty, and bodies is stressed. The waves of flesh and the abundance of desire install a queer-normative pornutopia, which is attributed a regenerative and restorative function.

Queer pornographic art is not innovative in its use of wet aesthetics. Art and visual culture show many instances of wet aesthetics; its success lies in its visceral effects on the body of the viewer. Queer pornographic art, however, has radicalized wet aesthetics in promising ways; it realizes its visceral, motoric, and tactile potential in a liquefying, emancipatory, and sex-positive project. The viewer experiences queer pornography's wet aesthetics as heating by melting. It radically decenters our subject/object experience and our fixed sexual identities, orientations, fetishes, norms of beauties, and bodies. We are seduced into a sex-positive re-appropriation of bodily fluids, and our experience of desire and pleasure is reconstructed as dispossession, abundance, and surrender—an oceanic dance.

References

— Berger, John, *Ways of Seeing*, London 1972.
— Eaton, Anne W., "What's Wrong with the (Female) Nude? A Feminist Perspective on Art and Pornography," eds. H. Maes and J. Levinson, *Art & Pornography*, Oxford 2012, pp. 277–308.
— Levinson, Jerrold, "Erotic Art and Pornographic Pictures," *Philosophy and Literature*, 29, 2005, pp. 228–240.
— Maes, Hans, "Art or Porn: Clear Division or False Dilemma?" *Philosophy and Literature*, 35 (1), 2011.
— Prinz, Jesse, "Emotion and Aesthetic Value," *The Aesthetic Mind: Philosophy and Psychology*, eds. E. Schellekens and P. Goldie, Oxford 2011.
— Prinz, Jesse, and Van Brabandt, Petra, "Why Do Porn Films Suck?" eds. H. Maes & J. Levinson, *Art & Pornography*, Oxford 2012, pp. 161–190.

…schule * Vorträge und
…gen Wintersemester 2016–17

* **Birgit Megerle**
Transparented
12 Jan, 19 Uhr, Aula

* **Amalia Ulman**
Privilege
17 Jan, 19 Uhr, Aula

* **John Roberts**

Problems. Deskilling and Reskilling in Contemporary Art
18 Jan, 19 Uhr, Aula

* **The Value of Critique**
Symposium mit Luc Boltanski, Sabeth Buchmann, Rainer Forst, Petra Gehring, Eva Geulen, Isabelle Graw, Klaus Günther, Rahel Jaeggi, Bruno Latour, Thomas Lemke, Christoph Menke, Juliane Rebentisch, John Roberts, Martin Seel, Beate Söntgen, Kerstin Stakemeier
Konzept: Isabelle Graw & Christoph Menke, eine Kooperation der Städelschule und dem Exzellenzcluster "Die Herausbildung normativer Ordnungen", Goethe-Universität Frankfurt am Main
19 – 20 Jan

* **Judith Hopf**
Up
24 Jan, 19 Uhr, Aula

* **Jumana Manna**
A Magical Substance Flows Into Me
1 Feb, 19 Uhr, Aula

n Exhibiting
es

uratorial Studies

December 7, 2016
Willem de Rooij and
Philippe Pirotte

Dutch artist Willem de Rooij and rector Philippe Pirotte host a public talk on the occasion of De Rooij's solo exhibition Entitled *at Museum für Moderne Kunst in Frankfurt in 2016–17. Subjects of museological orthodoxies and the value of physical exhibitions arise, alongside recurring themes of collaboration and exploitation, image and content use, and the process of collecting objects. De Rooij discusses creating the video* Junks *and the political implications of his slide projection* Orange, *both made with his former collaborator Jeroen de Rijke (1970–2006). Reflecting upon his interests in pan-cultural fantasy, most notably shown in the workgroup Fong Leng, De Rooij positions himself an archeologist of the recent past, committed to questioning modes of representation.*

PP Good evening, everybody. Good evening, Willem de Rooij. Tonight, we are at the Museum für Moderne Kunst and the exhibition *Entitled* is all around us. Willem, perhaps you could start by introducing the three main works that are presented here.

WdR This exhibition combines three groups of works and each group has a slightly different status. The area that we are seated in now is an archive of newspaper clippings, which I collected from 2000 until 2002. It is existing material that is brought into this particular context by me. Another group of works is a three-dimensional collage of existing objects created by the Dutch fashion designer Fong Leng. The tracksuits that you see presented in the spaces around you were all produced from the mid-1980s until the early 1990s. Over the past nine years, I have collected around two hundred objects made by Fong Leng, a selection of which is presented in this exhibition. The third group of works is the weavings that you see hanging on the walls. These are woven objects that I have been producing since 2009 in collaboration with a weaver in Potsdam.

PP While preparing for this talk, I came across something that I did not know, and that is that you started your career as an Art History student at the University of Amsterdam.

WdR Yes, I was preparing for art school and like many young art students I did not have a full portfolio of work that I could show to the committee. After high school, I took a year to produce those works and study art history. I knew from the outset that I would not finish my studies at the university, but I was interested in the subject matter and I wanted to understand how the university system worked. After that, I went to the Rietveld Academy in Amsterdam to study Art.

PP Art history remains an important factor in many of your works. In 2010, you made a book for your exhibition *Intolerance* at the Neue Nationalgalerie in Berlin. That book was motivated by an art historical desire and it contains a piece of art history that did not exist before. Could you tell us about that project?

WdR At the Neue Nationalgalerie, I created an installation in which I showed two groups of existing works by other artists. The exhibition included eighteen paintings by Melchior d'Hondecoeter—a Dutch bird painter from the seventeenth century—and twelve feathered objects from eighteenth century Hawaii. While I was preparing for this clash of objects, so to say, I found that there was virtually no literature available on either of these groups of works. So I produced the books that I myself would have wanted to read when I started that project. I made the first comprehensive publication about Melchior d'Hondecoeter, with essays by Marrigje Rikken and Lisanne Wepler, listing about two hundred of his works. Simultaneously, we produced a *catalogue raisonné* of all the feathered objects in Hawaii known to date, written by Adrienne

Kaeppler. With those two books I wanted to generate scholarly research that had not yet been produced. An important aspect was to highlight the difference between my expertise as a visual artist and the expertise of art historians or ethnographers: I do not want people to think that I see myself as an ethnographer or an art historian. These books have a very particular function in my thinking about art.

PP The exhibition here at the Museum für Moderne Kunst is called *Entitled*. "Entitled" as a verb refers to the act of naming something, but as an adjective, the word has a very different connotation. It means that one believes oneself to be deserving of certain privileges or special treatment. Were both of these meanings important to you when you came up with the title for this exhibition? Or is it rather a post-conceptual joke that mocks the self-reflexivity of giving titles to exhibitions?

WdR Probably all of the above. I find titles very meaningful. They are carriers of meaning that operate almost separately from the artwork. Sometimes I use anagrams as titles for my works. I will make an anagram of the name "Susanne Gaensheimer" for example, the director of this museum, or "Frankfurt am Main," which gives me the opportunity to hide contextual information in a title. Not long ago, I made an exhibition at the Kunstverein in München called *Untilted*. "Untilted" refers to something that is straight, not tilted, but it is also an anagram of the word "untitled."

For this exhibition, I liked the word "entitled" because it made me think of the word "untilted," but it is just a little different. And as you said, it means "having a title."

PP The word "entitled" sounds very sovereign, almost arrogant.

WdR Well, that is one possible reading of the word. I do not believe the word "entitled" contains arrogance in itself, but it refers to arrogance. It refers to that very specific type of arrogance that is fueled by the belief that one can lay claim to a particular position by right of birth, by right of location, by right of physical properties, and so on and so forth. There is a woven wall piece in the show, called *Pink*. It is made of ten different threads of synthetic sewing thread. All those threads are made into a new thread that produces a shimmering shade of pink. When I made the piece, I was thinking of how schoolchildren always draw a white person in pink. Obviously, we are talking about a cliché, a culturally coded commonplace of how to read a skin color, but for me, the color pink has to do with my own physical properties. There are a number of other clues in this show that refer to these kinds of questions.

PP Color definitely has great resonance in this exhibition. At the entrance of the museum, we encounter *Bouquet 4*, a gigantic flower arrangement of white flowers with a wonderful scent. Knowing that most of your objects function as catalysts that mobilize different contexts of meaning, what meaning do you want your viewers to read in a white bouquet of flowers?

WdR I wanted to make a white flower piece for a very long time, but I found it difficult to do that. I was always afraid that the work would look like a flower arrangement for a wedding or a funeral. I have spent quite some time thinking about the scale of the bouquet and the kind of flowers it should contain. When I finally created the piece, as it is on display in this exhibition, I liked the fact that it consists of so many different flowers. No two flowers are alike and yet all of them are white. There is difference and there is sameness, and that for me is the spine of that piece. Of course, when I think about the color white, I also think about "white-ness." Whiteness is important in the spaces that we are in, the so-called white cubes. It is also a theoretical trope that is used in the field of identity discourse. Basically, the white piece is the counterpart of the pink piece. They are two different ways of looking at how to talk about a color that both of them are not.

PP Clearly, meaning cannot be inherent in the object itself. When we talk about the artwork as a catalyst, it is all about how things have been arranged, put together, juxtaposed, or in which context they are shown. The exhibition includes the slide projection, *Orange*. The caption suggests a whole variety of possible interpretations, some of them overtly political, others not at all.

WdR I do not want to impose a specific recipe of how

to think about a color. I have very strong associations with certain colors, and I attribute a number of specific meanings to colors in the same way other people do. For Jeroen de Rijke (with whom De Rooij collaborated from 1994–2006) and me, *Orange* was a particularly pressing and important piece to make. In 2004–05, nationalism in the Netherlands became an important social phenomenon and orange, the Dutch national color, became more and more visible in the public sphere. Companies started to use orange in their logos and commercials. There was an understanding that the concept of national pride was magically projected onto any object that was colored orange. To me, that was extremely oppressive. Orange can be a very alarming visual marker in a field of other colors. The increasing presence of orange in the public sphere was a highly problematic and very unwelcome development in my visual world, so I was trying to understand what that meant for me. At the same time, I was aware that for the prisoners in Guantanamo Bay, the color orange has a very different connotation. That is why I added such an elaborate caption to the work—I was trying to outdo the first interpretation by the second.

PP Wasn't there also a reference to skin color, in the sense that the color orange is impossible to represent in certain photographic media?

WdR That is right. The eighty-one monochrome orange slides projected in this exhibition are analogue photographs. Now, most analogue photographic and slide material that was used at the time—from Agfa or Fuji let's say—was specifically designed to make the skin of white people look good. The color orange was excluded from the spectrum of photographic materials to avoid the risk that a white person would look orange in a particular light. Jeroen de Rijke and I did not know that. We tried to photograph different shades of orange and our photographs always came out yellow or pink, never orange. Then we performed all sorts of tricks with filters, lights, and other colors, to get the orange color out in a spectrum that did not actually provide it. That is how we discovered the notion of exclusion within the material that we wanted to use.

PP When you talk about exclusion, it might be interesting to move to another subject matter that is very apparent in your work: the paradoxical reflection about concepts such as exclusion, extraction, and exploitation. Ironically, extraction and exploitation seem fundamental to the creation and production of culture, when culture is defined as the adaptation of natural, cultural, or other resources towards the creation of symbolic value. In your work, you approach this paradox in a rather referential way, but sometimes also—and I am thinking about the weavings here—in a more formal way. The whole idea of extracting an aspect or an affect out of a broader set of materials or a broader set of things, and setting it apart in order to focus on it, seems inevitable. Is it possible to produce culture without exploitation?

And isn't every collaboration somehow a form of exploitation? Today, it is impossible for an artist to make use of appropriations and extractions without a thorough reflection of who is represented, who might be exploited, and who might be the owner or the co-owner of that subject matter.

WdR I have collaborated with many people in my work. I think everybody does. There is no artist who works alone. In my case, these collaborations have taken on many different forms. My collaboration with Jeroen de Rijke lasted for twelve years and it was one where we shared authorship. We both had equal status within the collaborative relationship. When I work together with the weaving workshop in Potsdam, there is a completely different form of collaboration. I go to the workshop with a very particular idea and although I develop it together with the weavers, I will be the author of the work. There are collaborations with filmmakers and photographers, who document my work. What is a collaboration? What is an appropriation? When does an appropriation become exploitation? Or when does collaboration become exploitation? Collaboration and exploitation are two sides of the same coin, which is interesting and exhausting at the same time. Like in any relationship, the interaction between an artist and the people surrounding her or him has many different aspects, and the boundaries are often blurred. I am interested in those grey zones, rather than in the extremities.

PP For me, a pivotal work in this exhibition is the video piece *Junks*. It is small, but extremely effective. The junkies are being filmed while we hear you and Jeroen give them instructions—stand still, hold your pose, etc. What is the status of the protagonists in that film? What level of agency do those junks have? And is there not a serious level of objectification going on?

WdR Of course there is because there is a camera between us. Whenever there is a camera in the room, you cannot avoid objectification. A camera is a very powerful tool. No matter where it is in the room, it has a very strong presence and its implications—whether you are the photographer or the model—are always very impactful. When Jeroen and I made this piece, we wanted to talk about exactly that. What happens to people when that powerful tool is between them? What happens to the photographer? What happens to the model? The way that you hear us talk to these models will not be different from any other set where photographers talk to their models. Models cannot see themselves, so they have to be told what to do. That is how photos are made, and there is usually no time and no budget for pleasantry. The difference with our models was that they were drug users, living in the red-light district in Amsterdam. That is where we depicted them. We produced a set in the middle of the night on the street where they moved around, either having just scored some drugs or on the lookout for it. Jeroen and I were students with very little money, so we offered them half a liter of beer for three minutes of their work. We asked them to stand still for three minutes, which is not so easy, especially not when you are in a state like that. The video registers a push and pull between us and them. We wanted them to stand still, and they wanted to get that beer and cut the three minutes in half. What you hear is that negotiation, which was one of the things that we were particularly interested in.

PP A lot of your work, or rather the way that you install many of your works, is a direct reflection on the museum and on what you call the "mutual exploitation" between the artist and the museum.

WdR Yes, making this exhibition, for example, has been a fantastic exchange. It is a collaboration, if you wish, or perhaps even a mutual exploitation between myself and the Museum für Moderne Kunst. I have received a lot of space and a lot of opportunity to do with these spaces as I wish. There were also restrictions, which is always the case if you work on an exhibition in a museum. In this case, we have discussed different ways in which to show the works. What will be on exhibit, how many works will be included, how much empty space will there be, and so on and so forth. This is very important for me because I not only show the works but I also show the institution where they are presented. In the end, I came up with a scenario where these three groups of works form an even pattern, almost like a wallpaper that feels similar in every corner of the exhibition. It was an explicit wish from the museum that we break this overall grid and stick a pin in this hermetic idea that I had. It produced another sense of balance in the thinking about the work on display.

PP There is a very early work in the show called *Hut*. It was created in 1993, and you have never shown it before. For me, that piece can be understood as a premonition of a reflection on museological ideologies, how they function, how they create and erase contexts.

WdR I was a second-year art student and I was interested in museological orthodoxies or structures. Nowadays, students travel far and beyond, but in those days we stayed pretty much in Amsterdam and we looked at what was around us. I was interested in the institutions that were there: the Rijksmuseum, which shows old Dutch art, the Stedelijk Museum, which shows international contemporary art, and the Tropenmuseum, which shows ethnographic art. *Hut* was inspired by a postcard from the Tropenmuseum depicting a traditional hut from West Java in Indonesia, as it was displayed at the museum at the time. The hut was reconstructed within the museum building, so it was a house within a house. The piece *Hut* consists of two postcards: the original postcard, as well as a copy of that same card on which everything surrounding the hut (the exhibition room in which it was reconstructed) is covered with black gouache. I tried to imagine what that hut would look like if it were not in a museum.

Then, I imagined what West Java would look like because I had never been there before. *Hut* was basically an imagined study of the context and the origins of the object.

PP In a lot of your work, appropriated or not, there is a desire to infuse self-evident, normative western culture with ingredients from somewhere else. We have this wonderful weaving here, called *Taping Precognitive Tribes*, an anagram of Andy Warhol's *Big Retrospective Painting* of 1979. It seems as if you want to overrule a possible, self-proclaimed icon of western art—the art-historical concept of the retrospective—and confront it with a more problematic concept drawn from the history of anthropology.

WdR I am trying to study those orthodoxies, but at the same time, I am indebted to them. I was brought up in them. They mean a lot to me. However, in the course of growing up, I have come to understand that they are mere orthodoxies. We have to learn what is interesting about them and revise what is flawed. How do we categorize objects that are not from this cultural sphere? Why do we categorize them at all? Why are they even here? I also think about the status of the art space. What does the space that we are in mean without art? What are these spaces and why do they look the way they do? I am trying to look at many different sides of the museological industry because it harbors my work. I do not see myself as someone who criticizes museums. Museums are terribly important. Their core business is to take care of the artwork, and I hope that will happen to some of my works when I cannot take care of them anymore. However, it is a job that is invisible to the greater public and it can be a very hard cause to raise funds for. I think many artists place their trust in museums, but the museological orthodoxies need to be looked at. Even if we do not revise them, we should consider them, analyze them, and finally, understand that they are orthodoxies.

PP What was your motivation to collect the sportswear by Fong Leng? This is the first time that I have seen so many tracksuits in one of your exhibitions. Was this collection inspired by a museological impulse to save this cultural production from oblivion?

WdR I collected these tracksuits for the same reason that I bring other existing materials together, such as the paintings by Melchior d'Hondecoeter and the feathered objects from Hawaii. The tracksuits form a crucial part of Fong Leng's *œuvre* that has not been collected, not been written about, and not been shown until I started to do that. In the 1960s or 1970s, Fong Leng was well-known for making high fashion: unique pieces for very particular clients. In the 1980s, she started making tracksuits. These objects were made for huge groups of people, as tracksuits are, and they are quite different from the couture objects she made before. I became interested in them because they contain a host of cultural markers, and I think that now, thirty years later, we can observe them and try to understand them for what they really mean. On the other hand, I have always been interested in cataloguing objects that are not canonical. Fong Leng's tracksuits are not *haute couture*, just as Melchior d'Hondecoeter is not Johannes Vermeer. I have no interest in telling everybody that Vermeer is a great painter. That is not a statement that I need to make. Similarly, Yves Saint Laurent was a more innovative designer than Fong Leng, and Fong Leng's leather couture pieces are more innovative than these tracksuits. I am not here for us to state what we already know. What I try to investigate is what is exciting about these tracksuits.

PP They were actually quite popular in the Netherlands. The signifiers she mobilizes on those prints are very strange. They go from African to Navajo to Chinese embroidery.

WdR Yes, there are many cultural signifiers that are rather unspecific, so you get a fantasized meaning, a pan-cultural fantasy sphere. That must have appealed to buyers at the time. What I find interesting about that, is that I could not imagine the same thing happening today. Multicultural markers have gone out of fashion. But I am still very interested in the idea of multiculturalism and I detect a very commercialized ideology behind these tracksuits. That is one of the things that I found fascinating about them. What I also like about them is that they have been created by a woman who started making objects for the few and then decided to make objects for the many. The difference between the individual and the group or the place for the individual within the group, are concepts that are hinted at in different areas of this exhibition. My aim was to bring these tracksuits together and suggest different social constellations.

PP The often-strained relationship between the individual and the group is especially present in the newspaper clippings called *Index: Riots, Protest, Mourning and Commemoration (as represented in newspapers, January 2000–July 2002).* Basically, it is an archive of social uprising in that period of time. I must admit I have a bit of trouble with the work because it is so beautiful. The installation of the work in this long corridor and the way the clippings are laid out, somehow suggest a frivolous choreography. When you enter the room, you almost feel compelled to move along rhythms suggested by the layout of the photographs. That stands in stark contrast to the gravity of the subject matter, which would probably demand a more solemn contemplation from the viewer.

WdR If you feel there is a frivolous character in the work, do you think that it has to do with the composition and the placement of these frames in the room, or do you think that it has to do with the photographs themselves?

PP I think it probably has to do with the composition of each frame and the effect the multiplied frames have on you as a viewer. Clearly, they are not the same, they are all different, but the composition seems to neutralize the subject matter. At the same time, the succession of frames induces a movement, which is frivolous.

WdR These images were collected over a period of two years and they are organized in chronological order on eighteen panels. One of the things that fascinated me about these images was that they were all so beautiful. I was still living in the Netherlands at the time, which is a very image-driven society, and Dutch newspapers would hire very talented and active image editors. You would buy your paper with a stunning image on the cover and that image would sell the newspaper—not the headline, the image. I found it interesting that these images were actively used to sell the content, but why not? I am not here to police the aesthetic quality of an image and how that quality should relate to its content. I am here to question those relationships.

PP You have said that the work is about how people create strategies of appearing in the press.

WdR That is certainly how I look at these images. I was surprised by the similarities between the different images. Like you said, the multitude of images undermines the individual meaning of each picture. I totally agree. That is then, in the end, the effect. But what I found important is that the people depicted in these images, seem to copy each other as well. There appears to be an iconography of protest that all these protesters know about. Certain poses simply look better than others, and we remember them from images of previous protest marches. Even the press photographers that cover the protests seem to be aware of other kinds of iconographies. There are images of mourning that look like fourteenth century Italian paintings. Those iconographic traditions are still used in news media today. Therefore, I think the beauty and the relative frivolity that trouble you are produced within the images themselves, not just within the compositions that I made.

PP It struck me because the piece is made in 2003. A year earlier, documenta 11 produced a catalogue, in which the first fifty pages contained similar images. It forced the artworks in the exhibition to compete with the content of those images, which I thought was a very problematic competition. By investigating the beauty and the strategies of self-staging individuals, your approach is completely different. However, it is clear that these kinds of images became an issue in art discourse around that time.

WdR There was a renewed interest in protest at that moment. After the anti-globalization protests in Genoa and Seattle, there was an appetite for it. Protest was seen as a plausible mode of action and as such, it gained visibility.

PP My last question relates to your strategies for creating these compositions. It is interesting that you do not reconcile the heterogeneous elements with a discursive narrative. You bring them together through the medium of the exhibition, or through the medium of showing, or through the medium of the composition within each frame or a collage of pictures. What do you think about the possibilities of the exhibition as a medium today? A lot of art is brought together by narrative discourse, and the interest in the importance of the physical exhibition as a medium seems to be waning.

WdR I think it is important that an exhibition has an author. Nowadays, a lot of shows are based on a compromise and I think that is the end of the exhibition. It is very understandable that this should be the case and there are many factors that play into this dynamic, but I do think that an exhibition, just like an artwork, begins and ends with an author and the author needs to have the last word.

PP What do you think about the physicality of the exhibition? Do you think there is an urgency to the physical exhibition?

WdR I have been discussing this issue with Klaus Görner, the curator with whom I developed this exhibition. We have been working on the documentation because the installation of the artworks in the space became so important. When I make my work, I am very aware that I create it in order to be seen and experienced in reality. At the same time, I understand the importance of documentation. After the opening of this exhibition, people came to tell me how happy they were to see some of my weavings in reality, because to their surprise they look quite different than documentation circulating online. To me, that indicates that we have reached a point where people believe that the documentation is an accurate representation of the work. It will continue to be interesting to think about documentation in the future and to clarify that the image you see is not actually the piece. By experiencing the piece, there is something else at stake, something else at work, and there is another experience and another gratification to be gained.

Question

I have a question related to the orthodoxies you study. What methods do you use to research or question or investigate museological orthodoxies because it must be incredibly timeconsuming?

WdR That is a very broad question, but I can give you an example. There is a piece in this exhibition that was made in 1993 at the Stedelijk Museum in Amsterdam. I photographed the corners of a number of exhibition rooms where artworks were on display. I tried to photograph each corner in exactly the same way so that each corner was cropped in the same way, but they were all images of different rooms. That is how I analyze the space and the physical properties of the space. The piece highlights the differences between those rooms, but also their sameness. They are all distinctly different, yet made out of the same elements (wood and plaster), so the photographs become a scan of the orthodoxies of museum architecture. Of course, there can be different methodologies at work. When we talk about the orthodoxies of how to have yourself depicted when you are protesting for or against something, I use the same comparative method, but perhaps in a less systematic and more frivolous manner. They are two different ways of studying the different aspects of an orthodoxy.

Question

Many of your works focus on how different institutions select and represent artworks. How do you deal with selection and representation within your own work? For the newspaper clippings, you have selected images from hundreds of available images. In the bouquets, there is a totally different process of selection going on, and you have also selected the tracksuits by Fong Leng. How do you decide that you will use an object as a material for your work?

WdR Actually, you are talking about three very different examples here. In the case of a flower piece, somebody else made the selection. I will come up with the idea, go to a florist, ask for a flower piece with one hundred different flowers, and see what comes out. I like to be surprised by someone else's selection. In the case of the tracksuits, the selection took place over a period of eight years. As the collection grows, certain pieces are disposed of, while others are added to the collection. It is a natural process that only gets analyzed afterward. What is interesting about this process is that there is very little known about these tracksuits. Fong Leng does not want to talk about them. So my selection is based purely on what I see in front of me, which makes it a very strange exercise. I feel almost like an archeologist of the recent past, thoroughly studying all the objects. Is there a label? How are they stitched? What are similarities between different pieces? Might they have come from the same workshop? This is very speculative and interesting work, and it is an ongoing process. It is like working with materials that you know almost nothing about.

Question

Is it an initial impulse for you to use materials that you know nothing about? When I walk through your exhibition, there is a homogeneity of course, because you create all the works. But there is also a strong sense of detachment, opaqueness, de-contextualization, and even an act of abstraction. I was wondering if it is necessary for you to not know about these objects before you start working with them and do you wish to recreate that setting for an audience?

WdR I don't actively set out to search for something about which nothing is known. Clearly, I will find it more interesting. Like I said, I will not be able to add much to the discourse about Johannes Vermeer. There have been so many fantastic scholars publishing and investigating the work of this artist. I do not have a lot to add to that. Moreover, if I find existing materials, then that is what they are to me: materials. I need to be able to work with them and make them my own.

I need to be able to make them into something else. In the end, I am not a fan of flowers or tracksuits—I am after something else. That is why I find it so important that I can use these objects as materials, apart from what they otherwise represent.

Question

You use them in the sense that they remain loudly mute.

WdR I would hope so, yes. That sounds good to me.

St äd

22. April
Gabi Ngcobo
Künstlerin/Kuratorin
19 Uhr
Weltkulturen Museum

23. April
Zin Taylor
Künstler

24. April

28. April
Loretta Fahrenho
Künstlerin

29. April
Barbara Klemm,
Künstlerin,
Anne-Marie
Beckmann,
Kuratorin und
Barbara Basting,

el so

Sommer

11. Mai
Minouk Lim
Künstlerin

13. Mai
Minouk Lim
19 Uhr, Portikus
"United Paradox"
Ausstellungseröffnung

15. Mai

21. Mai
Bouchra Khalili
Künstlerin

26. Mai
Bisi Silva
Kuratorin

27. Mai
Paul O'Neill

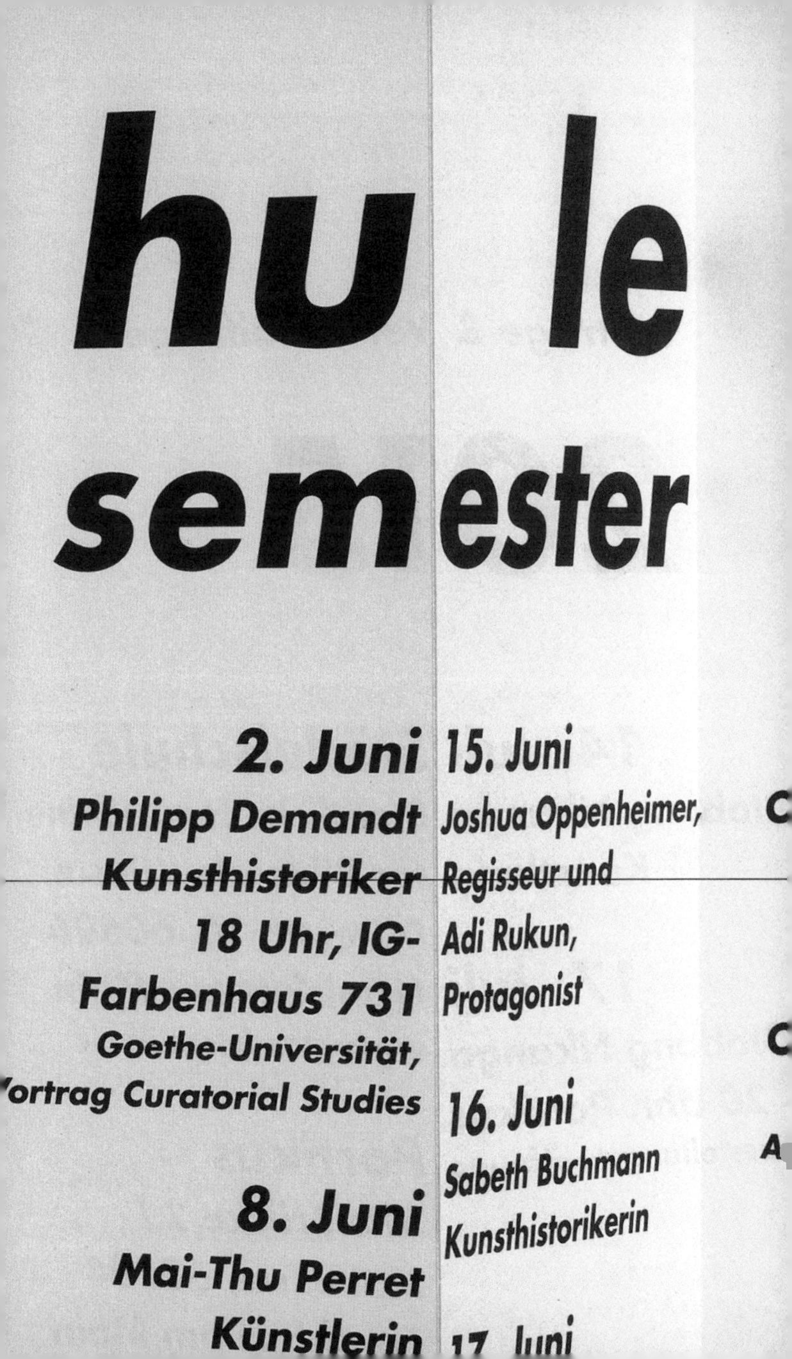
hu le
semester
2. Juni
Philipp Demandt
Kunsthistoriker
18 Uhr, IG-
Farbenhaus 731
Goethe-Universität,
ortrag Curatorial Studies
8. Juni
Mai-Thu Perret
Künstlerin
15. Juni
Joshua Oppenheimer,
Regisseur und
Adi Rukun,
Protagonist
16. Juni
Sabeth Buchmann
Kunsthistorikerin
17. Juni

Vorträge & Veranstaltungen

2015

14. Juli
Otobong Nkanga
Künstlerin

17. Juli
Otobong Nkanga
20 Uhr, Portikus
Ausstellungseröffnung

Städelschule
Staatliche Hochschule für Bildende Künste
Dürerstr. 10, 60596 Frankfurt am Main
www.staedelschule.de

Portikus
Alte Brücke 2 / Maininsel, 60594 Frankfurt am Main

June 15, 2015
Joshua Oppenheimer and Adi Rukun

American-British filmmaker Joshua Oppenheimer and Indonesian protagonist Adi Rukun speak in a panel discussion with rector Philippe Pirotte and event organizers Sung Tieu and Thuy-Han Nguyen-Chi at the preview of Oppenheimer's film The Look of Silence. *The documentary, and sequel to* The Act of Killing, *addresses legacies of the 1965 Indonesian genocide. Oppenheimer describes bearing witness to a collective psychosis of deception and witnessing how survivors continued living with guilt and fear. Moreover, he outlines the history of Indonesian cinema about repressed violence, reveals the influence of Rukun's video diaries, and affirms that his documentaries, which took a decade to make, should be seen in line with Direct Cinema and* cinéma vérité *as a translation, not as a report.*

Sung Tieu: Welcome Joshua Oppenheimer and Adi Rukun, thank you both for coming. Tonight, we will discuss your latest film *The Look of Silence* and its predecessor *The Act of Killing*. Both films focus on the Indonesian genocide following Suharto's military coup in 1965.

Thuy-Han Nguyen-Chi: More than one million Indonesians lost their lives. Joshua, you have spent almost ten years working on this project, perhaps you could tell us how the idea for the films was conceived and how you met Adi Rukun?

Joshua Oppenheimer: I met Adi at the very beginning of my journey in Indonesia when I first started working with survivors to explore the presentday legacy of the 1965 genocide. Adi's elder brother, Ramli, had been murdered in 1965 and I wanted to find out why virtually all the survivors are still living in fear today. What is it like for them to go on with their lives while the perpetrators are still in power? What is it like for the genocide never to have ended? When I began this work in 2003, Adi's father was not yet suffering from dementia. He was a central participant in the project, but what had happened was so traumatizing that Adi's parents, Rohani and Rukun, had never talked about it to Adi in detail. So Adi latched onto my filmmaking process as a way of understanding what had happened to his family, to his village, and to his country. He convinced other survivors to tell me their stories. Within three weeks the word got out of what we were doing. The army threatened survivors not to participate in our film and suggested that I go home. At that point, Adi and the other survivors encouraged me to continue. They told me to film the perpetrators and see if they would tell me what had happened. At first, I was afraid but once I overcame my fear, I found to my horror that the perpetrators were immediately open and boastful about what they had done. When I took the footage back to the survivors and to the Indonesian human rights community, they said, "You must continue to film the perpetrators. Anybody who sees this will be forced to acknowledge the terrible things that have happened and the awful regime of fear, which the perpetrators have built. Anybody who sees this will have to acknowledge that something is still terribly wrong today." I then felt entrusted by them to do a work that clearly they could not do safely themselves. I filmed every perpetrator I could find, working my way up the chain of command. In the beginning, I filmed the perpetrators by themselves but after about eight months, in January 2004, I started wondering if they were only boasting for me? If I confronted them with one another would they still speak in the same way? So I took the risk and brought two death squad leaders together—the scene I am referring to is the scene where the two men take me down to the river, taking turns playing victim and perpetrator—and I found that they were even more boastful when they were together. They were reading from a shared script. The boasting was obviously systemic, a sign of impunity. I could no longer cling to the illusion that these men were sociopaths or monsters. If there is a monstrosity here, then it is obviously a collective, political monstrosity. If these men are psychopaths, then they play their part in a collective psychosis. I realized that these atrocities had been committed in the name of anti-communism, but actually, they served corporate interests throughout the Cold War. The impunity of the perpetrators is what keeps people afraid everywhere across the Global South. That same fear prevents unions from being formed. It prevents the working conditions from improving in the sweatshops, where everything we buy is manufactured, and in the mines, where all the minerals we use are mined. In fact, this fear keeps everything cheap for us and it is a direct result of that impunity. Impunity is the story of our times. I decided to make two films. *The Act of Killing* would be about the boasting of the perpetrators. It is about the lies, the fantasies, and the stories that perpetrators cling to so that they can live with themselves. Note that this is inherently a film about the present, not about the past. It is not a historical film and inevitably it became a flamboyant fever dream of a film because it is about escapism and guilt, fantasy and guilt. It is not a documentary anymore. It is a new thing. I am not really sure what it is. *The Look of Silence* explores the effects of living for more than half a century in fear. What does it mean for Adi's mother to know that

Adi's schoolteacher was a member of the death squad that killed his brother, Ramli? She could not do anything at all. What was that like for her? What is it like never to be able to work through trauma and grief? Not only can the dead never be wakened but all the lives broken by fear and trauma can never be made whole again. Whatever justice comes in the future, it will not put Adi's father's life right. So I felt that the second film should be a retrospective poem in memoriam to all the lives that have been destroyed by fear.

Thuy-Han Nguyen-Chi: Adi, you became a very important partner to Joshua very early on in the filmmaking process. Why did you agree to work with Joshua on this project? And how did that collaboration transform you?

Adi Rukun: Thank you. First of all, I would like to express how moved I am that so many of you came to see the film today, thank you. During my childhood, only my mother would talk about what had happened in 1965 and she would only talk about the murder of my brother, Ramli. No one else would say anything. There was no information at all. My neighbors said nothing. My father never said a word, and our schoolteachers taught us things that were completely alien to my family's experience. When I reached junior high school, a propaganda film came out, justifying the killings and stigmatizing the victims. It is the same film that the two perpetrators are watching in *The Act of Killing*. It felt incredibly false to me and the question was: How to expose it? How could I reveal the truth and show that this film is a lie? In my neighborhood alone, thirty-two people were killed, including my brother Ramli, and this film presented an awful image of the victims. It claimed that all of the victims were communists, that communists were the embodiment of evil, and that they should all be exterminated. Yet, my mother would always tell me that my brother, Ramli, was different. He should never have been killed. So I was searching for a way to expose these lies but I did not know where to begin. I never imagined I would have the opportunity to participate in a film like this, and when Joshua turned up it was almost like a dream. It was the opportunity, which I had always hoped for but never thought possible, so I was very happy to get involved in the making of both films.

Joshua Oppenheimer: I would like to add that it was Adi's idea to confront the perpetrators in *The Look of Silence.* He said, "I must meet and confront the men who killed my brother." At first, I thought it was too dangerous. I felt we could not guarantee the safety of everyone involved. Adi proposed to meet the perpetrators, not angrily, not out of vengeance, but simply to show them that he was trying to understand and that he was willing to forgive. He hoped they would apologize so that they could reconcile and live together as neighbors again, not as victim and perpetrator, not afraid of each other. He believed that it was the only way in which his children would not inherit the prison of fear that his father, his mother, and he himself had been inhabiting. I suspected immediately that this endeavor would fail, but my crew convinced me to support and film the confrontations. To my knowledge, there has never been a documentary before where survivors confront perpetrators while the perpetrators are still in power. This unique situation allowed us to do something completely unprecedented, although I was convinced that we would not get an apology. I have worked with Anwar Congo for five years and even then he did not admit that what he had done was wrong. When he so much as glimpses at his own guilt, he starts to almost vomit. So how was Adi going to get these people to admit that what they did was wrong in an hour and a half? On the other hand, I realized that if you could show through the film how torn the society is by documenting sensitively and delicately the complexity of why we fail to get the reaction Adi is hoping for, then maybe we can make it impossible to ignore this abyss of fear and guilt, and fear of guilt, that divides every Indonesian from each other. Moreover, younger Indonesians would not have to raise their children in this trap of fear. That is why I agreed to do it. There was always a possibility that Adi would fail in the confrontations, but we thought we could succeed in a bigger way through the film as a whole.

Philippe Pirotte: Welcome, Joshua and Adi. Thank you so much for being here at the Städelschule tonight. I think that seeing the films made us all go silent. My question is for Adi—the films have been shown in Indonesia both publicly and in semi-secret gatherings, and although most of the other collaborators have wished to remain anonymous, you have gone to screenings many times. You have presented yourself as somebody who promotes the discussion of reconciliation. There is a fantastic moment in the film that explores if reconciliation is possible at all. What do you think happens now? What does this film instigate and what does that mean for the future of Indonesia?

Adi Rukun: The airing of *The Look of Silence* has had a very severe impact on my family. From an early rough cut of the film until its premiere at the Venice Film Festival in 2014, we had been planning to relocate to another part of Indonesia for our safety. We chose not to go abroad. We wanted to stay in Indonesia because I feel we have a role to play in the release of the film and in the movement the film has given rise to. I was a bit worried at first about whether my children would adapt to their new school but they have adapted much more quickly than I could have hoped for, and I must confess, much more quickly than me. They are in much better schools now and our life is better overall, mainly because we are not afraid anymore. We are not living near the people who have been extorting us and threatening us for the past fifty years.

Joshua Oppenheimer: There has been an outpour of support for Adi and his family. People have raised money so that the family could actually open an optic store. Before that, Adi was going door-to-door selling glasses, which was a very hand-to-mouth existence. There is a secure financial future for the family now, and resources for the children. They have access to better education, and so on and so forth.

Adi Rukun: I think the films have made a very big impact in Indonesia. *The Act of Killing* has changed the way the country looks at its past and present. It has paved the way for *The Look of Silence* to have an even bigger release. *The Look of Silence*'s Indonesian premiere was hosted by the National Human Rights Commission and the Jakarta Arts Council, both parts of the government, something which would have been unimaginable before. The premiere was held in the largest theater in Indonesia and about 3,000 people came. Since then, there have been more than 3,500 screenings throughout the country. These films make it possible for people to talk about some of the most difficult things that people could not talk about before. The younger generation has a right to know its own past and this film has made it possible for people to address their past.

Joshua Oppenheimer: What the film shows above all is that the past is always present. We can never run away from our past. The past will not catch up to us, but rather, it is us! William Faulkner said it beautifully when he said, "The past is not dead, it is not even past." It is here. It is all around us. The reason why the perpetrators boast, I think, is because they are haunted by these horrible, rotten memories that come to them in their nightmares as shapeless, formless fear. They seek to sugarcoat these awful memories with the sweet language of a victor's history, which is still available to them because they have not been removed from power. So the boasting is a way of trying to replace these horrific memories with words. It is also a means to construct some sort of psychic scar tissue around the wound through words and performances in an attempt to try and make it all somehow look heroic and okay. Of course, they fail miserably and that is why they have to keep on doing it, again and again, and again. That repeated recursive performance is the ultimate tragedy. It supports a whole mechanism of intimidating the rest of society because then neighbors are boasting to neighbors. Sometimes people say: "Joshua, your films have made a difference because they pull back the curtain and reveal a horrific nightmare lurking behind." That always feels wrong to me. If I had simply been exposing a genocide that no one had talked about, nobody would care. It would never have made this impact. We live in a time of frozen scandals. Atrocities take place all over the world. Simply revealing another one would not have drawn your attention. I think the reason that these two films have made this impact, the reason they function as a mirror in which we see something universal, is that they do not pull back the curtain to show the nightmare. They show that the curtain is the nightmare. The deception, the lies, the stories that are told at school, which Adi was referring to, they are all part of the nightmare.

I believe that my two films have exposed two complementary aspects of impunity that everybody in Indonesia already knew about. The first film exposes a regime of lies and fear, which everyone knew they were living in. Even if people were not aware of the details of the killings, they knew that there were certain subjects that were too dangerous to talk about. Other people knew about the details of the killings but pretended they did not. That became clear to me when Indonesia's leading news magazine, *Tempo*, responded to *The Act of Killing* by sending journalists to villages and towns all over the country in search of perpetrators who would speak like the men in my film. Everywhere they went, in every neighborhood, these journalists could immediately identify the death squad leaders because they were boasting publicly, which means people knew. So the first film exposes this regime of fear in which everyone is living, and now after it has been exposed, people have to talk about it. The second film also exposes something that everybody in Indonesia is familiar with: What is it like to live in fear of your neighbor? People must know that experience if their neighbor is boasting about murder and other atrocities. The second film did just as we had hoped: it has shown how torn the social fabric is and it has inspired people to take the struggle for truth and reconciliation further. My films reveal that all the stories told about this subject are lies. Writing a new story is the work of activism. It will be extremely difficult because of those in power, both the perpetrators and the oligarchs who became very wealthy through their close relations to the perpetrators, know that if the story changes, their billions and their power will be seen for what they really are—the illegitimate spoils of atrocities and the illegitimate spoils of plunder. These forces are lined up against genuine truth and reconciliation, so it will be a struggle. The first chapter of this story has opened the space for discussion, for the acknowledgement that this nightmare is a present-day nightmare. The second chapter has shown how torn society is and inspires people to struggle for change. The third chapter will have to be written by the people of Indonesia in the future.

Syafiatudina: Good evening everybody. My name is Dina. I am from Indonesia and I have two questions. Adi, you appear in the film and you confront your brother's murderers. Therefore, this struggle inherently becomes your personal struggle. How do you inform your children, for whom these events will inevitably become a part of their history? And Joshua, why do you not show yourself in your films, although oftentimes the informants are addressing you directly?

Adi Rukun: It is essential that my children understand the meaning of this film. They are in the film. We were relocated as a result of it. So clearly, the film is of tremendous importance to my family. But I think the film is very important for Indonesia as well. I keep a close eye on how it is received in Indonesia and on the political developments that the film gave rise to. Survivors today are still being intimidated and stigmatized. Recently, there was a gathering of very old survivors, people of seventy years old and older. They are without exception very poor, and when they came together to discuss ways of improving their economic situation, thugs physically attacked them. Old people were simply knocked unconscious. That is unacceptable! When *The Act of Killing* first came out, a local newspaper in West Java published an article with the headline, "The World Condemns Pancasila Youth," about a paramilitary group that is featured in the film. Right after the publication, five hundred paramilitary thugs from Pancasila Youth attacked the newspaper office and beat up the editor of the newspaper.

Joshua Oppenheimer: I would just add that these attacks, including threats of attacks on screenings of the films, are not spontaneous, they are organized by the military and the police. What is happening is not simply that Islamic organizations are attacking the screenings. Islamic organizations—or rather, random groups that claim to be an Islamic organization—are paid by the military and by the police to threaten and attack screenings. That in turn, is used as an excuse by the military and the police to demand that the screenings be canceled. It is a collaboration between the state and the paramilitary shadow state, and that has always been the mechanism of intimidation in Indonesia since the 1965 killings. As a result of these threats, thirty screenings have been canceled out of a total of 3,500 screenings. That is not very many, but it means that screenings are driven underground. People are afraid. Instead of holding an open screening, they hold a closed screening and fewer people will see the film. The pattern of threats ended when a group of students in Yogyakarta barricaded themselves into the university and went ahead with the screening despite the threat of an attack. This was so positively covered in the media that—and this is my theory—the army abandoned that strategy. There is a consistency with which the threats disappeared, providing further evidence that they are part of a central strategy and not just spontaneous eruptions of violence that happen when local groups get wind of a screening.

Adi Rukun: These elder people that I was talking about earlier were beaten up for the same reason. Some groups strongly object to the idea of survivors coming together. This is a very serious problem. It is a struggle for the future of the country. The government does not want change because a change in the story will render their power illegitimate. These people are still in power and I hope that anyone who sees this film will get involved with this struggle inside Indonesia. Especially the media will have to put pressure on the Indonesian government to address its past. I think it is very important that the media takes an active role in this.

Joshua Oppenheimer: To address your second question: the reason why I am not in either film is very simple. As a viewer, you are immersed in very uncomfortable aspects of human experience. In *The Act of Killing*, you approach Anwar Congo through my intimacy with him. You recognize his humanity. You feel a certain familiarity with his uncomfortable, ugly emotional reactions. You identify with him, through my closeness with him. It does not mean that you sympathize but you emphasize, and that would not happen if I were in the film. If I were in the film, I would immediately become the protagonist who delivers a glimpse of remorse to Anwar. It is very important that together with Anwar, you immerse yourself in the evolving nightmare of his guilt and his increasingly futile efforts to run away from that guilt. In *The Look of Silence*, it is equally important that you are immersed in Adi's family's situation. Rohani becomes your mother. Rukun becomes your father. Adi becomes your brother if not you, and his children become your children. The films are not windows onto faraway places, but rather mirrors in which we see ourselves. That would not happen if you had a foreign filmmaker guiding you through the film. Moreover, in both films, it is the filmmaking process itself, which generates the central drama. The confrontations in *The Look of Silence* are not taking place because Adi is going around knocking on people's doors. They take place because the camera is there and Adi has been able to prepare himself by studying the footage. Similarly, the dramatizations in *The Act of Killing* are for the film, so the film itself becomes the dramatic motor.

Question

I was very fascinated by Adi's courage and determination to confront his brother's killers in *The Look of Silence*. However, it also demonstrates that each survivor deals with his or her past differently. Some want to forget, some are in denial of the past, some are unable to move on. Even a person like Adi, as much as he has strength and perseverance, is incapable of reliving the past. His confrontations have nothing cathartic about them. That is why for me, one of the key moments in the film is the scene where Adi's father is crawling around in a room, looking for a way out. Could you tell us more about that scene?

Joshua Oppenheimer: The scene of Adi's father crawling on the floor is perhaps the most important scene in the whole film, at least for Adi and me. It is the only scene in the film that Adi shot and it was how Adi explained to me that he wanted to confront the perpetrators. I was reluctant, as I have told you earlier because I thought it was too dangerous. Then, Adi said, "Let me explain why it matters to me." Back in 2009, I had given him a camera to use as a sort of notebook to record visual metaphors that might inspire a second film. He had been sending me tapes throughout the editing of *The Act of Killing* and he said, "There is one tape that I did not send you because it is so meaningful to me." It was that scene, where Rukun is lost in his own home. Adi told me that this was the first day Rukun—his brain destroyed by dementia—could no longer remember any of them. It was the end of the Ramadan so the whole family was together, but nobody could comfort Rukun because they were all strangers to him. It became unbearable to Adi to see his own father crawling around, looking for a way out of his own home. So he picked up the camera and realized—this is the day it becomes too late for my father. He cannot remember the son whose murder has destroyed our family. He cannot remember his life, but he has not forgotten his fear. He is trapped in a prison of fear, like a man locked in a room who cannot find the door, let alone the key. That is when Adi told me, "I do not want my children to inherit that prison of fear from my mother, my father, and me." He thought confronting the perpetrators could be a way out. But it is a way out conceived in absolute desperation, right? How desperate do you have to be to take that risk to try and reconcile yourself with your neighbor? That is why *The Look of Silence* is more than just a political film about impunity and the coexistence of perpetrators and survivors. It is a film about memory and oblivion.

Philippe Pirotte: *The Act of Killing* and *The Look of Silence* appear to me as two dialectical parts of the same project. You were working very closely with Anwar Congo, almost mirroring the way in which you were working with Adi Rukun. Both films make use of the same tropes, like people watching and discussing pre-recorded footage. However, cinematographically both films are extremely different. *The Look of Silence* provides us with a very serene experience, while *The Act of Killing* draws us into a delirium. Especially to an international audience, the latter creates an image of a country that is delirious, weird, with a paramilitary group ruling the country. There are many moments when the documentary film morphs into fantasy and fiction, how much of that is purely Anwar Congo's delusion?

Joshua Oppenheimer: The image of Indonesia in the media is that it is the largest Muslim country in the world, the most moderate of all the Muslim democracies. Every night on CNN, you can see paid advertisements promoting Indonesia's business climate. I think what my film does, is it completes that picture and shows the truth. Indonesia is reigned over by a shadow state of oligarchs in collaboration with a paramilitary group. Certain scenes, such as the scene by the waterfall, for example, are absolutely Anwar Congo's own vision of redemption and the opening of the film tells you that. *The Act of Killing* begins with the scene by the waterfall, but instead of the beautiful choral music we hear later in the film, we hear the real sound, "One, two, three, four! More teeth! This is real beauty! This is natural beauty! This is peaceful, this is beautiful!" It is about the construction of false images of beauty. In *The Look of Silence*, we show footage that was broadcasted to millions of Americans in 1967, where a death squad leader—who also happens to be an archaeology professor with a doctoral degree—claims that Bali is more beautiful without communists. He literally takes the journalist to the edge of a mass grave, which he has helped to fill with bodies and says, "Now Indonesia is more beautiful." Americans accepted that delirium too, which means that these extreme visions are not unique to Anwar Congo. I hope that you do not come away from *The Act of Killing* smirking or feeling superior. All of our societies lie about their past. People in the United States will often ask me, "Is it not grotesque to let these perpetrators create cowboy scenes about a genocide?" To which I answer, "No!" The *raison d'être* of the cowboy movie is to glorify the genocide of the Native Americans. Fundamentally, I trust the viewer to be smart enough to know that this film looks at the world through a very dark mirror, albeit a very truthful one. In the uncut version of *The Act of Killing*, every sequence is brought to an abrupt cut and a haunted silence. Even the landscape is not beautiful and lush but haunted. Sometimes, it is no more than a derelict building with one person living or subsisting in it. These moments are abrupt shifts in perspective from the perpetrators to the absent dead, whom I hope haunts every frame of the film. So the image that we get of Indonesia is Anwar's nightmare. It is Anwar's fever dream, where the lush and delirious landscape and the haunted space of the dead somehow converge and merge into one space. These two dialectically opposed spaces come together at the end of the film when Anwar's fever dream and reality become one as we approach that final scene on the roof. *In The Look of Silence*, I wanted to immerse the viewer in any one of these haunted silences. What is it like to be a survivor and rebuild your life in the rubble, surrounded by the same powerful men that have killed your loved ones? Both films are formally joined. They are two parts of the same whole. By watching the second film you can enter into any of the silent spaces that were presented in the first film.

Philippe Pirotte: The notion of *sadis*, the Indonesian word for sadism, comes back very often. Is there a connection to a tradition of slaughter and gore movies that have been made in Indonesia? Is that a reference that informs some of the fantasy scenes, the masquerades, and the disguises?

Joshua Oppenheimer: From 1965 until the end of the Suharto regime, there was a political inability to talk about the violence that had ripped across this society. In addition to that, there was a return of the repressed in Indonesian cinema. Some fantastic films were made. Forgotten masterpieces like *Ferocious Female Freedom Fighters*,

Jungle Heat, and *The Intruder* are some of the most grotesquely violent and expressively nightmarish films ever made. They are horrible and they are magnificent. They are utter trash and they are beautiful. More recently, filmmakers like Joko Anwar and in a more subtle way, Edwin, have been producing films that give voice to this repressed violence. So yes, a genre emerged called *sadis.* I think the pinnacle of the genre is the propaganda film that Anwar Congo and Adi Rukun are watching in the film and which Adi was talking about earlier. Before 1965, there had been a vibrant Indonesian cinema coming up with its own cinematic language, experimenting with elements from the French New Wave and Italian neorealism. In 1965 all of the prints were destroyed, all of the scripts were destroyed, all of the negatives were destroyed, and virtually all of the filmmakers were destroyed. We do not know what that cinema was really about. There are a couple of copies of a couple of films but dozens, if not hundreds of films, are simply lost. One of the great challenges for the younger generation is to imagine the past, which has been obliterated.

Philippe Pirotte: One of the strangest fantasies in *The Act of Killing* is Herman, the sparring partner of Anwar Congo, singing and performing in women's clothes. Whose idea was that? And is there a tradition of travesty in Indonesia?

Joshua Oppenheimer: Drag has indeed a certain tradition in Indonesia. There was a television show a couple of years ago, where a drag queen would be presenting songs. It was like a nostalgic singing show for army officers. All the officers would show up in uniform and the transvestite host would sing. Now, Pancasila Youth had a theater troupe and in that theater troupe, men played all of the roles. Herman would always be this matronly storyteller in drag, which Anwar thought was delightful and funny. It was Anwar who proposed that Herman should play the femme fatale in the dramatization of his nightmares, which were written by the newspaper staff that you see in the film. I asked the newspaper staff to write the script for Anwar's nightmares because I felt it would show the collective denial of guilt. The nightmares are obviously a manifestation of trauma, which the newspaper staff is cheapening by turning them into trivial entertainment. They refuse to see what it obviously means. They refuse to say, "Are you alright? What happened?" They just cannot look at the core of the nightmare. So when Anwar proposed to have Herman play this femme fatale in his nightmare scenario, I did not question it for a long time. I did not dare ask because I did not want him to have second thoughts. Herman's travesty appeared to me like magic. It was an utter mystery. It was so strange. Gradually, I found out that Herman had been acting in women's clothing in Pancasila Youth's theater troupe before. I did not put that in the film as an explanation because I wanted it to come to you as the mysterious, beautiful, strange thing that came to me. Herman in that bright, pink dress, sitting there, as the sun blossoms on him, scratching his ear, right after Anwar has done his nightmares, becomes a metaphor for what the whole film is about. He is this beautiful, incandescent, lovely, seductive monstrosity! That is what the movie is about and I wanted it to be that for you as a viewer.

Thuy-Han Nguyen-Chi: You describe your work as a "documentary of imagination" and I am very interested in the interrelationship between fiction and fact in your filmmaking philosophy. Could you share your perception of *cinéma vérité*, or the fly-on-the-wall approach, and your own position towards documentary filmmaking? And within this context, how would you negotiate the terms of dramatization, performance, and re-enactment?

Joshua Oppenheimer: I would like to start by saying that I do not think there is a single re-enactment in *The Act of Killing* or in *The Look of Silence*. That might sound strange, particularly when you think of the simple demonstrations of killing in the films. However, those are not re-enactments but rather dramatizations of the present-day lies and fantasies that the perpetrators tell themselves so they can live with themselves. This is a crucial distinction. It is the difference between a film of the past that illustrates and visualizes the past, and a film about the present and the role of fiction and fantasy in making our present what it is. Re-enactment is a strategy that filmmakers use to make a past visible, which is no longer available to be filmed. I am not interested in showing you what the past looked like. People often ask me why I did not make some of the dramatizations more realistic. I think that would dishonor the dead. I will not trample on their ground and try to portray what they have been through. This same position is inherent in the film when Anwar says, “Now I feel what my victims must have gone through.” And I answer, “No, you do not. They were dying and you are acting.” These are two completely different things. There is a moral abyss that divides the illustration from what I think these men are doing. I have no desire to even approach representational adequacy or verisimilitude in my work. The parts in the film that are the most realistic, are also the most stylized. Those are the *film noir* scenes. The most realistic scene for Anwar—the scene that obviously pulls up the most horrific, true psychological dynamics—is a scene where the mother is played by an overweight gangster in a 1940s gangster outfit and the child is represented by a teddy bear. I think the more honest fiction films are, the more stylized they become. This is the philosophical core of my work. It is the core of what I am exploring between fiction and documentary.

In answer to your question about the fly-on-the-wall approach: whenever you film anybody, they will start performing. Most filmmakers will quickly try and get past that, or try to hide that by conniving or collaborating with the participant to get the participant to act natural. But what they are really doing is simulating a reality in which the camera is not present. When I say this, people often respond, "Yes, but will people not forget the camera after a while?" Now, think about that for just one moment and ask yourself: Is it really possible to forget the camera? Of course it is not. Imagine you are having an intimate conversation with your mother about something that you have been too afraid to talk to her about before. Well, perhaps you would never find the courage if there were no camera. Secondly, if you do have that conversation, do you really believe that you could confuse that experience of talking to your mother alone about something very painful, with the experience of having exactly the same conversation while you are being filmed by a group of people with lots of equipment, who have the power to shape how you are perceived by the public and how your relationship is understood by the public forever more? Of course you could not confuse those two things. It suggests that the fly-on-the-wall technique and the story about Direct Cinema as observing and documenting a pre-existing reality, is perhaps a good story to get audiences to appreciate the masterworks of Direct Cinema, but it is not a good description of how those filmmakers made those films. If you look at the masterworks of Direct Cinema, you will find that they never attempt to overcome the self-consciousness of the participants. Look at the

Maysles brothers' film *Grey Gardens*. The mother and daughter who are at the center of the film are positively competing for the attention of the camera throughout the film. They are performing the entire time and that is one of the central dramas in the film: Who gets the filmmaker's attention? A film like Frederick Wiseman's *Titicut Follies*, one of the greatest documentaries ever made, where a film crew enters a psychiatric hospital, proves that even if the responses of the patients are not rational, they are still responding. Suddenly, there is a camera to record the patients' delusion, to record the patients' complaints, and complain they do. This is not a manifesto against Direct Cinema. It merely suggests that if we want to understand how the best works of Direct Cinema are made, we better understand documentary or non-fiction for what it really is. First of all, Direct Cinema is the cinema where people play themselves. Second of all, a series of collaborations is created by the filmmaker and the subjects in which everybody is hopefully within the safe space of making a film, and within that safe space, everybody is being pushed beyond their comfort zone. That is how good non-fiction cinema is made. In the editing, the moral obligation for having taken everybody beyond their comfort zone is not to create a faithful report of the journey that the filmmaker takes with the participants. The obligation is to do justice to the painful truths that come out through those occasions, which are indeed every single important scene in the film. I work very hard, despite what it may look like, to ensure the safety of everybody in my work. It may look like there are children that are being traumatized and there are villages that are burned down in *The Act of Killing*. But it is a film set and the children who are crying are actors who were auditioned for their ability to cry. Similarly, in *The Look of Silence* I am very proud that none of the confrontations ended with us having to run away. I am very proud that Adi Rukun is safe. We worked very hard for that. There was a team of twenty-five people working to ensure Adi's family's safety. So instead of trying to get past the moment of self-consciousness, I use it as the insightful moment that it really is. In that moment, people are not acting or performing. They show or act out how they wish to be seen and how they wish to see themselves, from which you can infer how they really see themselves. Most of the stories and fantasies that become visible in that moment of performance are often drawn from television, cinema, manga, game shows, and advertisements. We are constantly imagining ourselves through second-hand, often third-rate, stories with which we escape from the most important aspects of our lives and from what it means to be human. So, performance is escape but performance is also the very stuff of what we are. Therefore, a non-fiction film camera is a prism that makes visible the kind of myriad, the spectrum of stories, fantasies, and fictions that make us what we are, and that make the world what it is to us. In that sense, I see my work as creating the conditions, particularly in *The Act of Killing*, for what I call the "documentary of the imagination." I am standing on the shoulders of a filmmaker called Jean Rouch who coined the term *cinéma vérité*. For Jean Rouch, *cinéma vérité* was about allowing people to stage themselves and act out their own fantasies as a way of showing the imaginative conditions of people's lives. That is something that I am building on and certainly taking in new directions.

Sung Tieu: There is a lot of repetition in the way you set up your scenes. I am interested in the scene where Anwar Congo, together with his grandchildren, reviews the *film noir* scene featuring himself as the victim. There are so many layers of repetition in the way Anwar looks at how he plays the victim of his own act and then challenges it again by viewing with his grandchildren on television. I am interested in how you stage this repetition of events and use it to confront Anwar with the horror of his own actions. It seems that this repetition is almost necessary for Anwar to realize what he has done and what has actually happened.

Joshua Oppenheimer: I would distinguish between repetition and recursion. Recursion is a process that repeats but in new conditions each time, so things change and develop. One thing you see clearly in the uncut version of *The Act of Killing* is that the method was indeed a recursive process.

Anwar Congo was the forty-first perpetrator I filmed. I lingered on him because on the very first day I met him, he took me to the roof to show me how he killed with wire. I went to his house with cameras ready and right away he said, "My wife has guests, why don't I take you to the place where this all happened so I can show you?" And he thought to bring some wire, and he thought to bring some wood, and he thought to bring his friend who could play a victim, and off we went. Yet, as we walk up to that roof in the beginning of the film, he lets out a sharp sigh, which is a kind of little moment where the mask slips for him. Then he starts to talk about ghosts and he shows us how he killed, as though he were compelled to demonstrate or put words to these awful memories. After showing how he killed, he says, "Now, I must show you how they died." Of course, that was the thing he had to watch hundreds maybe thousands of times. Every time he murdered somebody he had to watch that person be strangled, which haunts him still. I think he had to get it off his chest, he had to share it, and he had to show me. He says that if he thinks about it, he will go crazy and he has spent his whole life trying to forget. He goes out drinking, taking drugs, dancing. He even boasts what a good dancer he is, and he starts dancing right there as though to banish the pain that he has just experienced himself. That lead me to realize that the boasting, which I had already spent two years filming from forty different perpetrators, is not pride. It is the banishing of pain. I lingered on Anwar because I wanted to explore that a little further and I dared to do with him something that I had been too afraid to do with others—I showed him the footage to see if he would recognize, in the mirror of the footage, the meaning of what he had done. He looks very disturbed in that first scene, when he is watching himself on the roof. But he cannot even say that this makes him look bad. To say that would be to admit that it was bad, and he has never been forced to do that. So he does the natural, human thing that everybody would do and that is to lie to himself. He comments that the footage is good, but it could be better if he could just change this one little thing. As though, if he could fix the scene aesthetically, he could fix his life morally. He proposes what he considers an improvement. I agree to go along with it, not because I understand that this will be the start of some five-year collaborative process but because I recognize that the improvement will provide even more powerful material for this exposé of impunity that Adi and the other survivors from the village in North Sumatra had asked me to make. I knew the next scene would be even more outrageous. Through this simple recursive—not repetitive—process of shooting one scene, watching it, him proposing the next scene, then shooting and watching, and shooting and watching, the scenes gradually evolved into the surreal genre and styled dramatizations that they eventually became. In hindsight, I think it is not surprising that those fiction scenes, which are a recursive enactment of the boasting, become a prism through which Anwar recognizes and experiences the full meaning of what he has done. He definitely sees it in the scene where he watches himself with his grandchildren, but he starts to see it much earlier in the film. In fact, it is on his face from the very beginning, which is why he lets out that sigh on the roof when he first gets there. What is motivating him from the beginning is his conscience, his need to run away from guilt, and his fear of guilt. That is the engine of the film. That is the engine of every Indonesian perpetrator who boasts, except for the few who may be monsters. Gradually, through this recursive process, these performances become more and more threadbare. They no longer have the strength to protect him from guilt. So guilt starts rupturing through, breaking through.

Question

Taking into account your history as a documentary maker, I would like to know how you ended up in Indonesia. How did you come across this subject? Could you have made this same film somewhere else, in Cambodia for example?

Joshua Oppenheimer: I went to Indonesia because of a film I was involved in called *The Globalization Tapes.* I was experimenting with the idea that documentary or non-fiction film should be collaborative and that it should involve performance. A friend of mine knew this and invited me to make a film exploring the violent underbelly of globalization by making a collaborative film with plantation workers about their struggle to organize a union in the aftermath of some totalitarian regime. So I found myself at twenty-seven years old on a plantation in North Sumatra, where foreigners never came. No one spoke English except for a crew of Indonesian labor activists, who could translate for me somewhat. I found myself in a place where the conditions were truly diabolical. Women workers were given the task of spraying pesticides and one weed killer, in particular, was so toxic that if it would spray in their faces they would go blind. The mist of the poison would get into their lungs and in their bloodstreams and livers, killing them in their forties. During the six months I was filming there, two women died and two got very sick and died later. This left a very big impression on me. The union approached the company and asked not to make them spray this particular herbicide anymore, but instead of giving in to their demands, the company hired Pancasila Youth to threaten and attack the workers. The workers dropped their demands immediately, and I asked, "How is this possible? Is this not a matter of life and death for you?" They replied that it was, but they were terrified of Pancasila Youth. Their parents and grandparents had been killed in 1965, simply for being in a union, and Pancasila Youth had been the main civilian death squad organization in this region.

At that moment, I realized that what was killing my friends was not only poison, but also fear. So after the plantation workers and I finished *The Globalization Tapes*, I went back to make my own film with this survivors community about their fear and about why they are still afraid today. Almost immediately, I was introduced to Ramli's family because he is the most well known victim in that region. His name has become a synonym for the genocide as a whole because his murder was one of the only murders that had witnesses. Everybody else was taken away from prison, killed, and left in a river to drift out to sea, but people knew Ramli had died. They knew he was buried on the plantation where I had been filming. To speak about Ramli was more polite than to speak about the other dead of whom there was no proof that they had died. It was also an act of resistance in a community where everyone was traumatized by events that the army had threatened them never to discuss. In answer to the second part of your question, I could not have made this film in Cambodia because the perpetrators were removed from power in Cambodia. Although the United States tried to turn a blind eye to the Cambodian genocide as long as they could, eventually they had to condemn it as a genocide. I did suggest earlier why I could have made a film like this in the United States. You need to only look at cowboy movies to realize that they exist for the sole purpose of glorifying genocide.

Question

Thank you, Joshua, for sharing two hours of brilliant filmmaking experiences with us. My question relates to what was said earlier about the interrelationship between truth and fiction. In your "documentaries of the imagination," exactly how concerned are you with the concept of truth and the true chronology of the filmmaking process?

Joshua Oppenheimer: Mark Twain famously said that we sometimes have to lie to tell the truth. I believe that to be true. Very often, films that take on orthodoxies about the chronology of the shooting are the same ones that repeat the moral lies, where we pity the victims and view the perpetrators as monsters so that we can reassure ourselves that we have nothing to do with them. That is a sentimental catastrophe. If you feel there is a human truth in this film, you should recognize it in your own humanity, in your own self, in your own experience of your existence on this planet. My role is not to create a film, which is a report of the events that happened during the shooting. I could do that, but it would sacrifice the much bigger truths that I would like to show you. For example, in *The Look of Silence*, we began by shooting the confrontation with the man with the red glasses. We did that because he had no power. We knew that we could film him safely and have some footage to show Adi's wife and mother about what we were doing, so they could consent to making the film. In the film, we only show that Adi tells his wife and mother what he is doing and they respond as you see in the film. Then we showed them the scene, which you do not see in the film, so they could see what kind of material it generates. Now, in the film, those two moments come much later after Adi has already been threatened. However, I felt in those two scenes that their fear is very honest and it shows how dangerous it is for this family. You could say that this is a lie and that you are being lied to. But the fact is that in order to protect the family's safety, we shot everything very quickly. All of the confrontations were shot in six days so that there would not be time for the word to spread. And yes, we were afraid. The family was at the airport every day while we were shooting, ready to evacuate if anything went wrong. We worked our way quickly up the chain of command and the order did not matter. So I am not giving you a faithful record of what happened during the shooting. It is out of sequence because that is the way of showing you the real danger and the real truth. The two films took a decade to make. They are the product of a long exploration of misery and pain, and some of the most awful aspects of what it means to be a human being and some of the most beautiful aspects. All I can hope to do in the editing is not show you the story of what I did while shooting, but to condense into a single poetic experience as much of that misery and horror and beauty as I possibly can. In that sense, you could see this film as a translation, not a report.

Question

Could you talk about the way you edited the sound for this film?

Joshua Oppenheimer: *The Look of Silence* had ten weeks of sound editing, which is far more than you would normally have on a documentary, and it had a five-week sound mix. If you would listen carefully you would hear crickets, engines, all of the sounds that one hears in Indonesia. I feel it is my task to immerse you in a certain landscape and to re-haunt that landscape with sound. In the confrontations, what is speaking is the silence between the characters. All the sound is removed except for the dialogue and the whole soundtrack is recreated from scratch. Like I said before, some purists would call this film a lie, but it is actually the truth. Those silences would not speak in the same way if they were cluttered with sounds of cars and horns and screaming children. The landscapes would not be haunted if they were permeated with day-to-day sounds. What the recreation of the soundtrack allows me to do is choose very carefully from the sounds we have recorded and build a whole score out of those sounds. Robert Bresson, one of the key influences on this film, said, "Do not use a score, do not use music. Let the sounds themselves be the score." When you hear a cricket sound, you actually hear sixteen tracks of crickets. One is just a solo cricket, there is a whole chorus of crickets, there are foreground and background crickets, and there are many tracks in between, depending on whether it is a whole haunted landscape or a very intimate scene. When Adi is washing his father you hear one single cricket with almost no reverberation, as if a ghost is whispering in Adi's ear, whispering in Rukun's ear. In the landscape shots, there might be a whole chorus of crickets playing a symphony. If in one of the confrontations, there is a car passing by or a child crying, then it is placed there to remind you of the outside world, at a place where I feel that you should be reminded of the outside world. For example, in the scene where the daughter of a perpetrator apologizes on her father's behalf—she is the only person who responds in the way that Adi is looking for—we hear a child crying, reminding us also of her duty as a mother. When we were filming, there were actually children there, but the sound you hear is a sound that is cleaned up and placed back.

On some occasions, people have mentioned that we conducted the confrontations as interviews. I would like to stress that they are not interviews for the same reason that the dramatizations are not re-enactments. Interviews are about trying to get information about the past or feelings about the past. These are confrontations. Adi is trying to encourage or invite the perpetrators to acknowledge that what they have done was wrong, and instead he receives threats in the present.

Question
When *The Act of Killing* came out on DVD, the director's cut turned out to be much longer than the version that was played in the movie theater. Will there be an extended version of *The Look of Silence* on DVD?

Joshua Oppenheimer: The story of the short version of *The Act of Killing* had to do with the situation in the United States. I had no name at that point. No one knew of my work. No one had heard of the Indonesian genocide. No one cared about it. I was advised that if I wanted this film to come out for a week in New York and a week in Los Angeles, I could show the long version. However, if I wanted more people to see and discuss it, I should make a two-hour version, which is the maximum a documentary can really be in the cinema in the United States. Then Werner Herzog called out of the blue to say that he had seen the film. He said beautiful things about it and when I told him I was shortening it for American cinema, he became furious. He said it was a crime to shorten this film and put down the phone. That was horrible for me. I went into filmmaking because of him. I was inspired by films like *Stroszek*—this is why I am a filmmaker today. Then, ten minutes later he called back to say that he had spoken to his wife, who had said that she could see the value of *The Act of Killing* getting a wider audience. If people like the film, they will seek out the long version that is available on DVD. However, in many other countries—in the United Kingdom, Australia, New Zealand, Japan, Korea, and the Scandinavian countries—the long version of *The Act of Killing* became the main version that was shown in the cinema. There was a great moment when we were at the Berlin Film Festival for the premiere of *The Look of Silence*, Werner Herzog said to the audience, "You have not seen *The Act of Killing* until you see the director's cut." So he still feels that way, but he understands the need for a shorter version. And I swear this is the only version of *The Look of Silence* and it is complete.

Philippe Pirotte: I would like to thank Joshua Oppenheimer for having spent so much time with us tonight. Thank you for sharing your thoughts. I would also like to thank Adi Rukun—*terima kasih*, Adi. And finally, thank you Sung Tieu and Thuy-Han Nguyen-Chi for organizing this event.

VORTRAG

Dan Graham &
Mark von Schlegell

Künstler / Schriftsteller

23. Oktober, 14 Uhr

VORTRAG

El Hadji Sy & Philippe Pirotte

Künstler / Rektor Städelschule

4. November

VORTRAG

Tom McCarthy &
Clémentine Deliss

Schriftsteller / Direktorin Welt-kulturen Museum Frankfurt

6. November

VORTRAG

Gabriel Lester

VORTRAG
Elif Erkan &
Fabian Schöneich
Künstlerin / Kurator
2. Dezember

VORTRAG
Josef Strau
Künstler
3. Dezember

AUSSTELLUNGSERÖFFNUNG
Konzentration der Kräfte
Elif Erkan
5. Dezember, 20 Uhr, Portikus

VORTRAG
Franz Erhard Walther

December 3, 2014
Josef Strau

Application for Turtle Island and a School Cannot Move

Austrian-born artist and writer Josef Strau continues his 2011 lecture about the "nonproductive" attitude, describes moving from Europe to the United States, and recounts producing his first solo show at The Renaissance Society, along with two new books. Strau uses this opportunity to pay tribute to the American continent and extends his interests to Mexican history and first encounters with Europeans. Following a phase of intensive research, Strau relates his findings. He tells stories of Spanish conquistadors meeting Montezuma, the king of the Aztec Empire, outlines events that led to the Mexican Revolution, and interprets The New World, *a contemporary film about Pocahontas.*

First of all, I'll explain a little bit about what my idea was for coming here after I got the invitation. My idea was to repeat something I did three years ago. Maybe there are a few people here who heard me then? I don't think it was a great performance, or a great lecture either, and in some ways, when I was invited here again, I thought, well, I would like to do a sort of apology for what I'd done last time. On the other hand, since I've arrived here, I was thinking, well, I don't want to repeat or correct what I said last time. I would like to actually do the same procedure again, and the procedure is that I'd always had the same situation with lectures like that, that I would bring photographs on my computer, I would show all the different projects I did, my so-called production, but then, I sometimes have this weird ambition that I won't do anything like that—an ambition which is very personal and that won't help you at all. And it is, basically, that I start talking and I don't know where we'll go, or where I'll go, and I just decide as I go along what the aim of the talk will be, or if there is an aim. That is what I did here, and I was very thankful to this school as it was the first time I'd ever done that. Because I often came to lectures with photos and so on, and it's very easy to look at projects and explain the references, and the production situation, but then it always feels kind of empty. Actually, it is something else for me to talk and see where it goes, and build the references while speaking.

So, the last time I had a book with me; by coincidence it was a novel by Giorgio Bassani, *The Garden of Finzi-Continis.* I read parts of it, and when I read it then, it was such a great discovery for me, I think I explained last time, why. But I'm very glad now that I have brought one thing with me at least. This time, I brought my own book, my own text. I hope I don't have to read it now, but the thing is, I should introduce myself, what kind of artist I am, what kind of production I do. For me, it's more interesting to try to explain that without photos, although I'm very aware that most people would not know my work here since it was just shown here and there, but never in Frankfurt, in Cologne once, but that was long ago. Anyway, I will try to start this evening by explaining a little bit why I did this book and how it happened to be here now. I was invited a year ago or more to make an exhibition at The Renaissance Society. It came like nothing, actually, like everything. Usually I was thinking that to have a show at a big institution like that is something you'd only get if you'd had dinners with the curator and knew each other very well, but nothing like that was the case. It was just a sudden e-mail coming, and I thought that someone was trying to play a joke on me, or deceive me, or had hacked my account or something, that this e-mail came that I should show at The Renaissance Society. But that's because a long time ago, for many years, I lived as an artist who had no production at all. I had always tried to do things and had huge ambitions, but I wasn't capable of producing to the point that I could show it. That was like the late eighties, early nineties when I lived in Cologne. And all these great years in Cologne, I made some exhibitions, not many. Usually I worked as an assistant for a few artists. The greatest experience I had was when I worked for Isa Genzken for some months; I also worked for a year or more for Georg Herold. The thing was, then, I wasn't very productive. It was sort of like a joke. For instance, Georg Herold realized that I'm not so good with handcrafts, or even the kind of person who could really help an artist achieve things. I have learned now, myself, since I have an assistant sometimes, and was invited to The Renaissance Society, that I have to explain myself in a more practical way.

I didn't know much about the art world when I arrived in 1987 in Cologne. But I learned very quickly. At that time, I learned that The Renaissance Society was like an exhibition place where European or German artists had their first big one-person show in the United States. After this exhibition, things in their lives changed a lot. They could suddenly sell their work, or even have some success, and so I maintained this kind of Renaissance Society mythology in some way. And as I said, after I got this email, I believed it was a deception or something, or a joke. And then I answered them in a quiet way and got this response, and I do an exhibition in the United States, as my first one-person institutional show. Maybe it's time for something I've never tried before, which was that I do an exhibition, which is based on very personal stories, and based on something which is very positive. Let's call it, something to do with an excitement about the country where I would do this show, which was the United States.

I lived for some years in New York, and I often had this issue that I was telling friends, sometimes late at night, that I love living in the United States and it's such a great experience. And they always dismissed that, and made jokes, and would say, "What, do you love Ronald Reagan?" or asked if I am, "A right-wing patriot or something?" But then I tried to explain that patriotism is a condition of liking the country where you come from without any kind of experience of the other. You just assume from the very beginning that the conditions you live with and where you come from are the good ones. When I was saying that, it was in an actual anti-patriotic political way, but then in a personal way, in a communicative way, that it's an unbelievably great experience for a person who came from the suburbs of Vienna, who went through certain things and always had to change the life, that there is an incredible kind of support there, turning even my little ideas into something, which I never experienced before.

So, I decided when they asked me to do this exhibition, that it was actually time to go public with this thing about the US. But what attracted me most was probably this idea, that since almost all kinds of American artists are always critical about the American condition, about everything, to come instead with something that describes the simple old immigrant narrative, which is, well, "We came over here by boat or plane, but we're very happy to be here," which I also heard from many other immigrants from all different countries. Of course, most of them had come in illegally, like barbers or taxi drivers or whatever, but they would tell you this story that they came and could never leave because they were illegal immigrants. It's a very common thing in New York, but they sacrifice this thing, that they can never leave the country, but they know why.

All these people that grew up in New York, with fathers, and mothers, and grandfathers who were already American, for them, of course, it's a simple and clear issue to be very critical about government, and about the culture. To be critical about the government is easy.

Anyway, so I asked The Renaissance Society if I could do two books. One, because always with every exhibition there's the production of a publication connected. So, we'll do one typical sort of art publication with photos from the exhibition, an introductory essay and so on. But also, I wanted to have a second book, smaller, or whatever, where I could just try to basically write a very personal statement about who I am, and how I relate to the issue of having moved to the United States.

I was hoping somehow that this might be an issue that isn't provocative, but that might produce discussions of different opinions, maybe it's not, I didn't know. The thing is, I will quickly try to explain my last project before going back, so this book just came out, and actually it's called, *The New World,* subtitled: *Application.* Because application means you have to go through this process, to get the green card, to get the visa to get into the United States. Which for me, is a really difficult thing because I'm not very good at paperwork. So, I kind of delayed, delayed, and delayed my visa application. And I was always wondering what would happen if I just write to the government. To write what I want to tell them, like look at me, I came from there and there, I've experienced this as a young person, and later that, and to just take me for that reason, and not because I did an institutional show, or that I did lectures and so on. The kind of problem involved in a visa application, to live somewhere else—that is what I tried to solve here.

The other point was that, when there was this idea, to have the opening with the book already there, proved a real challenge. Because I'd worked hard on the production, and during that time, the print deadline came closer and closer. Then, when there was only one week left, I had still not written at all. I hadn't even started. And what happened was a little bit the same thing that I am trying to do here now, that basically, the deadline came for a whole book, at least 100 pages of text promised, and you have nothing really, and you start thinking, maybe there's some old text I could use, hum, but no there wasn't and it's the same sort of condition coming here to the lecture. You know, that's why I won't show photos or go back to them, because I'm trying to show you how my own production is. Because I think the main issue in the last ten years, at least, it's not so much about how things are in the art world, it's not so much about what you do, what you prefer to do, but it's more about how you find a mode of work to present in a space or in a publication, which shows the production in itself, and how production becomes a kind of metaphor or narrative for the production as a narrative or reference.

I was always thinking there were all these great artists in New York who were working in this kind of way, almost like the manufacturing of how to manufacture a sculpture, which is in a way, how to present the manufacture of a certain kind of production that becomes the narrative or the expression of what the work is about. I love this very much. This idea … and I admire lots of artists like … no, I won't name him now. But I cannot achieve this same great manufacture, for this, one needs a big production place, you need a studio, you need assistants, you need a whole machinery for communication and production. I was not ready for that, to say it like that.

That is another point where I should introduce myself. I'm the kind of artist who never has any sort of studio, so I basically work at my house, and then, always, the exhibition gets closer and closer, and since I'm an artist who is more of a writer than a non-writer—I'm not a writer at all actually, but rather, I'm someone who writes things—and so by writing them down, I try to get to a point where I can get close to a mode of production. But then it ends up, always, like I come to the gallery, like I've come here and I have nothing so we have to do something quickly. Let's take this cardboard box over there. Maybe we can do that. Or, I'll wrap it and print out some text. It's very low, but something like that.

The other idea, for why I talk to you like this, and I'm apologizing to you, because you all came here for this tonight. The thing was to be that the lecture itself is kind of a metaphor for the pressures of work. With all the pressure of the production I can change my work. Probably my work has different periods. There was a period when I believed that it's not so interesting to just show the production as a very personal issue, but more for instance, to organize an art space, which shows other artists, to show that to be an artist doesn't mean to be only a productive artist who makes only paintings, sculptures, photography or something, but that the artist exists in-between. Like in the second-order issue, which isn't about the production. It's about how you actually establish yourself as an artist to the public and how you try to change the role of the artist as it is traditionally applied. In that way, a long time ago, we started a little art space in Cologne that was called Friesenwald; later I did another art space in Berlin, called Meerrettich.[1] And so, to come back to this, I have to apologize again, because I just arrived here from Mexico, and I've traveled the last five days through seven airports or something like that, I don't even know why. It's great, but I still kind of had the idea that when I was in New York or Mexico, that I would do what I just told you, this kind of immediate, improvisation to explain my work. But then I came here and was deadly jet-lagged, and I missed two days, almost, because I flew at night, and then woke up the next night, and now I'm a bit confused, to say the least.

The thing was, that some years ago the idea to be in the role of the artist without a studio was a new way of life for me, because it wasn't possible for me to

1 Meerrettich (Horseradish) existed from 2002–06 at the Rosa-Luxemburg-Platz, across from the Volksbühne (The People's Theater), Berlin.

maintain a studio. It wasn't something I chose really, but something that happened. Because, well, I had a very nice small room in Brooklyn, and tried to find a studio but it was difficult. The thing was, that I had developed, slowly, something more than a survival strategy, but something that is almost an attitude, which involved this kind of traveling situation. That I come to a place where I do the exhibition, but then I have to confess when I'll arrive, and I'll ask if I can come a week earlier, and they'll say, "Yes, sure," and then there is no transport or anything for the show, but then I have to develop something. But usually what I developed before was like text posters, and I connected them quickly to some kind of sculptural production that I can make in one week. What happened is that in time, the exhibitions became a bit bigger, and I learned that it's a great strategy of survival to exist like this, traveling, that I do not occupy a space, that I not only don't have a studio, but that I don't have an apartment as well. And now, when I come here, I'm a bit at the end of that, because for the last two years I had no address and kept traveling. And so, I extended. For instance, I made the production for The Renaissance Society in Mexico, since I have very good friends and a gallery there with a house who supported this project. So I suggested that I extend this kind of story, and that The Renaissance Society project becomes the place where I tell this story of tribute to the whole continent, to the United States, to Mexico, how they took me in some years ago, and how they helped me with this production, and many other personal things along with it. So anyway, that's about the book, the problem is that it isn't really distributed here, but it might be soon.

So, what actually was my method, was a kind of conceptual vein. For many months before my invitation to The Renaissance Society I wanted to tell this story of gratitude. But then, how do you talk about gratitude, of course, you can try endlessly. I'd go over to the deli, meet this guy, this guy tells me about his life about his grandmother. I'd go to the post office—there are these little things that happen to you in New York or Brooklyn—well, that's not really a story I can publish or anything.

But by coincidence I stumbled upon this total hippie story. I read a story about the first encounter of Europeans in Mexico, which was about Hernán Cortés, the Spanish conquistador and about the then King of Mexico, Montezuma. And well, so the thing was, when I was five or ten years old, I was always interested in stories of first encounters of Europeans and the First Americans. And I always believed, when I would ask teachers about it in school, they'd always say, "We don't know much about them. There are a few images. There are some broken temples, paintings of Gods, but we don't know anything about it." And so, since I didn't consider it for many years, I kind of started looking for this information on the Internet, and I realized that it isn't nothing. There is so much told about these stories and what happened in the beginning of what is called the genocide, which was the destruction of the pre-Columbian American cultures. And it isn't at all that there was no culture, as I had learned of it in school, but there were so many huge cultures, and actually there is much documentation about them. The first thing I read about was the king or ruler of Mexico, his name was Montezuma, as I said. I started to really like this four-volume book, which was full of descriptions by the conquistadores. You all know the story so I shouldn't tell it, but there is this tale about how they came there. They brought a writer, a Franciscan monk in the beginning, but then they had to bring in more, two or three writers, and they began this diary about how they arrived, and how they came to Mexico City. I was very impressed, not only by the incredibly detailed descriptions they used, but later, I was impressed to discover that there were Mexicans who also put all this together in books called the codices,[2] which is an image language in books that still exist. The codices, which describe almost every day of these first encounters of the first two years are still not all published and so on. Some of them are in Florence in some church or something, not available to the public. But, anyway, there are some details that came through. What I liked very much was this description, about the king of the Aztec empire, when Montezuma met Hernán Cortés there was a thing where they met in the street in Mexico City. You should know that it was really well described in these books by the Spanish, who had been in Rome and Moscow before. They knew the world a little bit, but they came there. They said they

2 Aztec codices are books written by pre-Columbian and colonial era Aztecs. These codices provide some of the best primary sources for Aztec culture. The codices consist of images and pictograms. (en.wikipedia.org/wiki/Aztec_codices)

had never seen such a big city. They had never seen such a well-organized city. Such a city of schools and everything. They said this is certainly the biggest city in the world. But they had this strange purpose of going there to destroy it, just to get the gold for the Spanish Empire to pay back their debts. My point was to describe the moment of this description of the first half an hour, where Montezuma meets Cortés and his friends after they had come a long way on horseback. Imagine the American President meets the Chinese President—it was a very ritualistic thing. But the conversation was about Montezuma being quite an elaborate man, but polite to a degree, or what I think is a kind of politeness, because he made himself very small, he said, for Cortés, who was just somebody who arrived with 1,000 people, but for him (Montezuma) that was nothing. So he said, "I'm nothing, I haven't done anything in my life, and you come here, as if you came from the clouds, from Heaven, you are such a great man." And he gave him this golden plate, which was very fine with these handmade carvings. So he gave him this calendar plate of gold, and said to him, "Yes, you came from the clouds," and so on, and made himself very small, while Hernán Cortés just said to his translator, "Where is your palace?"

He took that golden thing and gave it to somebody and had it melted down to one piece of gold to sell later. He did this again and again. There are endless stories of how these 1,000 people destroyed an entire city in only one year, and only a few people survived. This seemed almost inconceivable, how such a thing would be possible. But it was possible for thousands of reasons, like the lack of politeness of the conquistadores. For example, the Mexicans had this idea that before you have a battle you tell each other about it, and explain why you are fighting against one another. The Spanish or Europeans didn't care about that. They were only there to take.

Anyway, while I read that, and then later I started reading more, I discovered the Mexican Empire was such a culturally distinguished empire. I later started reading about the first encounters in the United States, like in Florida, Georgia, and Texas and so on. These are unbelievable books. Now I've read my whole life, but these are some of the best stories I've ever read for many reasons. For instance, there is one book from a guy named De Vaca.[3] He was one of the first to arrive in Northern America, in Florida. They came with a big boat of like 300 people, and the boat shipwrecked in Florida and only a few survived. They came to these Native Americans who had a completely different culture from the natives in Mexico. In the beginning they were very friendly, and took care of them. But the Europeans were not very friendly, they were always focused on fighting, or power. There were four that survived, and during their whole journey—they walked from Florida to Mexico—they had a lot of first encounters along the way. All these reports talk about these cultures that I had formerly believed were not documented.

My point was that when I did this project, the best way to somehow describe my own gratitude

3 Álvar Núñez Cabeza de Vaca

would be to take these kinds of adventure stories and first encounters, and to mingle them with my own story, because, actually, the De Vaca story is quite the opposite of the Cortés story. It is a story where the person arrives there and clearly he is a military man, but as he walked through the land, he has these experiences with different tribes. He describes quite well how he himself has actually changed, how this journey has made him someone different than who he was before. The book, I think, at least the end of the book, is one of the most intense endings I've ever read. He arrives in West Mexico, in the Sonoran Desert or somewhere, and there he discovers these very highly developed cultures, unlike what he'd found in Texas, where they didn't even have gardens, and were more of the hunter-gatherer type and they were rude, and he became a slave for a year.

But then, he comes to this culture where they have these gardens and he describes them. As part of the Spanish Navy he'd seen the entire world, but he'd never seen people as beautiful, intelligent or communicative ever in his life. What happened to him at the end of his journey is that he changed so much that they started projecting on him, that he possessed the potential to heal. And he always ignored this suggestion, but then they really almost forced him to use it, and they brought him sick people, and asked him to heal them. So, he pretended to heal them. Because he'd seen so many medicine men and they were always smoking, and sort of blew smoke on the body of the sick or whatever. He tried that and he tried again, and of course there were lots of other things involved, but the weird thing is that he healed the people for real. They might have been really sick and then a few hours later, they were running around celebrating. It came to the point that once they even brought him a dead person. They asked him to fix the man and of course he did the same thing, to pray and so on. And it worked. The dead person was suddenly alive and celebrating his life again, but he describes it unlike I do, he describes it in a way that completely rejects the idea, but insists that he was forced into it. And when he was successful it wasn't because they told him just to do it, but that they saw in him the potential to do it. They said, "We see in you that you have the possibility to heal and you should use it." He was forced through coercion, and basically he took on this position, almost against his own will, and what happened was that they followed him around and when he was walking there were always thousands of people following him.

He describes them as the most communicative, beautiful, and intelligent people. Then it so happens that he finds a horseshoe in one of the villages. Now this was something that didn't exist in America before Columbia, and he was in something like 1538, but 1532 was the beginning of the occupation of Mexico, so it must have been a few years later, but it wasn't. He asked them, "Where did you get that?" They said, "Oh yeah, we met these people and they have beards, and they look really different, they come from somewhere else." And he realizes that they got the horseshoe from some Spanish people, while he'd thought he was completely lost in this endless continent and would never get back to Spain. Then he says to them, because he knows how they are (the Spanish) and was afraid they had not changed as much as he'd changed during his time there walking from Florida, that he'd become a friend and compassionate lover of First Americans, that he knew that there were quite evil conquistador types with bad interests and so he warned them, "If you ever see a white man again with such a beard, go away as far and fast as you can." But they didn't believe him, because they couldn't believe that people could be so bad. And so he walks down the Sonoran Desert and tells them always to go home, to go away. But they follow him, because they have this idea that to be a host means to always bring him to the next place. Then at one traumatic moment, he is walking and sees the first people on horses, the first Europeans with lances, etc. and he still yells at them (the natives) to please go. And he comes to the Spanish, they see him with his long hair and dressed like a Native American with his European features, and they described that they'd just come from Mexico City north and were looking to collect slaves. And they say, "What, you are Spanish?" Then the guy from the Spanish army is really happy, and says that for one week they couldn't collect any slaves but here he'd come and brought them 1,000 so they would put them all in chains and take them away. He goes back to the Native Americans and begs them to leave, to run away, saying that the Europeans would make them all slaves and kill them, that they would all die, but they refused to leave.

The chief of the Spanish army says to the leader of the Native Americans, come here. The guy says no. He starts putting them in chains. The Chief makes this big speech, which has been written down, and it is one of the best speeches, I think, because it says so clearly in an almost biblical way, "You cannot both be Europeans, you can't both be Spanish, because the one man heals and gives life, and when we gave him something he passed it on to someone else. But, you are European perhaps. You use, steal, you take away things, you go to other countries in search of more power." I can't repeat it so well, but I think it is a pretty traumatic speech at the end of this book. And how it ends? He describes how everyone was enslaved and later killed.

Anyway, I think what I've said is a bit traumatic, and I told you I would improvise, so I don't know why it took me so long to explain this little book. I'm sorry. Let me interrupt a bit, by the way if you have any questions I'd be very happy because it would help me, and lead me possibly to less traumatic, and perhaps, more interesting things. I just want to say, that actually what I did, what I attempted, was not at all achieved.

When I started writing the book one week before its deadline I was thinking about my gratitude, not only for my own experience in Mexico and New York, but I was grateful to have been able to read these great books and documents about how people who had grown up on the same continent as me could have done such things, and they've been nearly forgotten. We all know that, but I realized the absolutely infinite amount of genocide waged on people and culture, I don't think there is ever too much awareness for that. To say that its reasons are still relevant, and may I make another cultural reference here, which I didn't mention in the book, although it was my plan to write about these cultural references, but when I have to write very quickly, I can't include everything, so I ended up writing about how I grew up, and how my aunt grew up, and then I'm writing about how I met a friend in New York and we decided to start a sort of art group. And I described how I went to Mexico, and wrote a few things that really refer to contemporary America, and that we went to Guadalupe, near Mexico City, a place where shortly after the invasion of Mexico by Europeans, it happened that the holy Mary appeared to Native Americans and told them that she wanted to help them. And that she, even the church that had already been established in Mexico as part of the Spanish invasion, that she was against that. Anyway, if anyone has never been to Guadeloupe, it is a very special place. There is this huge church where the Pope has spoken, and many Mexican people go there with certain expectations about healing personal issues. But I was brought there by friends with a car. I wasn't too interested in it. But when I was there I was, let's say, in a stupid way, enjoying it. To see all these people being so devoted. Something about this church, I'd never seen before. And I suddenly realized that I'd never been too interested in Catholicism, and almost opposed it my whole life. But then I learned that in America, in a place like Mexico City, it plays a completely different role. And actually, it was always connected to a sort of revolutionary, and anti-European movement, like for Mexican people with Native American backgrounds. The most famous Mexican revolutionary, the one who started the whole thing was a Jesuit. He started walking from a little village and said, "We've had enough of the Spanish King, it is enough, we won't be slaves anymore." And he took the famous image of the holy Mary and walked out of the church, and he spoke to his village and said, "This is over, this government, this empire of the Spanish Europeans must end now." And so people followed him and were so excited about his speech with the holy Mary that they followed him to the next village, and within days an army of the people had formed and that was the famous Mexican Revolution. It is something I'd never much considered as a European, that there is an element, for example, even in American Catholicism, which is actually more revolutionary than the left-wing discourse I usually experience in Europe.

I have other good news. I was just in Mexico two days ago before I arrived here. Because I've now mentioned the revolution and the holy Mother, there is something very intense going on in Mexico and I don't know why no media has caught on to it yet. I don't know why if you read the German newspaper there is perhaps one article about the drug war or some such thing. But in the last few weeks there has been an insurgence and the entire city is often blocked and you cannot move freely. No one knows where this will all lead and all my friends, I've never seen them like that, are so enthusiastic and now entirely involved everyday in this political movement. They feel like it's some kind of historic moment, and it will probably change the government, and may change the implications about drug wars over the last three decades. Anyway, I shouldn't speak about that as a visitor only, perhaps this is too long.

I'll try to explain, I brought two little objects with me—you may have seen them already. [Holds up The Renaissance Society exhibition poster]

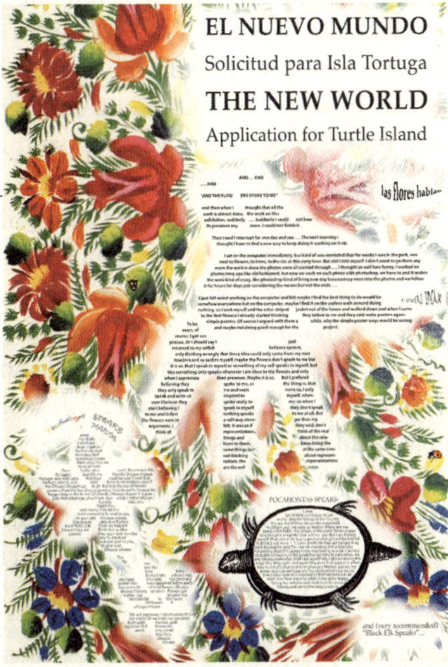

This is the poster. Here is a text of mine, which basically tries to tell you the same story I've just told you. That this is an exhibition, which is not clearly an art exhibition, but tries to tell a story simultaneously of my gratitude and my gratitude for all these first encounters, combined with the historic documents of these first encounters with the Americas. On the front there are texts that are mostly from me, and for the first time, I didn't do my kind of automatic first writing. I used preexisting texts, the main one is from the uncle of Montezuma who was a figure in the history of Mexico. He was not only a king, but also a poet. We still have poetry from him. There is one, which is reprinted here. There is one that comes from the movie, *The New World* (2005), with the same title by Terrence Malick.[4] I could recommend it, it is a movie, which in some ways could be considered a bit pornographic, but for me it was important to do this whole thing. Because what I did after reading all these references is, I was trying to download as many movies that related to these first encounters as possible. There are ten or maybe more, and one is called *The New World.* If you have seen it, I shouldn't talk about it. But what I like so much about the movie is that, in some way, I learned while I was working the complexity of this question: How can one explain this so-called gratitude? Because of course, you have yourself in mind. This is totally one-sided, like black and white. You cannot say all the Americans are great, or all the Mexicans are great, and Europe is very horrible. It's dark and it has such a dark history. Which of course I believe in some ways, but you cannot say that in public somehow. Because there are always all these "buts" and "maybes," and then I saw this movie from Terrence Malick, and this movie is, first of all, radically romantic. But it is romantic in a way that it romanticizes the Native Americans in a way that basically shows how a boat comes from England to what is now Virginia in 1601 or 1603, and they come there and just bring violence, power, animosity, self-hate, and hate of the other, while the Native Americans living in Virginia are living in a paradise compared to that. They don't understand what property means. They don't understand why you have this animosity against the other. So, the Spanish come in and there is this great first scene where you see the boats landing, an endless beginning, there is this music, and sun, and water. You see the Americans mirrored in the water, and they are all extremely good looking and so on. Then you see after the boats arrive, this park-like landscape with huge trees. It is America, trees are bigger, rivers are bigger, and then there are more rivers and more trees. Everything is abundant and huge. They go into the water and there is lobster and they have lobster and so on. But then they really walk into this place. They walk into this park-like landscape and you see this lens move through the whole thing and back, panning really slowly. You hear this narrative music, and then you see how it zooms off as they walk and on the other side off in the trees a woman is standing there, her name is Pocahontas[5] and she looks between these huge blades of grass because in America even the grass

4 Terrence Malick (born 1943) is an American film director, screenwriter and producer. Reputatably called by some as a "Poet of Cinema."

5 Pocahontas (born Matoaka, known as Amonute, c. 1596–1617) was a Native American notable for her association with the colonial settlement at Jamestown, Virginia. (en.wikipedia.org/wiki/Pocahontas)

is bigger, and she walks so you can hardly see her but everything is immensely beautiful. And well, she realizes that these people speak another language, so she tries to translate. They have metal things, big boots, and they don't want to translate at all.

She comes to them—this is really documented very well because this happened very often, that some First Americans were very capable of learning new languages quickly. They were very good at translating. They learned the Spanish language in just a few days. You have to know that most of the languages on the American continent were very different. So anyway, embracing the romanticism, in all their goodness, and intelligence, and beauty, there was even their ability to try and understand the other, to learn their language by making this dance. So she does this dance with her hands for the sun, but they don't react, they look angry, like she might be an enemy and so on. So the movie is really about her dance, and that of the other First Americans. But then it ends up that they come and immediately try to build a fortress so they block out the others. And when winter comes, they slowly die, because they made these big walls, and they are very European.

So, there is the very traumatic thing, winter, and the wall, and they start fighting and almost killing each other and then suddenly, of course, they together, with Wagnerian music, they come together with Pocahontas, her family and friends, they (the First Americans) bring food and fur and give them (the settlers) and put it down on the floor. Of course, the film continues because later she goes to Europe and becomes the most famous Native American. She goes to visit the Queen of England and so on. But what I learned from that film is that if there is a decision about what cannot be translated into writing or artwork, that it is better … not to hesitate. To say, "Well, I cannot say something radical, like that, that the Americans have a great heart, that they are very sweet, always very helpful, while the Europeans will destroy you." But if you ever have any problem like that, it could be a very different sort of problem, but the only way out of it, is to exaggerate, to exaggerate and not to hesitate.

What I tried to do in this project is to embrace and exaggerate this expression. What I try to do now is to exaggerate my own work because it is the first time I'm able to make this kind of sculpture, such as this bear that I bought in the middle of the night in a Mexican hospital [shows photo of big white bear on the back of his book] at four in the morning. What is happening in the hospital at four in the morning? Well, they had this little shop that sold these bears there. It was strange. But anyway, I bought that bear and then I bought this new camera and I wanted to try it out. So, I made this first shot, and I photographed this bear and the wolf. And then later I looked at this photo and, I didn't put this poster on the wall, it was Nora.[6] But then I looked at this photo that was very weird, actually, because the bear and the wolf are there, perfectly reading my text off the poster.

6 Nora Schultz (born 1975), German sculptor, friend of the artist.

I've made many text posters, and to be honest now at the very end, I've spoken about Europe and America, but there is something about it. Americans—in Mexico, in New York, in Chicago, wherever Guatemala, they read my texts. But in Germany, there are two people who do, and they always tell me when I do a poster on the wall in an exhibition. There are a few people only. But the thing is, it was a magic photo for me and I was thinking of the bear and the wolf, these two guys, they are reading my text and it is a little bit of an issue. When I did my first exhibition with text there were people coming in saying, "Higher, lower, but anyway, I don't read the text, why should I read the text? But anyway, it's strange, but I never read text." I don't know why that is, but there is a difference.

So when I was sitting in Mexico, I had a great graphic designer, a friend of my gallery, House of Gaga, and as always, they say, "Josef you have to produce the cover now," and I looked at my screen and said, "By the way, I have some stupid photos here," because I have many of them. But they loved the one photo too, and said, "Josef that's so great, let's make that the cover." Their enthusiasm, their laughter helped to do the book. It still looks a bit ridiculous, probably like my talk right now, but anyway, I think I tried to explain my mode of production a little bit. And I tried to explain the enthusiasm and greatness of being a traveler and going far away, like I thought when I was younger, some years ago.

This is the last story I'll tell, and it is somehow the same story. I was collecting for a sculpture and

I was looking for some chains. In Mexico, if you say chains, there are thousands of different chains, in all kinds of materials. Then I don't want to say this too often, but I think if you are an artist and haven't much money, Mexico is really the place for you. The whole city is beautiful, green, there is no winter, people are very concentrated, are very communicative, etc., and there is still cheap rent.

So I was putting these chains together, they were lying on the table, and hanging around me, and my Mexican friends said, "With those chains, what do you think? We could do chains for your opening?" I said, "Well, maybe, maybe we should name them after Montezuma. The chains of Montezuma stolen by the Europeans, and now we try to give it back. We keep that spirit in mind, to give things back." So, as I said it came from a lack of ideas, but I'd seen them on all the street corners, from people who do weavings on metal plates. Maybe I'll write a text because I cannot make chains, or do sculptures, or make paintings, I can't do anything. So I tried to write this text, sat down and put it all together for the show. In any case, it's almost impossible like that to write a nice sentence, but anyway, I started writing something like, "If you don't know where to go, follow your sheep, and follow them even if they go to a faraway land." I didn't know where the sentence came from. We went to this place and there was a guy standing there, and it's one of the sentences from the Bible, the Song of Songs or whatever. So, I took more of these sentences and said this example, "Follow your sheep wherever they go," as an idea for making productions.

ORTRAG
anz Erhard Walther
nstler
Dezember

ORTRAG CURATORIAL STUDIES
en Blumenstein
ratorin
. Dezember

Januar 2015

ORTRAG CURATORIAL STUDIES
chen Volz
rator
. Januar

RU
Jah
12.
Täg

AU
Me
13.

VO
Jor
Kür
TB

CURATORIAL STUDIES

olz

raw

ikerin

VORTRAG

Jordan Wo

Künstler

TBA

VORTRAG

Tala Mada

Künstlerin

TBA

VORTRAG

Isla Leaver-

Kuratorin Sc

TBA

tädelschule um 19 Uhr statt.

September 29, 2014
Lucy Raven

Motion Capture

American artist Lucy Raven provides an in-depth historical analysis of visual effects and animation in the film industry. Beginning on a tour of Base FX, a contemporary visual effects company in Beijing, and ending with the story of Hollywood Black Friday, also known as "Bloody Friday," a massive union strike-turned-riot at Warner Brothers studios in 1945, Raven traces the history of animation and the people who defined it. Detailing the invention of rotoscoping, celluloid animation, and the iconic work of Max Fleischer and Walt Disney, Raven examines how animation workflow has changed over time and the numerous battles with censorship, racism, and labor rights issues that have afflicted the industry through the years.

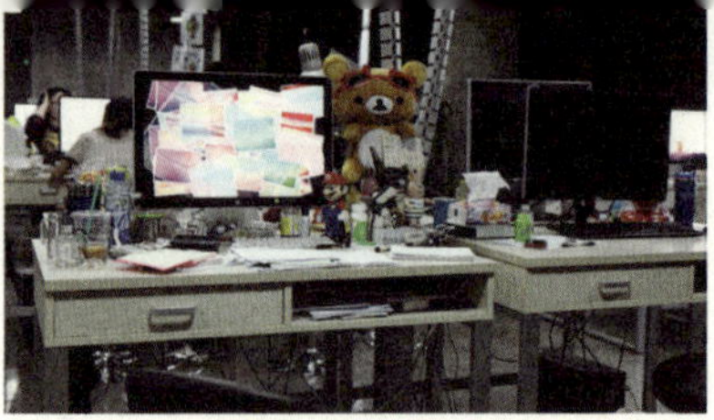

Most of today's films are digital, which means that more work is being done in postproduction. And most of Hollywood's postproduction work is being subcontracted to effects houses overseas, because of lower labor costs and the massive incentives given to movie studios in the form of subsidies offered by foreign governments to set up shop locally. The idea is that a lucrative industry will stay put in its new location, but in the last year, the governments that have tried this, most notably in Vancouver, Canada, have been going broke paying for subsidies, while the studios, like covered wagons headed West, are already moving on to the next horizon.

What we once thought of as special effects are now just called visual effects, or VFX, and nearly every film has them. In fact, some films are composed nearly entirely of VFX.

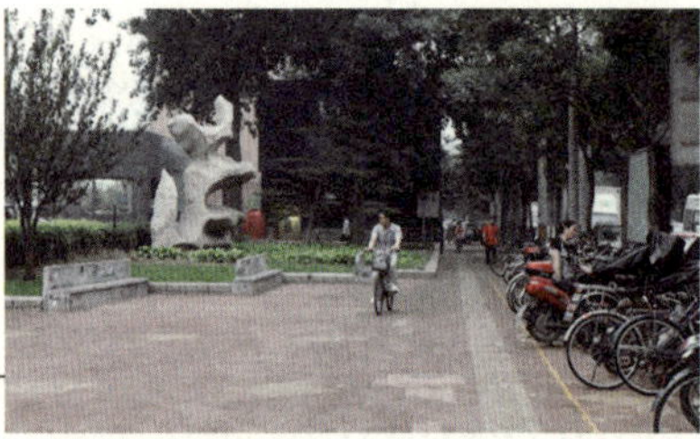

[01]

Last summer, I made a trip to some visual effects houses in Beijing, China.

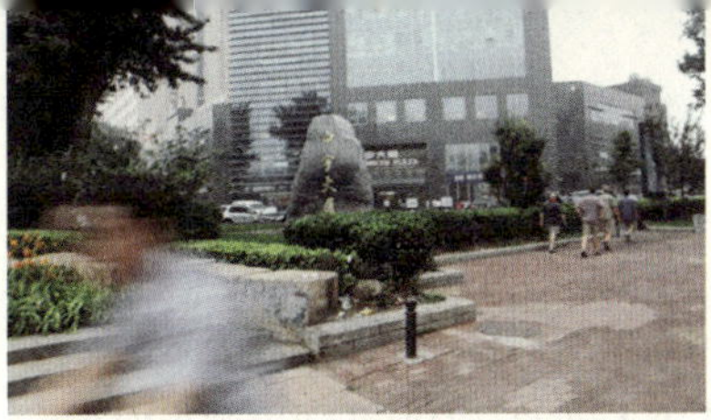

[02]

One company I visited, Base FX, was working on a new Metallica concert film, having recently wrapped work on a number of American blockbusters, including the last *Mission: Impossible*, *Looper*, *Pain & Gain*, and the recent sea creatures vs. giant robots epic *Pacific Rim*.

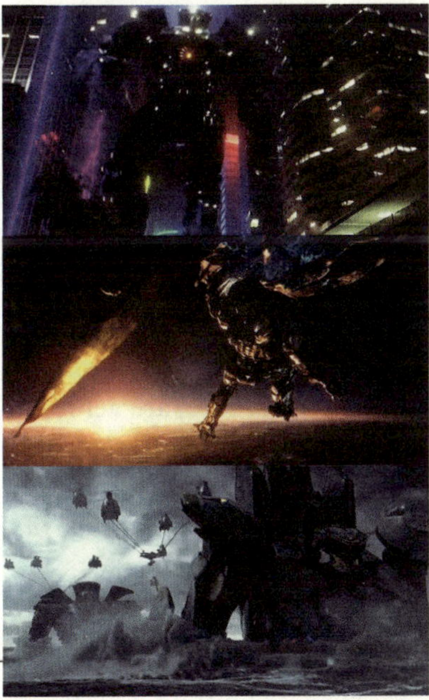

[03]

They were busy gearing up for the next *Star Wars* films, having just signed an exclusive deal with

Industrial Light and Magic (ILM), the visual effects company founded in 1975 by George Lucas to support production of the original *Star Wars*. ILM is a division of Lucas' production company Lucasfilm, which in 2012 was acquired by Disney. Base FX was operating as the conglomerate's backend.

The effects work I saw these technicians doing was new to them, and the company's boss, an American USC film school graduate, had brought over American, Canadian, and Australian supervisors to train each department. Every supervisor I talked to was newly out of a job in LA, and most seemed grateful for the work, even if it was halfway around the world, and even if the pollution levels the week I visited caused the US embassy to recommend not going outside unless absolutely necessary.

Visual effects, whether they're employed to create virtual weather, alternate locations, giant monsters, dust, debris, animal fur, or a heroine's hair waving in a nonexistent breeze, are achieved painstakingly. Films are broken up into tens of thousands of files—one for every frame in the movie—and worked on individually. Because of the exponential amount of work this makes, along with always rushed schedules, the default workflow is to break up and spread out the shots to a number of different studios—uploading and downloading the files from massive servers—according to who can do what, when, for the cheapest price, bringing the files back together in LA to be composited into the finished feature film. In this sense, the term postproduction is misleading; this work forms the bulk of how many contemporary films are created. When you look at this in the context of film history, it seems that we've basically reached its end. Instead, I've been thinking about the workflow of today's films as an extension of the history of animation.

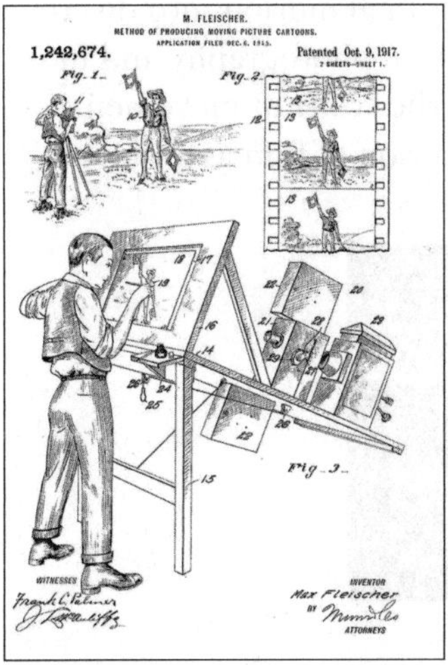

[04]

The first step of most visual effects work begins with rotoscoping, a process that hasn't changed much since Max Fleischer invented it in 1915.

Best known as the inventor of Koko the Clown and Betty Boop, and for his studio's animations of Popeye and Superman, Fleischer also held a number of patents, and his invention of the rotoscope is still the basis for today's digital character animation.

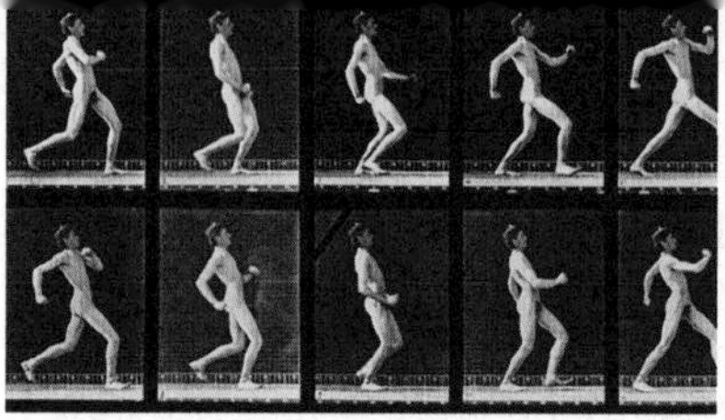

[05]

In the preceding century, photographer Eadweard Muybridge and scientist and chronophotographer Étienne-Jules Marey had figured out how to break up human and animal motion into discrete images. Their stop-action photography and motion studies reformed the study of movement and preceded the invention of film as a way to capture locomotion.

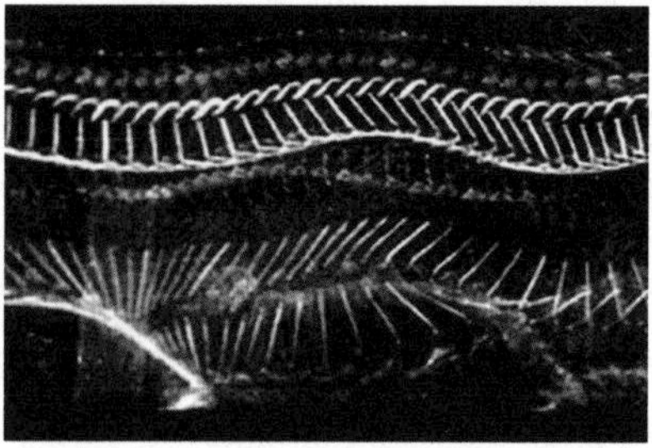

[06]

The camera could see things the human eye couldn't. It made possible the slowing down of movement to an impossible stasis. But how could you extract that motion? Dissect it from its maker and transfer it to another form?

For his initial experiments in rotoscopy, Max filmed his brother Dave dancing in a clown suit, then rear-projected the film frame by frame onto a sheet of frosted glass with a piece of paper affixed on top. Fleischer traced the figure's outline then advanced the film one frame at a time, making a new drawing as each frame advanced.

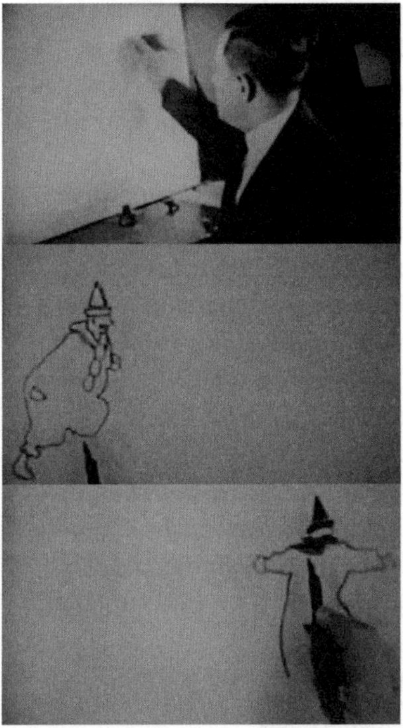

[07]

The rotoscoped version of Dave became the character Koko the Klown.

Around this time, Fleischer went to work for Bray Animation studios, using his engineering and animation background to produce training films for World War I. As the war ended, J.R. Bray and pioneering animator Earl Hurd invented a sytem of animating using transparent sheets of acetate. This system, known as cel animation (from celluloid), allowed the different layers of a cartoon to be drawn on different sheets then sandwiched together, so only the moving parts would need to be redrawn. This innovation, when paired with Fleischer's rotoscope, changed the scope and speed of what it was possible to produce.

But the Fleischers hadn't yet turned their studio into a factory. They were still very much improvising many aspects of their cartoons. They had no separate story department—individual animators developed gags as they drew. Especially unusual for the time was the Fleischers' work with African American jazz musicians, including Cab Calloway, Louis Armstrong, and Don Redman. (Less progressive, however, was the Fleischers' handling of race in the cartoons themselves; in all of these collaborations, the characters' appearance relies on traditional minstrel tropes.)

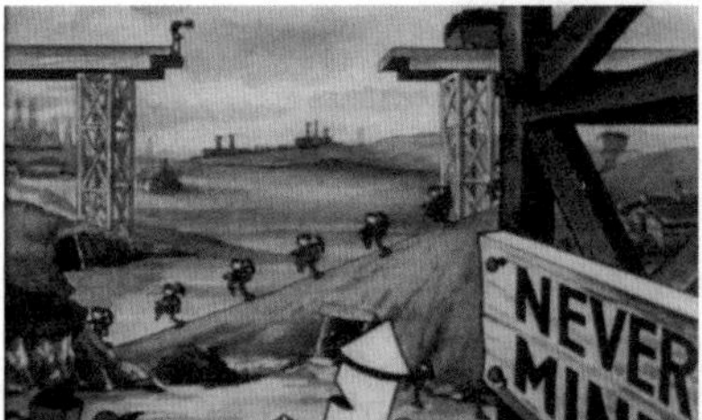

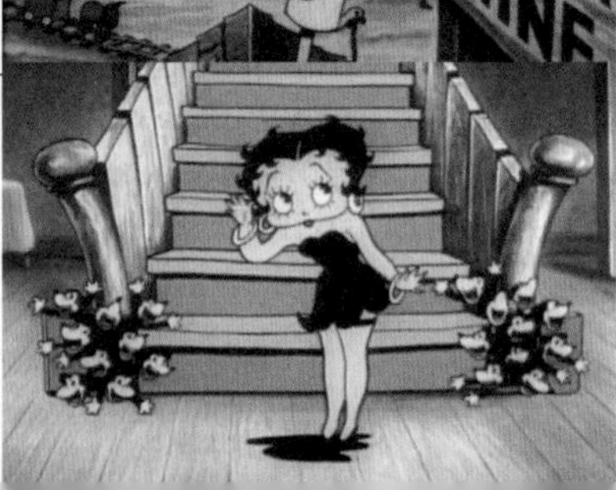

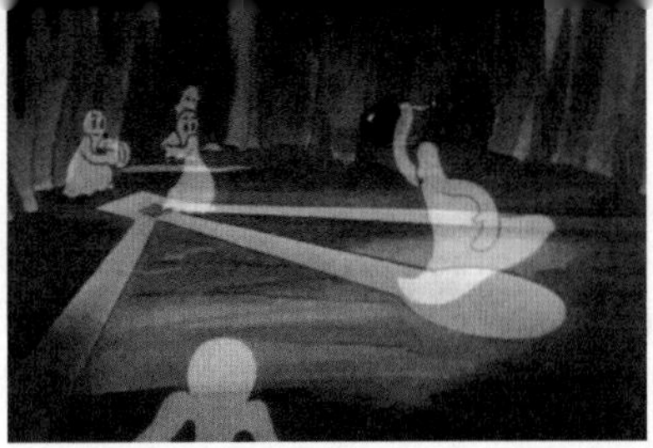

[08]

The studio's still lax approach to labor is evident in the Fleischers' 1933 Betty Boop cartoon *I Heard* (scored by Redman), which mostly takes place during lunch break at a coal mine. The mine is called the "Never Mine" and the work whistle is shown munching a sandwich. But the cartoon doesn't emphasize the operation's production line or the workers' toil; when the ore showers down into train cars at the end, it comes from the bomb a group of ghosts are using to play baseball. The mine scenes bookend the main event, a sultry song and dance number by Betty Boop in the mess hall.

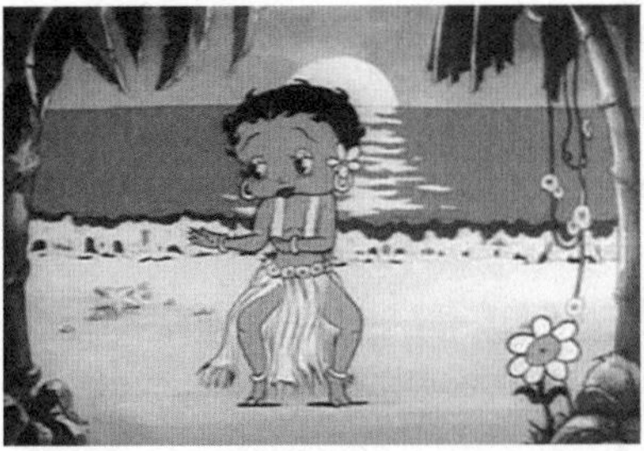

[09]

The film was made in Betty Boop's heyday as a popular flapper seductress. Two years later, the Hays Code, named for its author, Will Hays, began enforcing its code of moral censorship over motion pictures. Besides overseeing all plots that got produced, the Hays office prohibited profanity, miscegenation, licentious or suggestive nudity (in fact or in silhouette), and outlined many other stultifying edicts.

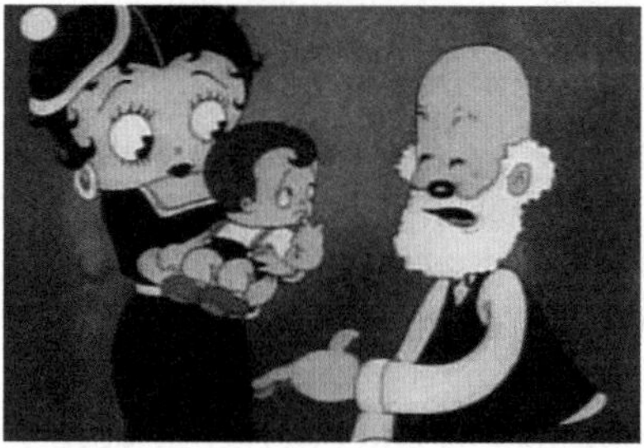

[10]

Even cartoons were affected and Betty Boop was made to turn in her garter for an old housewife skirt that fell below the knees, after which, she quickly faded from popularity.

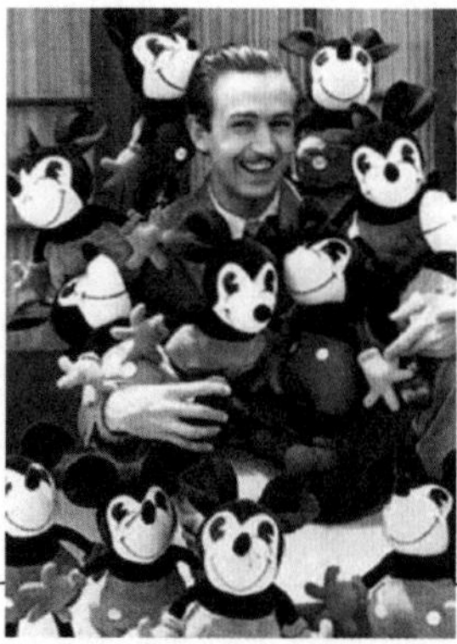

[11]

Meanwhile, another animator was much more in sync with the country's shifting morals.

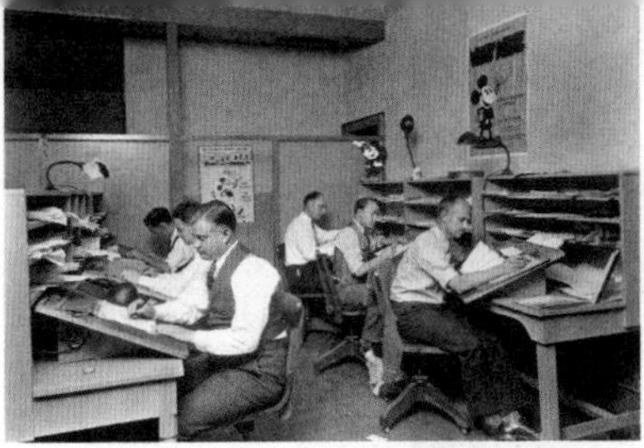

[12]

Walt Disney had been competing neck and neck with Fleischer on a number of innovations in animation techniques and color film developing and had made use of the rotoscope, most notably, in his first feature, *Snow White and the Seven Dwarfs*, in 1937.

Unlike Fleischer, whose characters stretched, morphed, blew up, and reemerged in rhythm with jazz riffs, Disney used the rotoscope to create ever more lifelike cartoons. He eschewed cartoons' inherent flatness and self-referentiality for *mise-en-scène* deep space, and a realistic sense of gravity.

To complete *Snow White*, Disney tripled his staff to about 800. The studio stayed open twenty-four hours a day, with workers rotating on three eight-hour shifts. More than two million cels were produced (250,000 were used in the final film) over three million working hours. As Esther Leslie noted in *Hollywood Flatlands*, the studio had become a factory for the mass-production of entertainment.

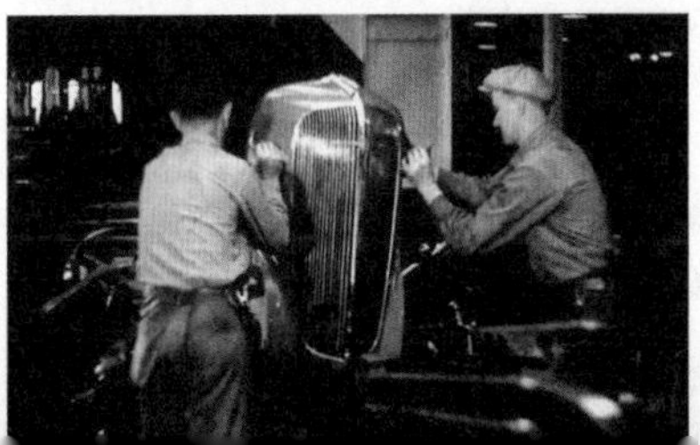

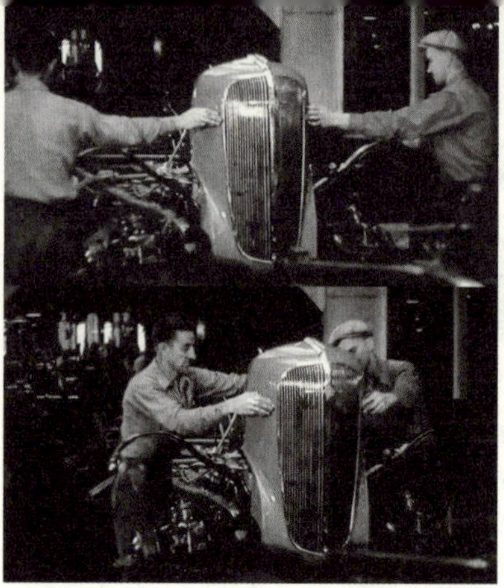

[13]

Around that time, Fleischer's first boss, J.R. Bray, began working at an industrial film company called the Jam Handy Organization, not just mass-producing films but making films celebrating mass-production. Their 1936 GM tribute, *Master Hands,* shows a Chevrolet being made from foundry to finished car at the Fisher Body plant in Flint, Michigan, with a score by the Detroit Philharmonic.

Just months later, the Fisher plant was the site of the first sit-down labor strike, where workers protested unfair working conditions and demanded union recognition.

The bodies that had done piecework on the assembly line now physically occupied the factory. Their unwillingness to move effectively halted production.

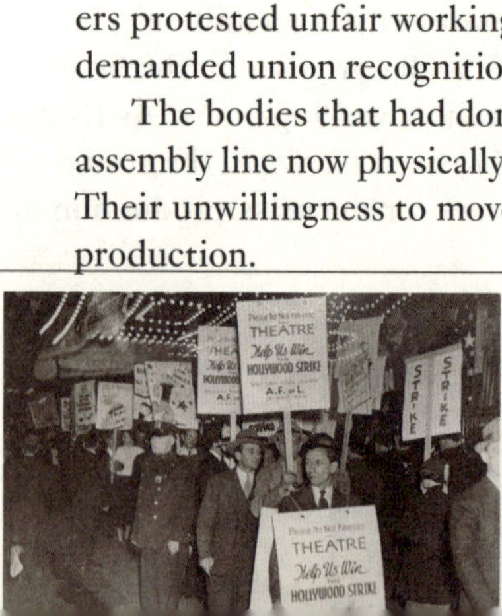

[14]

At the same time, animators at Fleischer's studio went on strike.

While the Screen Actors Guild had formed in 1933, and other guilds had formed of projectionists and musicians, there was not yet a guild for animators. As they protested uneven pay structures and increasing workdays without fair compensation, Fleischer's employees explored forming a union. Some of the animators had already organized under the larger Commercial Artists and Designers Union (CADU), which had helped put pressure on Fleischer Studios for better working conditions. The Fleischers, however, were not interested in negotiating with CADU and when their distributor, Paramount, increased their quota for Popeye cartoons, the animators responded by slowing down work. Fleischer pushed back, placing armed guards at the entrances to his studio to intimidate employees. In May 1937, he fired thirteen cartoonists, explicitly because of their union involvement. It was the final straw: that week, CADU voted for the animators to strike with the goal of forming their own union. They were joined in solidarity by union projectionists, who refused to project Fleischer films, and musicians, who would not play on their cartoons. After five weeks, desperate for the strike to end, Paramount pressured the Fleischers to settle with CADU. It was the first union contract to be signed for animation.

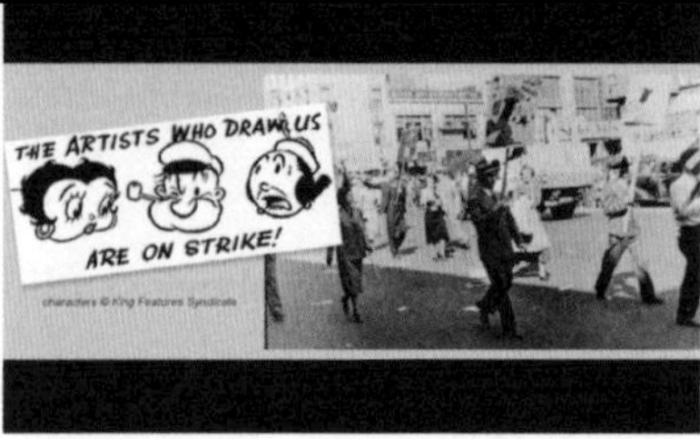

[15]

Many of the cartoonists had returned to work when the Fleischers received the offer of a major tax credit from the state of Florida, a right-to-work state that banned union organizing. The Fleischers accepted the offer, made plans to move their studio to Miami, and volunteered to pay relocation fees to animators willing to move down with them. The studio relocated in 1938, and soon after, a number of animators, dismayed by southern society's widespread prejudice and segregation, returned to Manhattan. Forced to recruit and train new workers, the studio eventually went over budget on nearly every project. Paramount ended their contract in 1942, seized the studio's assets for money owed, and moved them back to New York to make shorts. The Fleischers filed numerous lawsuits to try to recover their company, but far from succeeding, they ended up costing the brothers dearly.

Fleischers' workers, meanwhile, were gaining momentum and support in the workplace. A year after their victory, in 1938, they were chartered by the Painters, Decorators and Paperhangers Union as the Screen Cartoonists Guild, Local 852. With union organizer Herb Sorrell at the helm, they successfully organized and signed contracts with MGM, Walter Lantz, and Screen Gems.

In 1941, two big studios loomed large for the union—Looney Tunes and Disney. Early in the year, Leon Schlesinger of Warner Brothers locked out the guild animators, but he folded in just six days and signed with the union. Disney would prove significantly more difficult.

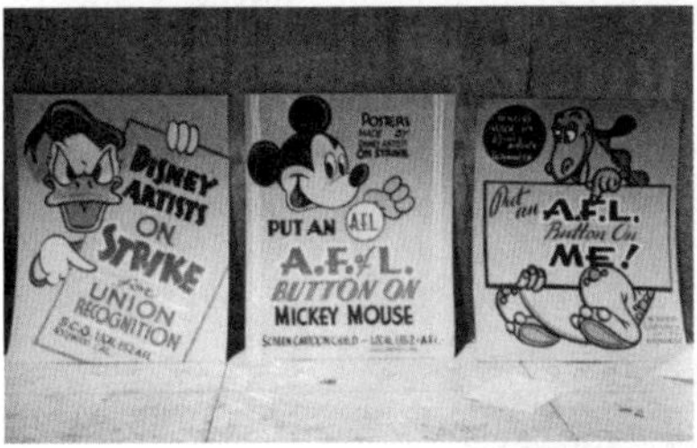

[16]

Walt felt personally betrayed when his highest-paid animator, Art Babbitt, resigned as president of the Disney company to join the Screen Cartoonists Guild. Disney fired him, calling him a troublemaker and a Bolshevik, and three days later, on May 29, the strike began.

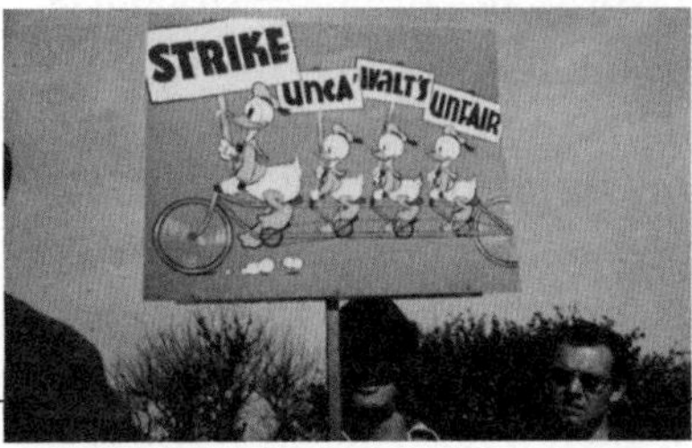

[17]

Though the studio had ballooned during the making of *Snow White*, many employees were promised profit-sharing bonuses and worked free overtime in the push to complete the film. But despite the film's success, Disney didn't pay them. He also didn't credit them—only Disney's name appears in the film's credits. On top of this, the weekly pay scale was so uneven, a top animator might make $500 a week, while a cel painter got $12.

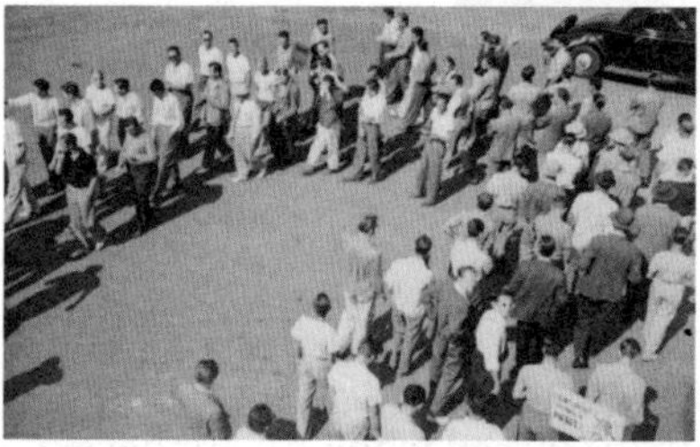

[18]

Disney lost a huge amount of its foreign sales market during the war, particularly to Germany, which was the largest international importer of US films at the time. Although *Snow White* was reportedly a favorite of Hitler's—Goebbels gave him a print of the film for Christmas to be screened in the Führer's personal theater—the film was banned in Germany.

The strike dragged out over five weeks. Unable to settle the terms, and still refusing to recognize the union, Disney was persuaded to go on a press junket and research trip to Latin America for what would become his live-action/animation musical *The Three Caballeros* (1944). While he was away, President Franklin D. Roosevelt brought in a federal mediator, who sided with the guild on every count.

Dumbo was the film Disney was producing during the strike. The film, incidentally, takes place in the labor law free land of Florida.

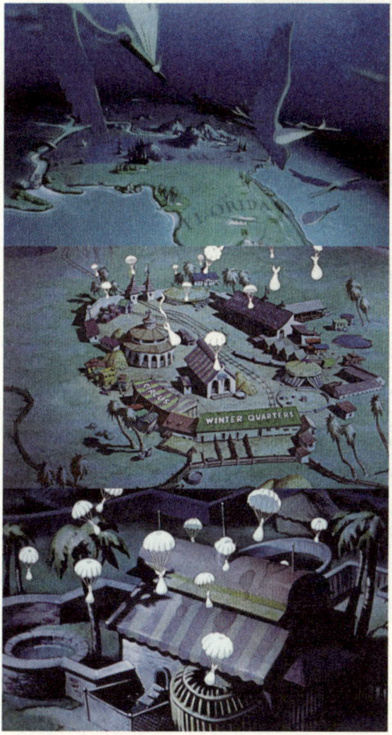

[19]

Dumbo tells the story of a baby elephant with giant ears, who eventually learns to capitalize on this strange trait by flying.

Early in the film, we see a mixed crew of elephants and black workers (making their only appearance in the movie), working to mount the circus tent.

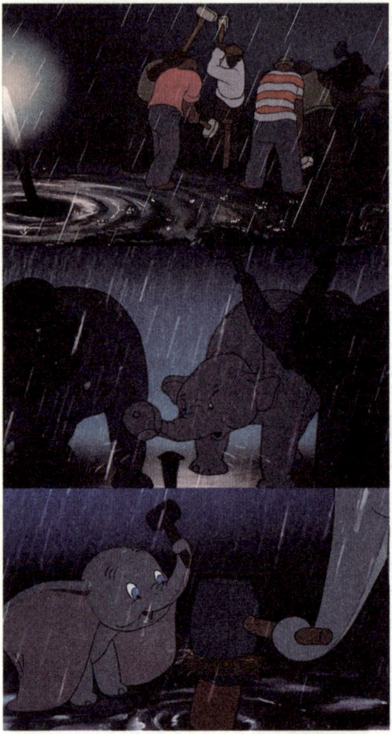

[20]
Here's what they're singing:

We work all day, we work all night
We never learned to read or write
We're happy-hearted roustabouts

When other folks have gone to bed
We slave until we're almost dead

We don't know when we get our pay
And when we do we throw our pay away /
We get our pay when children say
With happy hearts, "It's circus day today"
(Then we get our pay, just watching kids on circus day)

Muscles aching
Back near breaking /
Boss man houndin'
Keep on poundin'
For your bed and feed
There ain't no let up
Must get set up
Pull that canvas! Drive that stake!
Want to doze off
Get them clothes off
But must keep awake

Swing that sledge! Sing that song!
Work and laugh the whole night long
You happy-hearted roustabouts! /

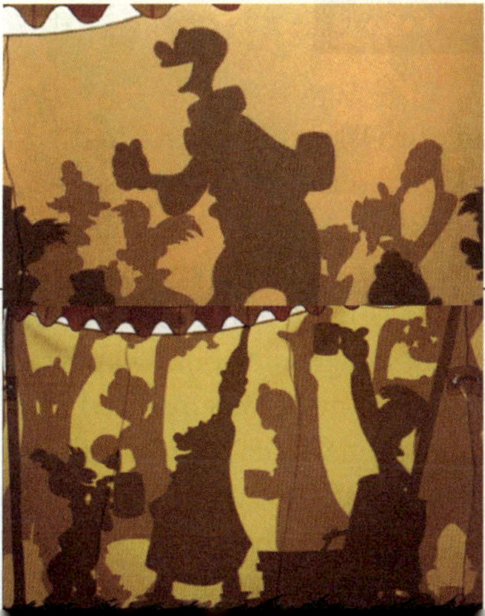

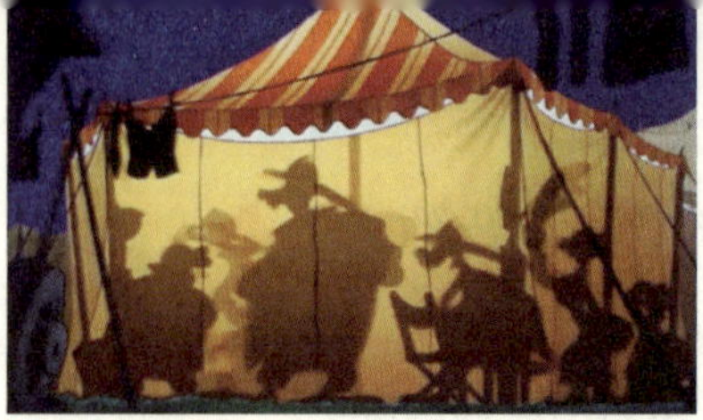

[21]

A later scene is even more explicit, caricaturing the strikers as clowns asking their big boss for a raise.

While Disney's rank and file marched outside, the Disney compound itself became the set for a live-action movie called *The Reluctant Dragon*. A publicity-ready gloss on what it was like to work at the studio, it was made using mostly actors instead of actual animators, most of whom were striking.

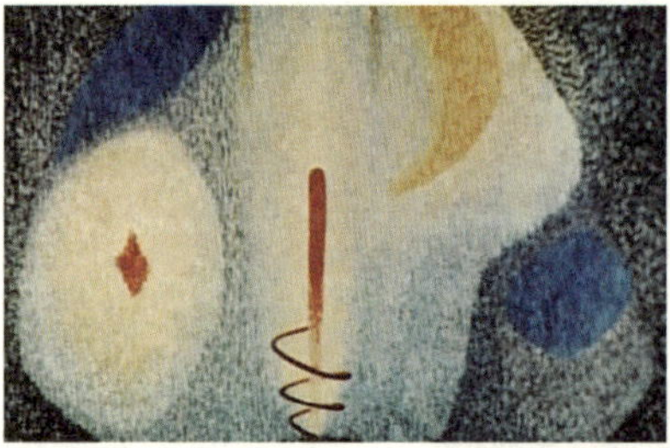

[22]

The German animator Oskar Fischinger had been hired to work on a scene of *Fantasia* soon after he'd emigrated to Los Angeles. As an abstract painter and filmmaker in Munich, and later Berlin, Fischinger had been working on his own, more abstract ideas of image and sound capture. His move to film from painting was inspired by the German filmmaker Walter Ruttmann's animation *Lichtspiel Opus 1*, which Fischinger saw in 1921.

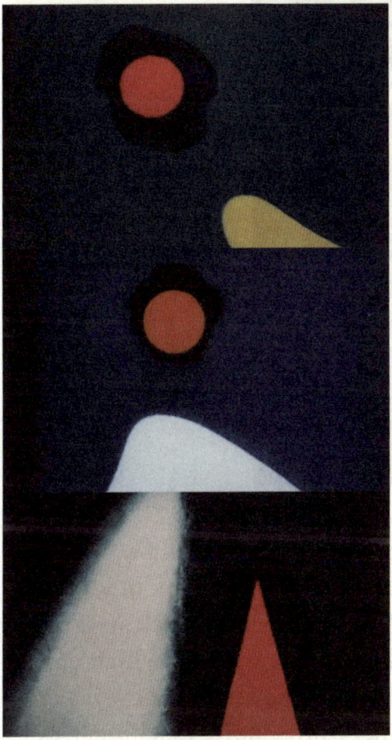

[23]

Ruttman, Fischinger, and others were making what they called absolute film—films with no objective representational imagery. This way of working also came to be known as "visual music." Often, the pieces were scored, but the term referred more to the complex visual rhythms produced by the films' combinations of image and form.

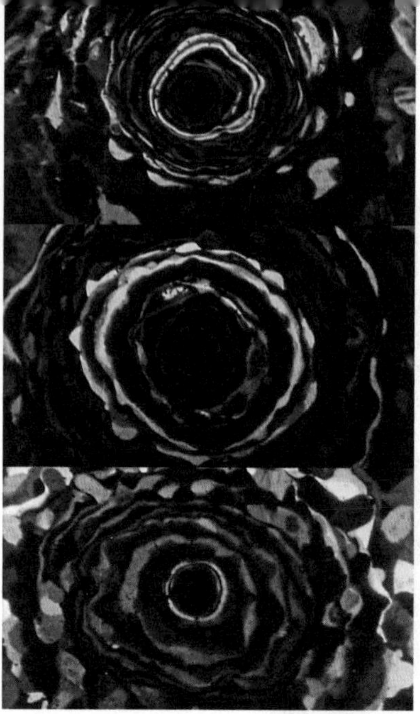

[24]

One of Fischinger's innovations was a wax slicing machine. A piece of wire cut a chunk of wax, one sliver at a time. As soon as the wire cleared the wax, it triggered a camera shutter, which captured a single frame of the slightly new façade. As with many of his works, here, Fischinger explored a mode of movement outside of narrative progression.

Walter Ruttmann was enthralled with Fischinger's invention and licensed the wax slicing machine to make backdrops for Lotte Reiniger's *The Adventures of Prince Achmed*. (Though his initial tests were a success, the hot studio lights melted the wax, and the machine could not be sustainably implemented into the film's production.)

As the Nazi party came to power, the German film industry was nationalized. Abstract art of all kinds was vilified, and Fischinger emigrated to America.

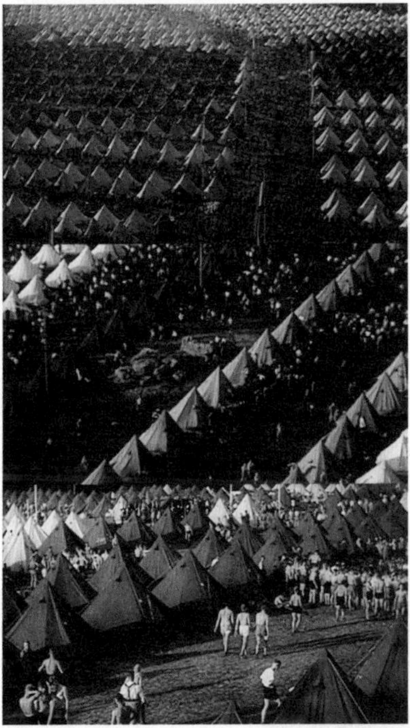

[25]

Ruttmann took another path, making documentaries under the Third Reich, and working as assistant director for Leni Riefenstahl's *Triumph of the Will.*

In the movies, through various modes of animation, you can make something inanimate seem alive. But, as suggested in the militarized, synchronized movements of bodies in *Triumph of the Will*, the perfect registration between mechanical and human motion can also be turned around to deanimate and control the body.

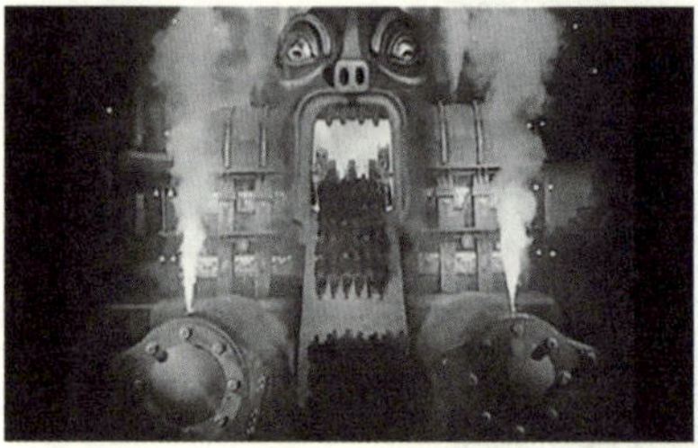

[26]

Already in 1927, the image of a factory of mechanized bodies was part of the popular imagination, as in Fritz Lang's *Metropolis*. Nearly a decade later, the idea of this hell presented by Lang became, for Riefenstahl, a blueprint for utopia.

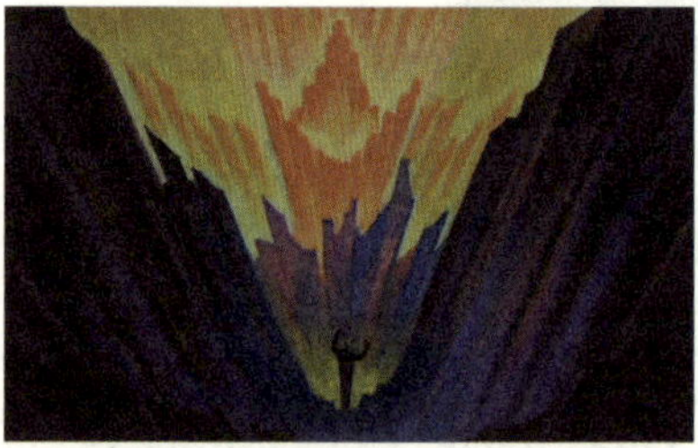

[27]

Fischinger's section of *Fantasia* never made it into the final film—Disney had added a sky behind the animations and other figurative elements, which he insisted the audience needed in order to take in the scene's meaning. Fischinger had emigrated to the States, only to have his animations censored again. In response,

Fischinger wrote:

Now a few words about the usual motion picture film, which is shown to the masses everywhere in countless moving picture theaters all over the world: it is photographed realism—photographed surface realism-in-motion ... There is nothing of an absolute, artistic creative sense in it. It copies only nature with realistic conceptions, destroying the deep and absolute creative force with substitutes and surface realisms. Even the cartoon film is today on a very low artistic level. It is a mass product of factory proportions, and this, of course, cuts down the creative purity of a work of art. No sensible creative artist could create a sensible work of art if a staff of co-workers of all kinds had his or her say in the final creation—producer, story director, story writer, music director, conductor, composers, sound men, gagmen, effect men, layout men, background directors, animators, inbetweeners, inkers, cameramen, technicians, publicity directors, managers, box office managers, and many others. They change the ideas, kill the ideas, before they are born, prevent the ideas from being born, and substitute for the absolute creative motives only the cheap ideas to fit the lowest among them.

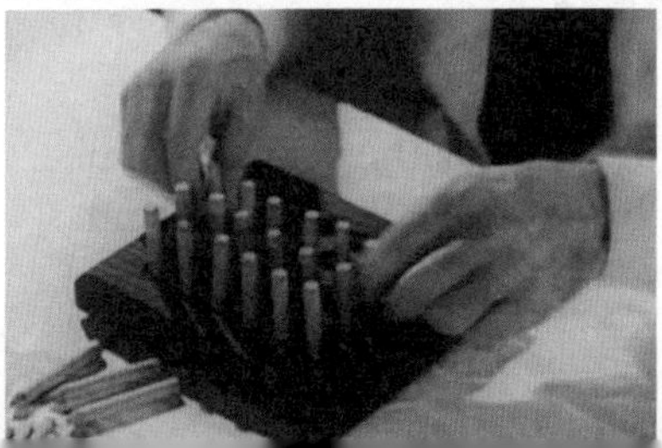

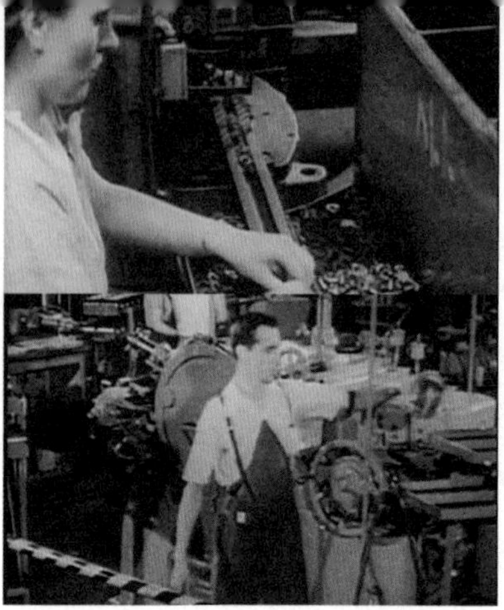

[28]

Meanwhile, Max Fleischer, out of work, went back to work for his old boss, J.R. Bray, at the Jam Handy studios in Detroit. This time, Fleischer's approach to capturing human movement was much more straightforward, and in step with the times. *The Easier Way* is a motion control study dressed up as a domestic dinner scene. Its aim is to motivate innovation in streamlining assembly lines, increasing each individual's productivity, so that the moving belt can move faster.

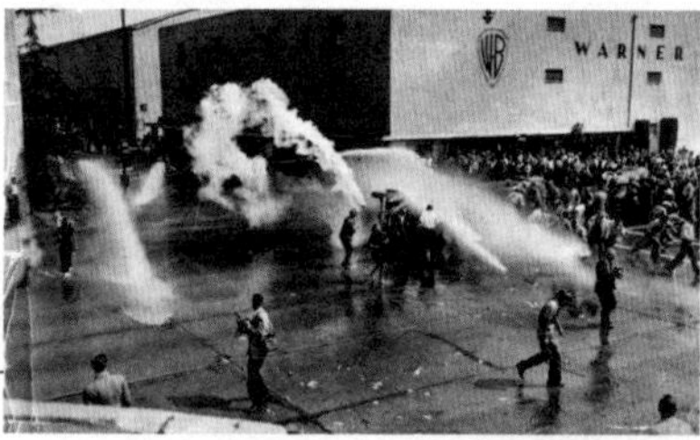

[29]

GM had been unionized by the year the film was made, 1946, but with soldiers back from

World War II, during which time women had joined the workforce, and with nothing left to produce for the war, there was a new wave of strikes across the US. It was kicked off by what became known as Hollywood Black Friday, a six-month strike by the Conference of Studio Unions—including set decorators, painters, carpenters, and cartoonists—that culminated in a violent riot at the gates of the Warner Brothers studios in Burbank, California, on October 5, 1945. The strike began in March with an estimated 10,500 CSU members walking out. While several studios went on to negotiate with the union, most did not, and by October, money and patience were low when 300 strikers gathered outside the gates of Warner Brothers. When non-strikers attempted to enter the building, barricades went up. Reinforcements arrived on both sides as tensions flared, with mutual aid coming to Burbank police from nearby Glendale and Los Angeles departments. A riot ensued, with strikers mobbing non-strikers, and strikebreakers fighting back with nightsticks, hammers, pipes, chains, and tear gas, and Warner firefighters spraying the strikers with fire hoses. National coverage of the riot forced both parties back to the bargaining table, and though the strike ended a month later, the CSU's resources were effectively exhausted, and solidarity among other unions, such as the Screen Actors Guild, broke down. The drawn out negotiations and the bloody images of Black Friday paved the way for the Taft-Hartley Act in 1947, passed with support from the studio's lobby, alongside accusations of CSU leader Herb Sorrell's Communist affiliations. Taft-Hartley, or the Labor Management Relations Act, greatly restricted the activities and power of unions, including bans on general strikes and secondary boycotts, and is still in effect today.

Toward the end of his life, Fischinger wrote: *And so we cut out the tremendous mountains of valueless motion picture productions of the past and the future—the mountain ranges of soap bubbles, and we must concentrate on the tiny golden thread underneath which is hardly visible beneath the glamorous, sensational excitement, securely buried for a long time, especially in our own time when the big producing and distributing monopolies control every motion picture screen in an airtight grip.*

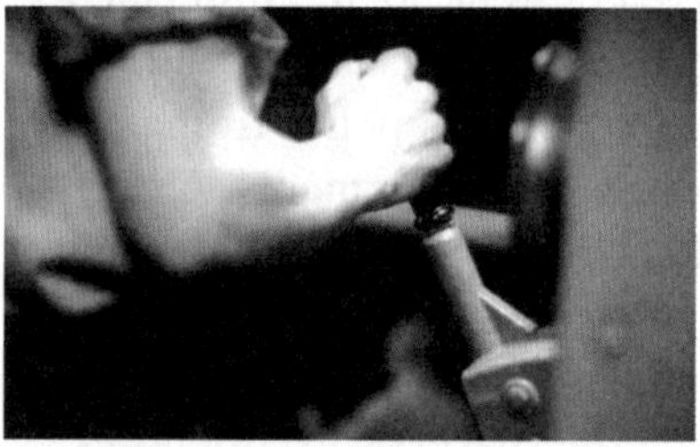

[30]

Finally, is the fist clenched around the lever controlling the machine, or is it the other way around? Today, it's harder to see or hear what sort of motion is being extracted or captured, and how, when the only things moving in the factory of mass entertainment are the fingers and the glittering lights of the servers.

…ting a Body of Work

Vortrag

Her?"

Vortrag
Vortrag
Vortrag
Vortrag

10 - 20 Uhr

McCarthy

Ausstellungs…
Portikus, 20

McCarthy

Performance

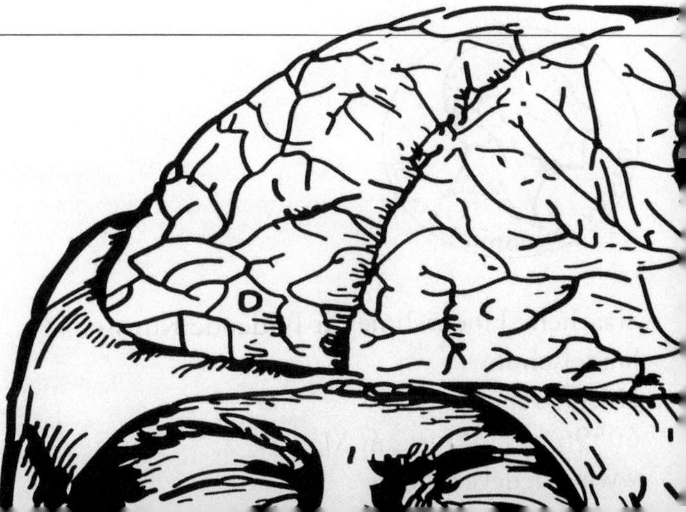

On, Abou

10.	Dezember	Georgia Sa *“What’s Th*
17.	Dezember	Ray Brassi
16.	Januar	Mark von
tba	Januar	Carissa Ro
3.	Februar	Klaus Thev
14 - 16.	Februar	Rundgang
14.	Februar	Mike Bouc
15.	Februar	Mike Bouc

Die Vorträge finden, wenn nicht anders angegeben, in der Aula der Städelschule jeweils um 19 Uhr statt.

JOHANN FRIEDRICH STAEDEL

Staatliche Hochschule für Bildende Künste
Städelschule
Dürerstraße 10
60596 - Frankfurt am Main
www.staedelschule.de

013-14

Vortrag

Vortrag, 18 Uhr

Kunstfeld" | Campus Westend
und Kritik

Vortrag, 16 Uhr
Ausstellungseröffnu
Portikus, 20 Uhr

Vortrag, 18 Uhr

Ai Weiwei, Romuald | Campus Bockenhei
Dayanita Singh"
und Kritik

Vortrag
"

Vortrag

Vortrag

Vortrag
Vortrag

Vorträge
STÄD
Winters

2. Oktober Pedro Cesarin

28. Oktober Christian Kra
"Postkoloniale
Masterstudien

31. Oktober Michel Auder
. November Michel Auder

5. November Susanne Gaen
"Der Deutsche
Karmakar, Sa
Masterstudien

5. November Chris Kraus
"Jason Rhoade

2. November Stefan Tchere

9. November Anne Imhof
"to Parade"

November 27, 2013

Douglas Gordon and Philippe Parreno

Scottish artist Douglas Gordon and French artist Philippe Parreno conduct a rare public talk and discuss their collaborative film Zidane: A 21st Century Portrait, *featured in Parreno's solo exhibition at the Palais de Tokyo. Parreno describes choreographing exhibitions and working with spatial relationships and interventions, the differences between the audience and public, and questions of authorship and collaboration. Together, Gordon and Parreno recount how a football game with artist Olafur Eliasson inspired their film of famed footballer Zinedine Zidane; touring the Museo del Prado with their film crew; and how they began with a portrait, and ultimately achieved the veracity they desired.*

DG Good evening, everybody. I would like to welcome Philippe Parreno here tonight. Philippe and I have done quite a lot of talks together. We have also agreed that neither of us would do it again unless we were getting married to each other. However, sometimes the best gigs in the world are the ones that happen unofficially, so let this be a great unofficial welcome to you, Philippe.

PP Thank you. Douglas is right. This is the first lecture I have accepted in almost fifteen years. I do not like lectures. I do not like the format because it contradicts the type of commitment I have towards art. I think art is essentially a conversational practice. It engages in a very fundamental notion of the other. The project or the exhibition has always been more important to me than the objects composing that exhibition. When I started studying at the École des Beaux-Arts with Pierre Joseph and Dominique Gonzalez-Foerster, we believed that there was nothing but the project. I found it very strange to see all these art students focus entirely on their own work, so I started talking to friends about the possibility to reshape that subjectivity into a project. We agreed that we would share and discuss our ideas and reformulate them, each time we found a new idea. After all, artworks are constantly being re-negotiated by their authors, by the geography of the space, by the political context in which they appear, and so on and so forth. Things are not given. They have to be re-invented all the time. That is the idea of modernity. I still believe in that idea and I think our generation is probably more interested in the process of negotiation than it is in the object of those negotiations.

DG I agree. I was never very interested in what I did unless anyone else was involved. This may seem very normal in art practice today, but back then it was not. I found it quite amazing that there was a group of people in Glasgow working together, and at the same time there was a group in Grenoble working together, and there was a group in London, and over the years all these elemental groups went together and they started to ferment and distill their ideas.

PP Obviously, this way of working causes very specific problems. The question is always: Who is doing what? As soon as you dismiss the idea of the author as a singular person, it becomes confusing for people to define who does what in a project. It took me a while to address that issue myself and perhaps it is still a bit of a question to me. But today when I do a so-called "solo show," I always return to this fundamental idea that I want my exhibitions to be more than just a display of objects. The sum of those objects must surpass their mere accumulation. The show is about me, but it is always *me plus something else*.

DG One of the reasons why I wanted Philippe to come to the Städelschule is because of his exhibition at the Palais de Tokyo in Paris. The show is daunting in terms of the scope of the ideas and the scale of the presentation. It functioned as a huge hall of mirrors to me. It is a very specific reflection of that particular way of working, where artists are determined to be as promiscuous as possible in terms of their relationship to their peer group and the new works that are brought in.

PP When Jean de Loisy invited me to do an exhibition at the Palais de Tokyo, I wanted to discover the leading mechanism that causes the appearance and disappearance of forms. I was interested in finding the codex. How do things emerge? How are they negotiated and according to what? At the time, I was working with Carlos Basualdo, the curator of the Philadelphia Museum of Art, on another show called *Dancing Around the Bride*. It was an exhibition about the relationships between John Cage, Merce Cunningham, Marcel Duchamp, Jasper Johns, and Robert Rauschenberg. The exhibition focused entirely on friendship and on the group of people surrounding Duchamp. These people re-invented modern art. They were in constant discussion with each other. A motif from Jasper John's paintings would turn up in a silkscreen painting by Robert Rauschenberg. The boundaries between the production of art, its commencement, and its reproduction remained very unclear. There was no definitive moment in time when an idea became an artwork. This is illustrated by a beautiful anecdote. The *Bottle Rack* was one of Duchamp's ready-mades, which had somehow disappeared. Rauschenberg found a bottle rack, identical to the one Duchamp had used. He bought it and he asked Duchamp to sign it. Duchamp signed it but he added the phrase: "I don't remember the original sentence."

DG Did you curate that show?

PP No, I was not technically the curator because I did not choose the works that were put on display. I merely helped Carlos choreograph the works in such a way that they would correspond to each other. I created flickering labels so that the attention of the visitors would be drawn to the change of light. We would combine certain works in a very specific manner. At the very first moment, when the works entered the museum there was an atmosphere of awe. Here were all the masterpieces of modern art. But once the works were brought together, they became much more fragile and people were confronted with the fact that most of the works do not consist of much. *The Venetian* by Rauschenberg is just a piece of cable painted white, but linked to Duchamp's *The Bride Stripped Bare by her Bachelors,* it becomes something else. So people were gazing from one work to another, as Carlos and I created a "choreography of the mind." This is what I have always been interested in doing. One could say that I was creating my work, without actually making any work. I showed my work in an exhibition that had none of my own stuff in it. Douglas and I have talked about ghosts earlier on, and I can see ghosts operating in art. It is the very idea of modernity that things are not given but have to be reinvented. That is how history is produced. So when Jean de Loisy asked me to do a show at the Palais de Tokyo, I proposed to think about the space first. I wanted to find new ways for the public to walk through the space. I wanted people to experience those exhibition halls differently.

DG Philippe and I spend quite a long time together talking around things and I believe that for artists, talking around things is much more interesting than talking *about* things. I suppose there are other jobs in the world where people are supposed to talk about things. One of the things that we spoke around about a lot was the use of allopathic and homeopathic medicine as an analogy. Allopathic medicine is very concentrated and there are times when you need allopathic medicine. However, if you are on the right frequency then homeopathy and the use of certain plants is a much more interesting idea. But when I start to think about plants and gardens, we might end up talking about that for an hour and a half. So let me distract you no more.

PP Actually, it is interesting that you mention plants and gardens because when I first started to think about the show at the Palais de Tokyo, I thought a lot about gardens. The space is so vast and impressive that I tried to see it as a landscape. I hired a Belgian landscape designer, Bas Smets, and asked him to assess how the space is positioned within the city so that we would no longer see it as an exhibition space, but rather as one of many public spaces within a town. My concept for the exhibition actually began with the assessment of that landscape designer. Also, I drew heavily upon the dialectic between the audience and the public. There is a big difference between these two concepts. The *audience* is typically a problem. When you go to the movies and you want to cut off the head of the guy in front of you because you cannot read the subtitles, then that would be the audience. The *public* is the person you need in order to see or to experience something. The space at the Palais de Tokyo was so enormous that I felt I had to find new ways to attract a public. So I installed a lean-to roof in front of the building, which flickered day and night. It was completely ghostly but it helped to draw people's attention to the Palais de Tokyo. That was my first intervention. At the same time, I installed a huge, luminescent wall in the entrance hall so that anybody stepping into the building would see other visitors backlit as silhouettes. I thought that was a beautiful start of the show. You walk into the exhibition and you see the "other" buying a ticket, walking around, leafing through a book, but only as a silhouette. Inside, we covered all the windows with a blurry filter so as to obscure any views of the outside world, and there was a gigantic LED screen that was completely see-through. When visitors passed behind the screen they became part of the installation, as if they were ghosts in the picture. It was very important to me that the public would become part of the picture.

DG Can I ask you something about the philosophy of a silhouette? A silhouette is a mechanical structure, produced by a light at a certain position in front of a subject. In a way, it is also a self-supporting structure because essentially it shows moving images. When I think about that, it makes me wonder if some ideas have to wait for the right technology in order to be presented properly. It seems that sometimes you just have to wait for the right support structure to come along, or wait for a structure to be discovered that can support a specific idea. What do you think?

PP I think you might be right. The videos I selected to be shown on the screen were actually very old works. There was a piece called *Flowers* that I did in 1988, while I was still in art school. At the time, we had just received a video camera at the school and I shot flowers for over an hour, just to see how long I could hold out without changing the focus. As I did not know what to do with the video, I wrote a letter to the television channel Canal Plus TV and I gave them the images for free. They actually broadcast them as a generic for the weather report sponsored by Interflora or something. Now, this was one of the first artworks I ever made and I learned immediately that a work of art does not exist without its exhibition. You can create anything you want but the meaning of the work is only consolidated by its exposure to a public. Both are linked somehow. The meaning of my original video was changed precisely because it was broadcast on national television. So I guess you could argue that some ideas need the right technology in order to be presented.

For the last fifteen years, I have been trying to see how an exhibition can become an *automaton*, and in the case of automation and pictures, the tempo is of course the soundtrack by which the visitor will encode or encrypt the events. At the Palais de Tokyo, I decided to add an arbitrary soundtrack: the *Petrushka* by Stravinsky. So you walk behind the LED screen and you see a piano playing Stravinsky. Each time the piano plays, black snow falls into it. The piano is a piece by Liam Gillick and me. It was envisioned for another show called *Il Tempo del Postino*, which dealt with the paradox that the time a visitor spends looking at an artwork is basically encoded by the institution. The institution decides how long the works are on display and how the works are displayed. For example, people will spend more time looking at an artwork when it has a bigger label with more information on it.

DG The average time the average person looks at an average painting is around three seconds. The average time that the average person will look at a monitor waiting for it to work is about fifteen seconds. Obviously, when the monitor starts to work, people walk away pretty quickly but it interesting that our expectation or our desire to know what will happen clearly outweighs our fulfillment. That is probably one of the reasons why I drifted into working with moving images. Back then there was a perpetual desire to know what was coming next.

PP *Il Tempo del Postino* revolved around those issues of time and duration. The space was given: it was a stage at the Manchester Opera House, but it was entirely up to the artist how long (s)he wanted the public to view the work. When we invited Liam Gillick, he said: "You may experience a lot of problems, dealing with all these different artists. What I will do is, I will give you a piano and every time nothing happens you can play it." Later, I asked Liam if I could use the piano to play the *Petrushka* by Stravinsky for my show at the Palais de Tokyo. Now, like I mentioned before, the question is: Whose work is this? Is it a work by Liam Gillick or by Philippe Parreno?

DG Or by Stravinsky!

PP Or by Stravinsky, exactly. Another collaborative piece in the show is called *Clandestine Library*. It consists of a bookshelf with books selected by Dominique Gonzalez-Foerster and when you push the bookshelf open, you enter into a secret room that contains the re-enactment of an exhibition I saw at Margarete Roeder Gallery in New York. It was right after the death of John Cage in 2002. The show opened as an exhibition of drawings by Merce Cunningham. Every day Cunningham would remove one of his drawings and replace it with a drawing by Cage, who had been his partner for many years. So the show started with a living artist and it ended with a dead one. It was one body of work for one body of work, and for me that was one of the most amazing exhibitions about friendship that I have ever seen. I really wanted to re-enact that show, so I built the same space and replaced a drawing every day. Because of the length of my show at the Palais de Tokyo I went from Cunningham to Cage and from Cage back to Cunningham again. It is a revolving story of those two artists.

Another project that deals specifically with the issue of authorship is *Ann Lee*, a work I did together with Pierre Huyghe. We purchased a manga character from a Japanese cartoon company and offered the character to different artists. Basically, they were free to use it in whichever way they wished. I made the first episode. Pierre Huyghe did the second. Liam Gillick did the third. Dominique Gonzalez-Foerster produced another episode. Rirkrit Tiravanija did one, Tino Seghal, and so on and so forth. We wanted to explore how a sign, like Ann Lee, could become the sign of a collectivity or a community of artists, and we ended the project with a loophole. By registering the copyright to the sign itself no one would be able to use the sign anymore, only Tino Seghal could continue because he works without copyrights. He created a performance with young girls, aged eleven to thirteen, based on Ann Lee. That performance became part of the Palais de Tokyo exhibition and simultaneously I showed *Zidane*, a film I made with Douglas on seventeen screens for seventeen cameras.

DG Yes, Zidane …

I think Philippe and I are still in love with Zidane. Let's talk about how we made *Zidane*. It could be interesting, especially within a school context, because it has a lot to do with the idea of patience. I believe in the conspiracy of circumstance. Philippe, Olafur Eliasson, and I met in Jerusalem in 1996, as part of a fairly large group exhibition. It so happened that the exhibition space was underneath a football stadium and when we arrived the show had already been installed. So we found a shopping mall, bought a football, and the three of us started to play what we in Scotland would call "keepie uppie," where you keep the ball up in the air and pass it around between the three of you. Then Olafur went away and Philippe and I were left with the ball. As we were bouncing the ball back and forth, using our spare time without actually killing it—which I believe to be an extremely important skill—we came up with a scenario that would eventually end up in the provocation of portraiture.

Philippe and I passed the ball to each other saying: What if we were to make a film together? What would that film be? What do we like about the films we like? We spoke about *Le Samouraï* by Jean-Pierre Melville and the fact that the principal character, played by Alain Delon, is not always involved in the shot. How interesting is that, to make a portrait of someone who is never there? That was the "what if." Then came the "why not": Why not take this outside of the traditional narrative but put it within the exact time frame of a feature film, which is equal to the ninety minutes of a football match plus the halftime in the middle. So these are the things that you talk about when you have spare time. We said what if, what if, what if, and why not, why not, why not, and then when we met Zidane he said: Why me? And I think it was he who, through that question, made the film into a portrait. So the subject is definitely self-defining, and I think this is something that Philippe and I both took from the experience: if you choose your subject well, then that subject will define the palate you use to paint the portrait. Then our film crew arrived—seventeen cameramen with seventeen focus pullers and seventeen runners—and everyone started asking for the storyboard. Of course, we did not have a storyboard because we would film a live match. So we took everybody to the Museo Nacional del Prado because the Prado in Madrid houses some of the most incredible portraits in history. We basically used the museum as a filmstrip and we were shocked to learn that many of our crewmembers had never set foot in the Prado before. They had never seen *Las Meninas*, although that painting has informed photographic theory for so many years. We showed them Goya's incredible portrait of the Duchess of Alba, one with clothes on and one with clothes off, not done as a diptych, and painted from very slightly different angles. Meanwhile, we talked these people through our ideas of what was about to happen at eight or nine o'clock that evening. It was a very peculiar exercise.

PP One of our first ideas was to give one camera to each of the fans so we would have had 80,000 cameras and 80,000 points of view. We took that idea from a text by Pasolini where he talks about the assassination of Kennedy. He writes that a normal depiction of the assassination is always based on a limited number of perspectives, but if you multiply that by the infinity of possible points of view, the bullet never hits Kennedy. So our first idea was to include so many cameras that the recording was bigger than the event itself. But when we set out to work on the event seriously, we restricted ourselves to a reasonable number of perspectives. It forced us to come down from the fan level and enter the pitch level—eye level—so there was no dominant position anymore. All these decisions took a lot of time. They were never planned in advance.

DG That "postponement of the now" gave us the opportunity to take whatever time we needed to make a decision: from five minutes to two weeks.

Question

What about the members of the film crew, the directors of photography, did they understand what you were trying to achieve? What were their backgrounds?

DG Most of the DPs came from regular feature films or commercial advertising. It was easy for them. Philippe and I were sitting in our little cabin outside of the stadium with our headphones on, watching seventeen images at once. We would tell them: left a bit, right a bit, up, down, zoom in, zoom out, please get your battery changed because we can see it is about to go dead. For us, it was a frenetic exercise but for them, it was their job. All they needed was a little direction, I suppose.

PP In fact, the shooting itself was very brief but it took us nine months to cut the film. We could not find the right angle to cut it. It is very boring to look at a man running after a ball for ninety minutes. However, during the editing Douglas and I had long conversations about art and about certain aspects of portraiture that had never occurred to me before. I count those conversations among the most important moments of studio practice I have ever had in my life. I think we had told Zidane that after the shooting we would not see him again. That had been our intention. But as we got stuck cutting the film, we did visit him again and we ended up talking to him about portraiture and about the notion of the model by Robert Bresson. We discussed the idea of portraiture in time, and the difficulty to maintain the public's attention span for an hour and a half. We had to deal with the fact that without a narrative, people would become bored and drift in and out of the picture.

Question

Is there not an unavoidable narrative that is inherent in the portrait itself?

DG I don't think so. I mean, obviously, there is a narrative that runs from the first kick of the ball to the final whistle-signal, but there is no instruction about how to look at the film. It is a portrait that consists of images without instruction.

PP The context in which the film was to be experienced, was the context of the cinema. We wanted to bring the art experience to the movie theaters. That was our challenge. It is one thing to understand an idea, but it is another thing to experience it for an hour and a half on a cinematic screen. We wanted the film to appeal to people who do not necessarily go to museums or art centers so we tried to bring the exhibition feeling back to cinema. Most films are driven by a story. The story forces you to stop thinking. If you drift in and out of the film—like you do with *Zidane*—then generally the film is perceived to be a bad film. We decided that in our case the soundtrack could help to bring people's attention back to the film, so we asked Zidane a couple of questions about his perception of sound. Then, when we had a first little cut of five minutes, we showed it to him. At the end of the screening, he said something remarkable. He said, "It is as if I am looking at my brother talking to my mother." We had filmed Zidane playing football. He had been concentrated on the game and he had not paid any attention to the camera. He had been himself. Watching the footage he recognized himself and because his brother looked very similar to him, it was as if he saw his brother talking to his mother. We took that as a great compliment and said to ourselves, "Ok, let us go back to the studio and cut this film for another five months."

Question

Would you have considered making the same film using a different subject?

DG No.

PP The last time we met Zidane when we presented the final cut of this picture, he said, "It is true. That is me. I am like that." Now, I do not know if anybody remembers that fantastic *Portrait of Pope Innocent X* by Velázquez. Supposedly, this is the phrase the pope used when he first looked upon his own portrait. He said, "*Troppo vero,*" it is all true. Zidane had exactly the same reaction to our film. He did not mind that at the end of the game he received a red card. He said, "That is me. I am tough. It is the way I am, and the picture is true." So we went from portraiture to model, to veracity in an image, all the while encouraging the audience to stay true to itself as an audience. Because *Zidane* has no narrative, viewers have to rely on their own visual experience. They must put together their own opinion about Zidane's portrait and about portraiture in general.

DG When we had finished, we spoke to Zidane and he asked, "How do you feel about it?" And I said, "I don't know. Philippe, how do you feel about it?" And Philippe said, "I don't know." And then I said, "Well, I think it will take fifteen years to assess this and another twenty-five to have an opinion about it. Hopefully, all will be better in about one hundred and fifty years, but luckily, that is something that we do not have to worry about."

PP The film was not very popular with the fans. Universal Studios promoted it as a documentary about Zidane, although we had consistently said that it was a portrait. So when the film was presented at the film festival in Cannes, people expected a traditional narrative with a voice-over talking about football techniques. During the editing, we met Jamel Debbouze, a well-known French comedian of Moroccan descent. He was wildly enthusiastic about the fact that audiences around France would go to the cinema to see an Arab man for an hour and a half. For Jamel, that was an enormous breakthrough in itself. He proposed to shoot a trailer, where he would say exactly that, but the producers and the distributors refused. They tried to sell it as a documentary because they were afraid of losing their audiences. So when the film was released, it was not very well received, although it became quite successful afterward on DVD. I suppose it took some time for people, especially for the football fans, to warm up to it.

DG Again, the difference between the audience and the public became a very potent problem here. To this day it is a great regret for both of us that we did not do the first screening at the football stadium in Marseille.

PP I think *Zidane* was all about time and the process in time. It was basically a structure without structure. We set out with a timeframe but we had no idea what would emerge on the other side of that boundary. I think what I learned from *Zidane* is that the most important part of the project was not the film, but a by-product of the end result. It was all about the process. That is what makes you a better artist at the end of the day. I felt like a better artist after *Zidane* than before *Zidane* because I learned so much from the conversations I had with Douglas. I discovered how to use time and how to allow a project to take place in time. In retrospect, I realized that I have done a lot of portraits: *Ann Lee, Marilyn, Zidane, 8 June, 1968*. Only, I was not able to define them as portraits until recently. Even during the filming of *Zidane*, we did not speak much about portraiture. We spoke about models and Robert Bresson's notes on the cinematographer, so it took a while to understand the logic at work. What I am interested in is grabbing that logic. That is also why I am as interested in Pasolini as I am in Rauschenberg. I like ideas. For me, ideas are like continents. You can navigate through them, and I do not differentiate between a novel, a movie, or an artwork. There is something deeply human at work in all those art forms that I am extremely sensitive to. Again, what is interesting to me is not what Douglas does or what I do, but rather the operational process behind it all. That is the realm, or the planet, of sensitive ideas. It opens up temporary existential territories, and I think art is all about that. I am fascinated by a set of ideas in which I can recognize myself and in which I participate even if I am just there as a witness. I had the privilege to see the Cage-Cunningham show and I was happy to re-enact that show as part of my own solo exhibition. Perhaps I felt the need to see it again, like a "ghost operator."

DG Shall we end on that bombshell?

PP Definitely. Thank you all for coming tonight!

20.
21. Juni PETER GEIMER
27. Juni PATRIK SCHUMACHER
4. Juli BEATRIZ C
12. Juli ANNE IMHOF

HN KNIGHT & MICHAEL KREBBER, 14H

N 11. Juni SUSAN GRAYSON

NA MEYER-GROHBRÜGGE, ARCHITEKTUR

ENGANG KURATIEREN UND KRITIK

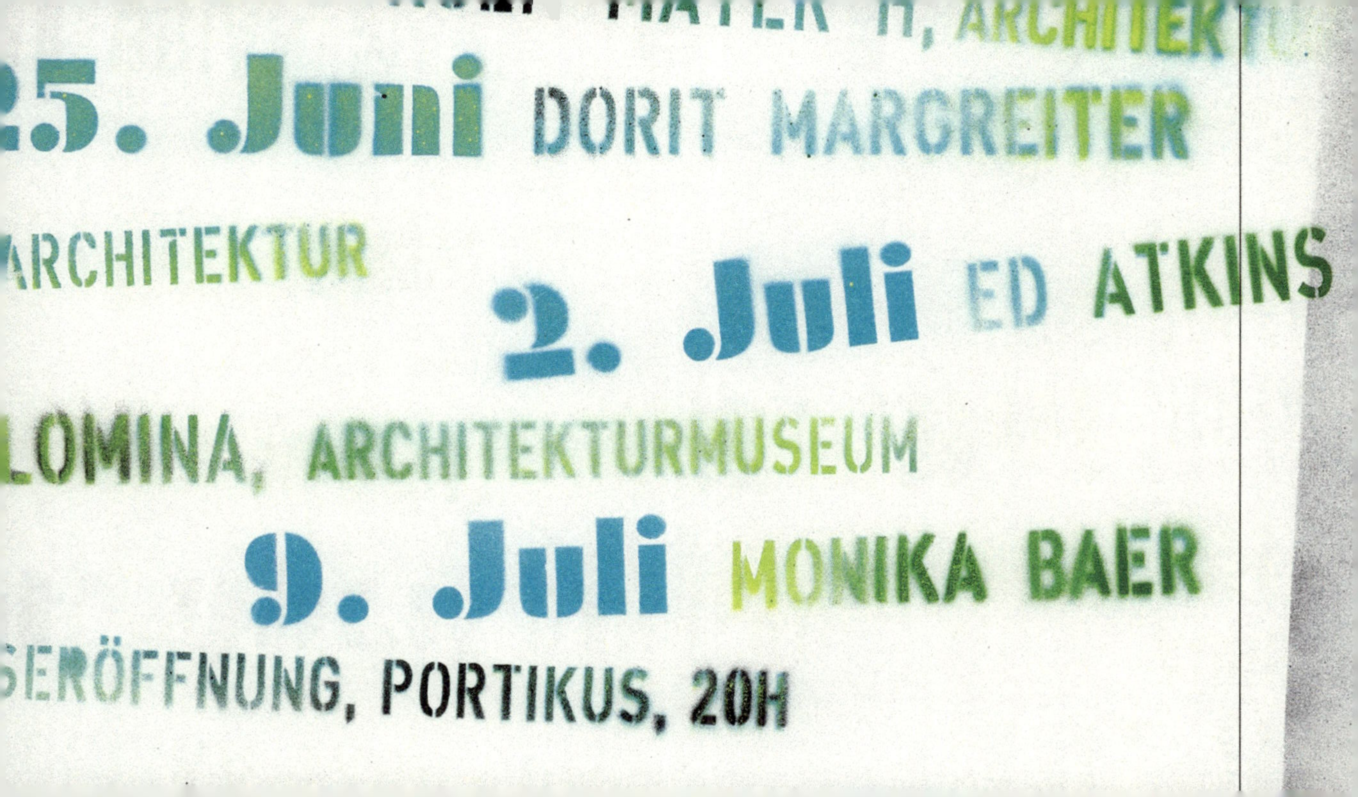
5. Juni DORIT MARGREITER
ARCHITEKTUR
2. Juli ED ATKINS
LOMINA, ARCHITEKTURMUSEUM
9. Juli MONIKA BAER
ERÖFFNUNG, PORTIKUS, 20H

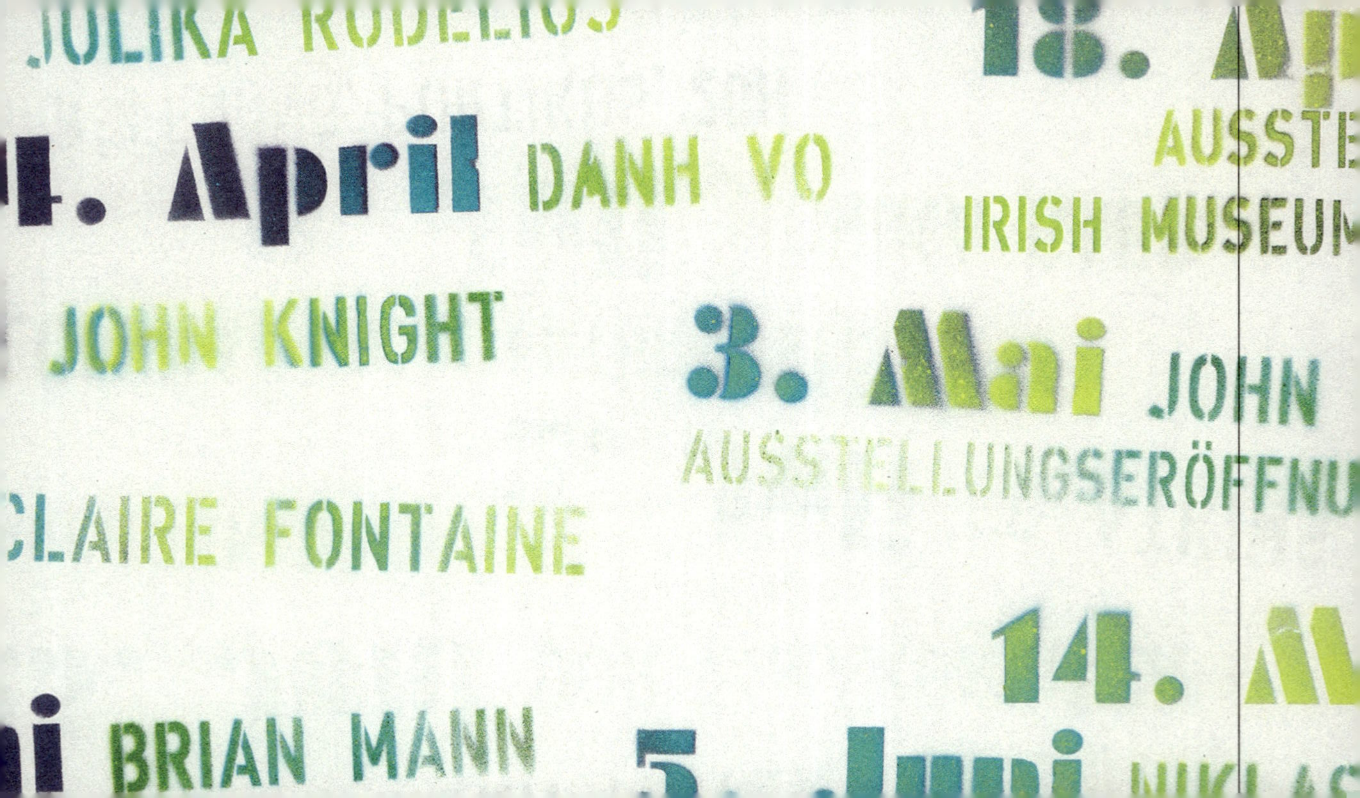
JULIKA RUDELIUS
4. April DANH VO
JOHN KNIGHT
CLAIRE FONTAINE
BRIAN MANN
18.
AUSSTE
IRISH MUSEUM
3. Mai JOHN
AUSSTELLUNGSERÖFFNU
14.
5. Juni

July 9, 2013
Monika Baer

The Artist's Materials and Their Use in Painting

German painter Monika Baer introduces essential concepts in her figurative and sensorial work. In this lecture, Baer speaks about studying in Düsseldorf with a lack of role models, feeling constrained by trends in conceptual art, and the popularity of ironic chauvinism. Avowing to break convention, she began building her own painting vocabulary of modular concepts. From hunters to huntresses, marionettes to breasts, and holes to mirrors, Baer questions the limitations and potential of borders. Narrative elements and disruptions of logic are expressed through movement, tension, and the activity of traces in painting, as subjects have transformed throughout the trajectory of her career.

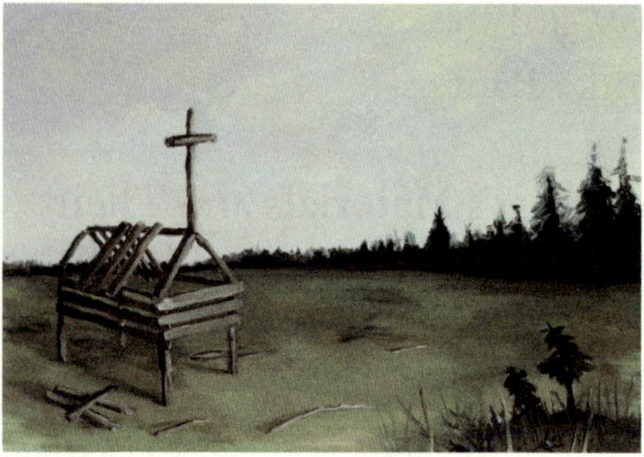

[*untitled*, 2015]

I'm going to start right away with this image. This is the most recent painting I'll show today. It's 250 × 220 cm. It takes its cue from a painting by James Ensor called *Ma mére morte* (my dead mother). What interests me in this painting by Ensor is the fact that, in the background, you do see the corpse of the mother, but he actually focuses on a still life in the foreground, consisting of an arrangement of medicine bottles—like an *Übersprungshandlung*, as if the bottles were more important. In my painting, there are bottles of liquor arranged just above the bottom edge of the painting, like bowling pins. Behind them a space rises, which is defined by various different painterly modes, from a painterly wash to a drawing in the background that depicts a cartoonish silhouette of a face succumbed to oblivion. The oil stick drawing was added last in the manner of graffiti on top of the painting, thus flattening the illusionistic space and nestling into it at the same time.

Staying with this image, I'm going to try and start with a constellation that forms the base of my considerations on painting, which articulates itself in my work. I studied in Düsseldorf from 1985 until 1992, and I arrived there wanting to be a painter. When I arrived, I was confronted with the heritage of art from the 1970s: Conceptual Art, Performance Art, and Minimal Art. This held a lot of influence in Düsseldorf at the time. For me, right at the beginning, Conceptual Art struck me as: "This is what art really is." That shattered my notion of painting. How could painting even be possible? After deciding to not leave that field, which would have been the most logical thing to do then, I spent years of my studies grappling with this problem.

In a way, painting was back again in the guise of Neo-Expressionism, as you all know, with Neue Wilde and so on. There were two other options within painting at the time—one was work like Gerhard Richter's, who taught at the academy in Düsseldorf. He established distance as constitutive for the work and employed different modes of painting and made different sorts of paintings, bringing them up simultaneously so that they would compete with each other and create a discourse. I took that for granted because it was so much a part of the academy discussion. On the one hand, I didn't see his work as a model because it was based on a concept that seemed closed. But on the other hand, his work did form a base for me. The other option at that time would have been the work of Martin Kippenberger and Albert Oehlen, but I could not imagine myself inserted into that kind of practice, as it was based on this kind of ironic chauvinism, which was not accessible to me for exactly that reason. That context didn't seem like it could have satisfied my ambition, which was certainly not to play a supporting role.

The main problem that presented itself then, and which is still active now, is that I had chosen a heavily gendered field in the first place. Even more agonizing was the fact that I thought painting as such was impossible. I saw no way forward. The first question was: How can painting be art *at all?* And then, the other question you all know yourself, I suppose: How can painting be part of any relevant discourse? And how should I deal with its historical baggage and also its depth? How can I cope with the fact that anything I do in painting is a convention in the first place?

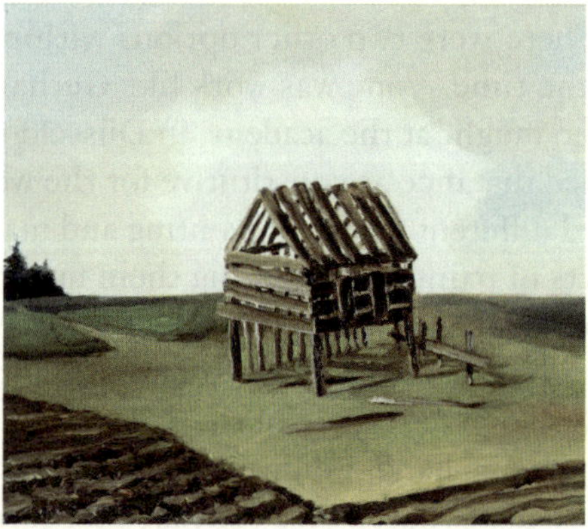

[*Ohne Titel*, 1992]

I'll switch to a very early image now. Here we go. This comes from the very end of my studies, so you can see how bad it got. This is one from a little series of paintings. They're small. I've got my sizes here in inches but I'll say small, medium-sized, and large. This is small. By imagining every brushstroke as constituting a board or a plank in this unconvincing architectural setup, I tried to depict the process of constructing a painting with shaky faith and against all odds, while enacting this at the same time.

The actual theme of this talk is something I've been wondering about recently, namely, whether that principal problem of painting that has remained with me is actually a constructive agent that can activate a painting and which motivates the work at large. This theme is not yet clear to me exactly. But my testing of painting's potential is a response to it. I wonder if I am vaguely applying the criteria I had spoken of before, those of Conceptual Art and Performance Art, let's say, and if my work within painting, therefore, moves between the poles of *mise-en-scène* on the one hand and the object on the other.

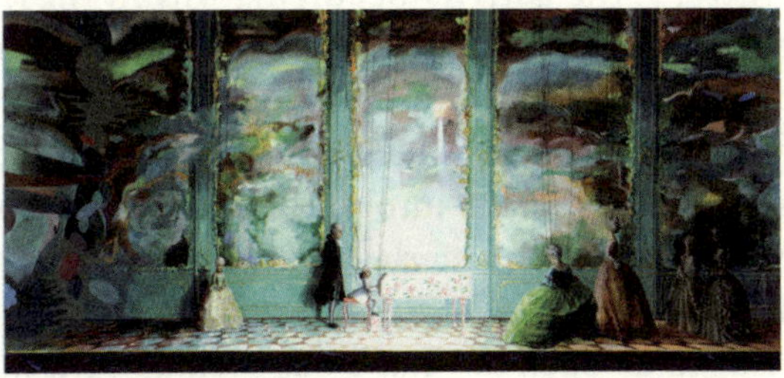

[*Ohne Titel (Nr. 2)*, 1997]

The ramshackle hut painting was from 1992 at the end of my studies, whereas this is from 1997. It's one of a series of marionette theater paintings that were shown at Portikus at the time. Do you see these little blue veins in the black at the bottom of that ledge? There's a border there, which marks the edge of the stage. For me, this edge defines the painting as an object. The painting itself mimics a marionette stage, like, how do you say, *maßstabsgetreu*? It's to scale. I think it's 300 × 160 cm or so. As well as actually hosting a narrative—in this case, a drama, which is something I have done often—the painting also displays the interactions of the conventions put into play with each other. This edge is the marker that places the viewer. What I'm thinking about at the moment is the way a painting directs the gaze so that it is not merely a passive object that is looked at, but an active thing that defines how it's looked at, and from which position. In this case, the painting defines the viewer as the viewer of a marionette theater.

This is another painting from this series, all of which are untitled. Here, the painterliness, *das Malerische*, is the activity occurring within these panels, thought of as mirrors in this rococo interior. Then this painterliness takes on its own life and moves out from the confinement of the panels into the space depicted and into the painting itself, confronting the other painterly trope, namely figurative painting.

But to go back to what I was saying, right now I'm wondering whether this constant itch or this constant concentration on a kind of impossibility is potentially what can keep a painting alert?

These are two from of a series of four.

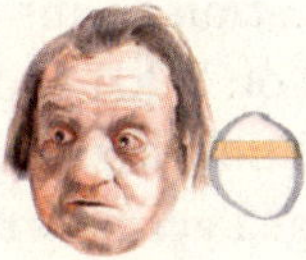

[*Ohne Titel (man with hole)*, 1998]

Right after the rococo stages, as a reaction *against* them, I started a series of white paintings—there were eight or nine of them from 1998. They are large, 300 × 190 cm. In terms of the idea of the activated painting, here the painting makes you trace the edges of the cut with your eyes—you repeat it. This is a real cut, a hole, it is not painted. In addition, the hole isn't just an indexical sign; it's also a narrative element. The face is connected and reacting to this intrusion. The face is taken from a still of the film *Greed* by Erich von Stroheim. The hole here is not merely indexical. The way that the wall is visible through the hole forces the viewer to realize that he or she is standing in front of a wall, constantly, while painting or looking at a painting, and the hole itself is not just a cutout, not just a hole, but suggests a decapitation within the narration of the painting—as I thought afterward—because I actually cut out a painted second head. Maybe now it's becoming clear, because these problems have stayed with me, why I find it very difficult to deal with painting as a medium that is taken for granted, painting in a default mode, where the question seems to be: What should I paint now? Instead of: What should I do with this thing? Or: What do I do with this situation? How do I deal with this thing? I actually think I'm constantly using disruption as a reminder of the impossibility of remaining in a coherent logic within a painting.

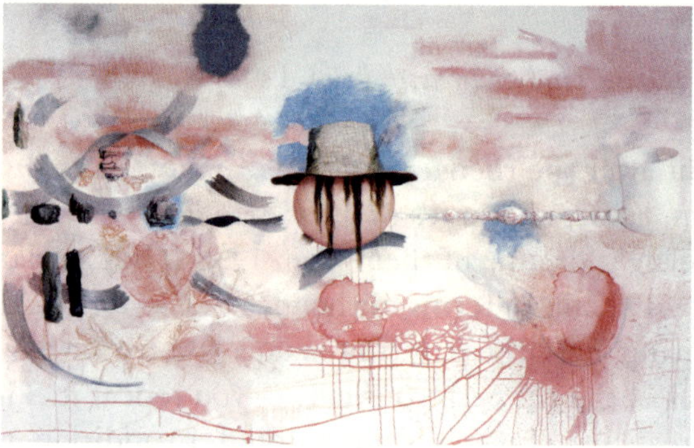

[*Jäger*, 2003]

This is called *Hunter*, a painting from 2003. It's again the same size, 300 × 190 cm, and is one out of a group of four in which the hunter turns into a huntress. I mentioned the topic of heritage and male genealogies before, as well as the lack of role models. I think finding or at least imagining myself outside these genealogies, especially in Germany at the time, generated a fair amount of aggression in me and placed me in a position of comparative freedom, a far cry away from a saturated or selfevident position.

Because I had experienced that as a female artist, especially as a painter, it was *meant* to motivate a joy in the aggressive ambition of an interloper, who wants to take over. What I was developing and defining for myself here is that painting is *all mine* and I can go wherever I am drawn to. So, I find in hindsight that this unkempt figure embodies this aggressive and somewhat primitive drive for expansion.

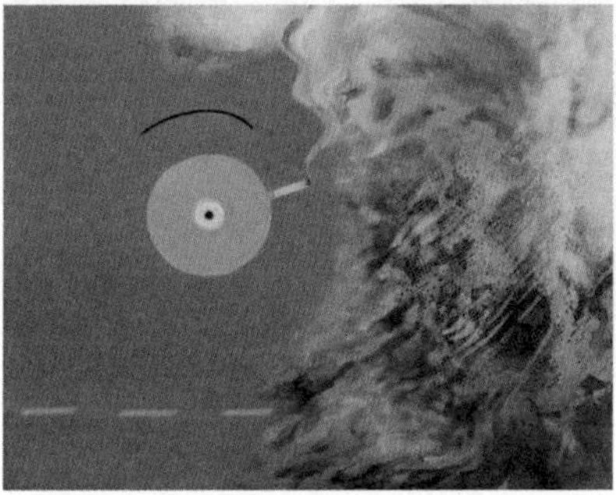

[*Kleine Spritztour*, 2001]

This is from 2001. It's smallish. The idea of expansion versus having to carve out a little niche for myself, or something that will reliably work—this provides opportunities for integrating various different practices into my own work. And not only that: allowing myself to wander off, while watching myself do so, brings me to places where I exceed the confines of my own taste—which I find a valuable and interesting aspect, although it can be embarrassing. So, I could end up doing paintings I wouldn't necessarily like.

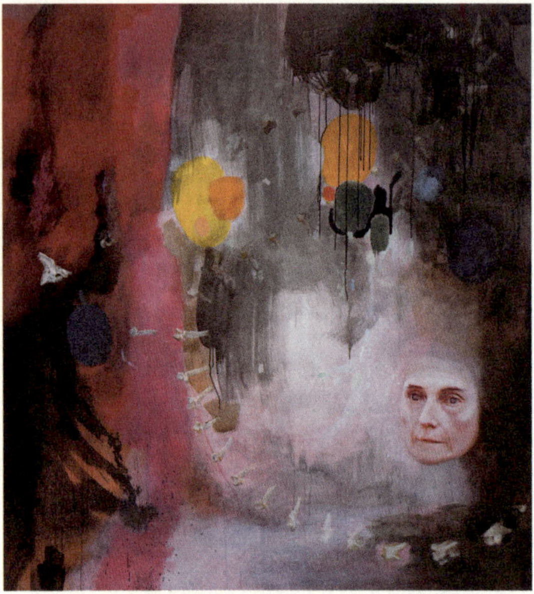

[*Vampir*, 2007]

The title here is *Vampire*, 2007. This is 280 × 250 cm. On the one hand, different painterly modes move into the painting, and on the other hand, it is as though the painting itself were wandering, as though you were holding up a frame and it were moving through certain spaces. To repeat what I said before, I find this aspect of crossing the boundaries of taste—not always and not as a rule, but time and again—I find that very interesting. In a way, I'd say, I'm testing painting continuously. It's an exclamation of: "No! But ..." And to be able to test this for myself, it must be possible to not always necessarily identify with what I'm doing in terms of taste.

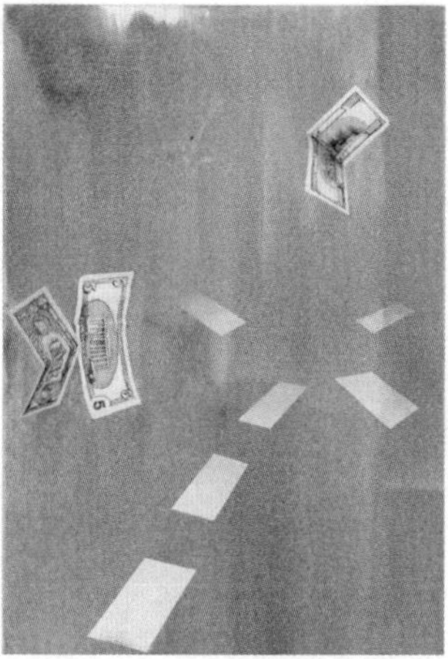

[*Ohne Titel*, 2007]

Again, this is one of a group of paintings on money. Back to expansion and wandering: as the work evolves and moves from one mode and setup to the next, I can observe a vocabulary being built up that has modular aspects. There are empty carrier forms that are layered with a *mask*. To explain this, I am showing you this painting of a banknote in a blue space. The base of the bill is a stenciled white rectangle that has had a banknote painted on top of it. It carries its surface like a character. I can compare this process to actors taking on a role. I employed the same method in the vampire paintings; I painted the faces on top of stenciled forms. And it's the case, as well with the breasts, ham slices, etc., these agents circulate in the work, they come together to form specific constellations and then are dismantled again to be re-formed, and so on. So, it's similar to a cast performing a play circling around this principle painting/art problem as well as the personal and political topics that emerge as relevant for me.

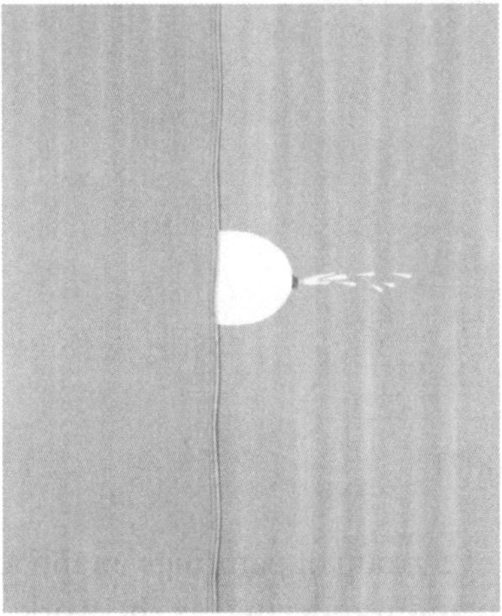

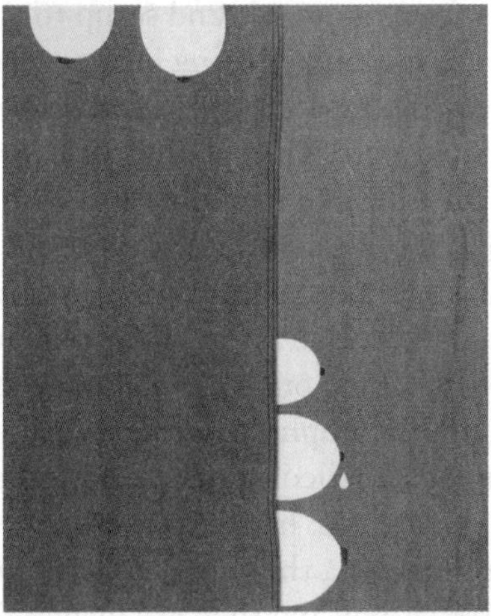

[*Ohne Titel*, 2008 and *Ohne Titel*, 2008]

These paintings are all untitled, small- to medium-format, from 2008 to 2010 or so. The blue of the money painting just now was cobalt blue oil paint. This was the last in a group on money, and right after, I developed the elements of the paintings depicting stylized breasts. Here, blue jeans are mimicked by a cobalt blue watercolor wash on unprimed canvas. Two pieces of canvas that were treated this way have been sewn together and show the seam like in a pair of jeans. The canvas is then primed with transparent acrylic and oil paint follows. So this is a real seam, out of which protrudes this painted breast. The seams in these paintings are similar in function to the stage edge in the marionette paintings. Along these lines, appearances take shape and disturbances occur. The painting interacts or collides with its own status as an object. And I wonder if these disruptions open the painting up to—let's call it—the *outside*, as they break the paintings' coherence and closure. In terms of the current discussion on *painting beside itself or beyond itself*, and the question of taking the painting outside, for me, the potential lies in the decisive edges and borders of the painting, in its limitations and the confrontational potential therein. A tremendous tension is located in the border between the logic of painting and that of *not painting*. For me, this is where the actual problems and challenges lie, and I try to bring these tensions into operation.

This series came right after the money paintings as well as the vampire paintings, also as a means to *recover* after that staged drama.

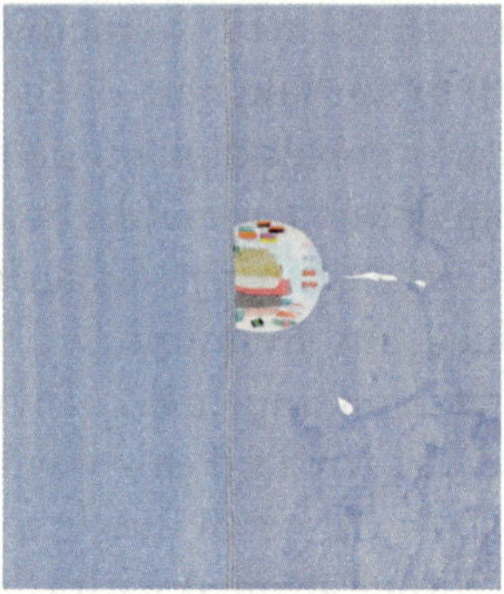

[*Bay view*, 2009]

Bay view is a medium-format work from 2009. The silhouettes of some of the breasts are filled with semi-abstract painting. Some are not. And I think of the fluids ejected as uncertain and manifold: water, semen, milk, sweat, etc. So, I'm obviously working on assumptions about gender. And they are a take on drip painting as well and the connotations around that.

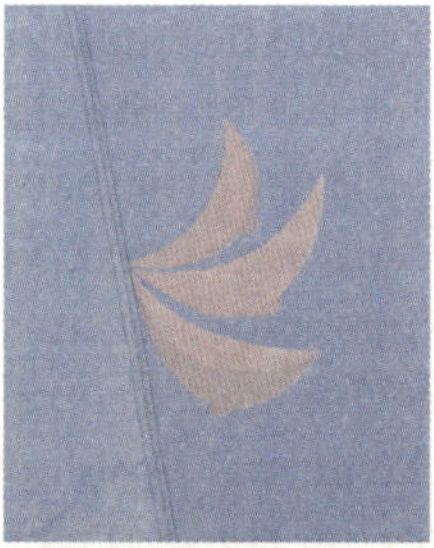

[*Ohne Titel (stocking)*, 2008]

In this painting with a diagonal seam, the breasts are on display as fanned-out slices. The first slice is painted with a sense of volume in contrast to all the other breast forms in the various paintings. The outline and the brick wall motif also turn up here for the first time. So, this is another example of motifs making an appearance, forming some kind of constellation, and then falling apart again. Later on, there will be a series of brick wall paintings, so you can see that a set of elements is developing into a repertoire.

[*monochrome*, 2009]

It took me some time to see the rhythmic process at work *within* my work. On the one hand, there is a to-and-fro between staged narration and the painting staged as an object. On the other hand, one series works against the other, either successively or simultaneously. For instance, the white paintings were the successors to and contestants of the rococo stages. And here, the pink monochromes were developed at the same time as the blue breast paintings. My experience in the studio is that a field opens in which I can work when there are two poles to move between, even if I'm concentrating on a single painting.

The paintings in this series, all titled *monochrome* have the appearance of monochrome paintings, whereas the cutouts are based on actual spider webs. The paintings teeter between these poles. I guess the cigarette on top defines the painting as a domestic object that you would just leave keys or a postcard on top of. Again, I see this as mirroring the edge of the stage. I was wondering if one aspect of the pink paintings was a kind of undressing of the blue ones, I suppose, because of the lace-like cutouts and sliding panels everywhere.

[*Ohne Titel*, 2012]

This process repeats itself in the next two series: *rear paintings* and *rote Wand*, from 2010 to 2012. They were shown in *Return of the Rear* at Galerie Barbara Weiss in 2012, and were all large-format. These are built up as follows: first a wash in a muted, matte, light earth or bodily tone, whatever that means. On top of that, pale pink oil paint is applied with a spackle leaving just the right sized gaps at the bottom of the painting, allowing the underpainting to show through. The thick, creamy paint around the gaps gives the impression of some tension on the material there, or wrinkle. Finally, there's a black keyhole on top of the pink, close to the gaps as the top layer, which is nail varnish-like and contradicts the logic of a hole. As in the earlier spider web paintings, the keyhole in its simplicity and literalness vulgarizes the monochromatic elegance and the notion of purity. These were painted alongside the second series of six paintings called *rote Wand*, which were also large-format.

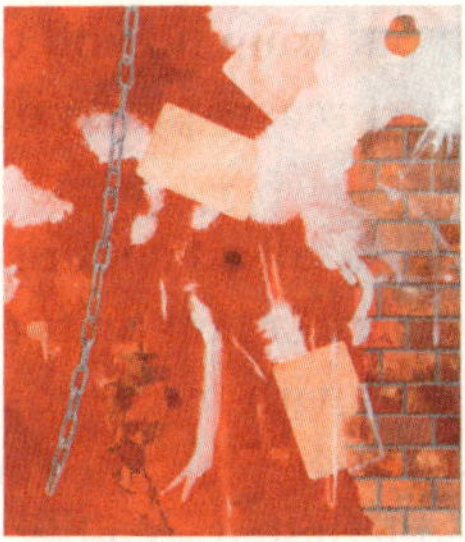

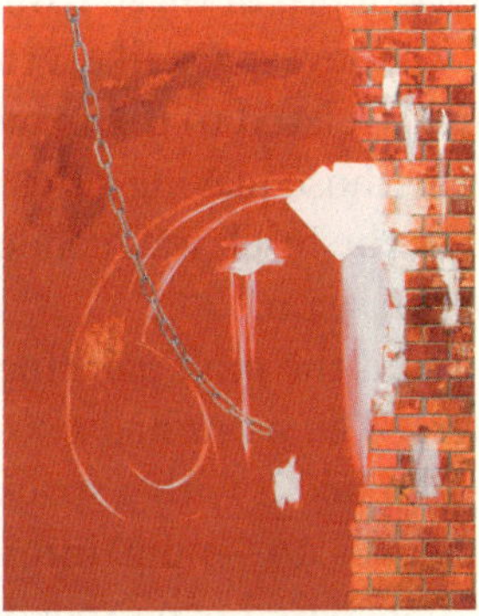

[*rote Wand*, 2010/11 and *rote Wand*, 2011]

Rote Wand refers not to the brick wall in the foreground but to the red wall in the background, which isn't defined as a wall other than by the title. The red carries no narrative charge except as a motif that stands for itself. The red is always shades of cadmium red oil paint applied in translucent layers with a pink underpainting for warm luminosity. The chain is painted on top of that, and as the last layer, the painterly interventions—strokes of white paint and other traces. This is a tricky move as it can destroy the built up red. Concerning the imagined activity depicted, the chain just swings to-and-fro. The tension builds up, I find, because of the materiality of the metal and the stone and the moment they could collide, as well as the curve moving towards the vertical of the wall. To get the curvature and the impression of weight, I hung heavy metal chains in front of canvases primed red in the studio and had them photographed to be able to paint them. The illusory depth of these paintings is maybe one meter—shallow space like a theater box. I see them as formally related to the breast paintings, because the way those playing cards fan out from behind that edge of the brick wall echoes the breasts protruding from the seam.

I find the pink paintings I just talked about seductive. The paint had a strawberry cream texture, and I applied it with a spackle and with my hands with gloves on—no paintbrush—whereas, the red paintings have been sanded and handled roughly, and the depicted materiality is metal and stone, and the red is poisonous. Here, the pastels only occur in the reflections in the metal chains. The red paintings make me think of clockwork, as though the movement of the cards were coordinated with the swinging chain. At the same time, the activity of painting is in operation too, and it manifests on the walls as if a handyman had left some kind of traces, like small samples of painterly conventions, as though the whole set up were to just get the traces on the wall.

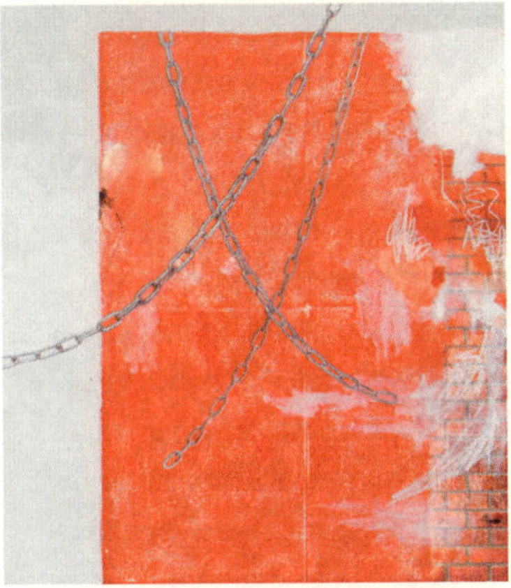

[*Extended Failure*, 2011/12]

In this painting, titled *Extended Failure*, I wanted the chain to swing from right to left for the first time, but I never managed it and had to give up—though I worked on it for a long time. You can see those white lines; it's been sanded about a thousand times; it just got worse and I had to give it up. A friend of mine, Thomas Eggerer, said the problem was the format, as there was not enough empty space on the left side for the chain to swing *to*, and the painting, therefore, couldn't develop its potential. So I took that failed painting to the restorer, and she sewed a piece of canvas onto the top and the side, which we now see as this light grey edge. And when I got the painting back, it looked so beautiful that I just left it as it was and primed the extensions. So this is a new format. The two chains—this one coming from the top and the other one coming from the upper left side of the red part—they're just painted over the mucked-up painting.

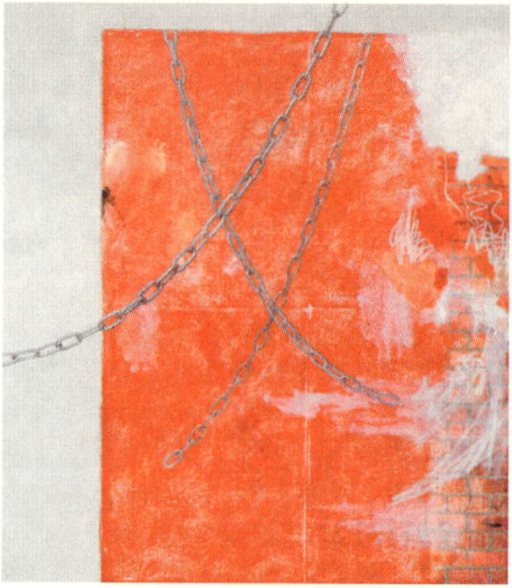

[*palette*, 2013 and *palette*, 2013]

Two paintings that sort of loitered around the others are called *Palette* and incorporate mirrors. The color is known as "flesh tone" and the oil paint bits, straight from the tube here, are behaving as paint would on a palette, sitting there, waiting to be mixed or applied. Well, it's a constant back and forth between the holes and the mirrors, the holes and a painted spot … shifting roles. I get the sense that the paint takes on the guise of certain materials—be it milk, chains, meat, money, breasts, or alcohol—as if they were shifting into each other from one to the next, to the next, to the next.

Question

At the beginning, you mentioned Düsseldorf in 1985 and Neue Wilde or something like that, as well as Albert Oehlen and Martin Kippenberger, but I know that you know Lukas Duwenhögger, because there's a photo of Thomas Ruff, him, and you.

MB Yes, I knew him. We began our studies at the same time and we were friends. He came from the Munich art academy. Another person whose work was fascinating to me was Christian Philipp Müller.

Question

Could you please say something about your use of the color pink?

MB That's a good question. As I said, I'm not quite sure. Let's have a look quickly. There we go. Let's take this painting as an example. As I mentioned it, pink could be some kind of undressing. Most of the things I say about the paintings, I think of afterward. I would never think: "I'm going to undress a painting and paint it pink." Never. So I wonder afterward while looking at it: Is this some kind of underwear, or what am I doing? And only now, having put these images together, do I really ask myself: Why all this opposition? Like with the blue breast paintings or the red chain paintings? How come so many are in these so-called "skin tones" or are really pink? What is this? I don't know, and I don't have to. It may be selected bait for the eye.

Question

Following up on that question, what was first—the blue or the pink?

MB The blue. What was first? The blue paintings, the breast paintings—they're untitled—then the pink ones.

Question

So the pink was in opposition to the blue?

MB Yes. It was maybe also complementary.

Question

Unconsciously.

MB Yes. I must say "semi-consciously." Not all planned out beforehand. I think about the paintings in the way I am speaking about them here only *afterward*. But in the case of these pink ones with the keyholes, I spent two years trying to paint them, alongside others as well, so I knew I wanted something specific but had trouble finding it. The paintings come from this place, you see ...

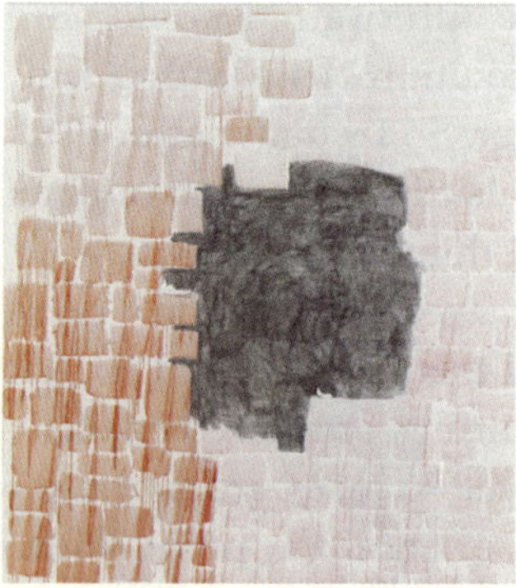

[*Hole*, 2009]

The title is *Hole*. This wall is fluid and there's this totally unconvincing gap in the middle and white turd-like bits of paint distributed around the painting. They're posing as mortar, as building materials. This painting, with its unconvincing mimicry, where the material poses as another material, is where the pink paintings with their strange, wrinkly gaps come from. Again, I think of stockings and stuff, you know, and this little Catholic keyhole. What can I say? I don't know exactly. They're clearly in opposition to the red paintings because I conceived of this combination as the basis for the Berlin show *Return of the Rear*, which featured the red paintings—which were this metal, stone, and this snaky-like chain, and then on the other hand, this creamy pink seduction in my eyes with these real gaps and a fake keyhole. *Tja*.

Question

There's this text by Lukas Duwenhögger in which he brings up the idea that there's always a fight between the color red and the color pink. I remember he was saying that pink would always be cool and red would be nowhere to go.

MB Pink would be cool and red nowhere to go.

Question

Cool is maybe the wrong word, but the idea is, as an artist, to talk about colors in terms of conflicts. He was saying you can go with pink, but you can't go with red.

MB Well, obviously not in my case. I don't think so …

Question

You can probably read it in the library here, but it's interesting that you came up with it too.

MB I haven't read it, but I understand what he was on to.

Question

I think it also comes from history and trying to find symbols for cultural phenomena.

MB Yeah.

Question

Because there are these gendered themes.

MB Yeah, there totally were and are these gendered themes and that goes right through the work. I take that as a given. There are paintings I haven't shown here because this could go on endlessly. The first keyhole paintings were black with this rather crappy acrylic gel pretending to be impasto oil paint, and on top of that, shiny little keyholes. You could potentially choose a white, a pink, or a light blue hole to peek through, depending on your personal preferences, for instance. Early on, there were these black paintings with pink holes. The title was *Slit Scene* and I thought of them as revolving around this Fontana move of slitting the canvas to provide access to the cosmos and to open up the Big Feminine ... Nope, wait a minute! There's just this black rag stuck to the back of the Fontana painting, a little backdrop, and it was like, [claps her hands], just turning it around. The rear view was the Fontana painting from behind.

Question

I have two questions. First of all, would you say a bit more about your use of mirrors and layers of elements like the chains? And also, there are these three levels coming out from each other that you are using. Can you tell us something about that? Do you think of this as part of the paintings' stage-like quality?

MB Yes, that's what I think it is. I more or less always think of these levels as two-dimensional stacked layers. It's more or less a simplified idea of the theater stage, where props are set up behind each other to create depth.

Question

Is this also why you include hyperrealistic elements in the paintings?

MB Well, that's a difficult question to answer. It's a method of seduction, a way of drawing the gaze into the painting, which can then be blocked or slapped back, for instance. Or it's a motif, which when painted in that way can take on the role of a protagonist in this play, in this construction. Maybe the keyhole isn't a good example because it hasn't got that quality of realism, but it denies a fleeing into painterly vagueness. The realistic elements stand for this denial. I mean, you look at them, and it's difficult not to recognize them. You're forced to see that this is a chain and it is metal. There's no way around it. It takes the position of a hard fact.

Question

For example, the blue painting with the seam—you could have painted it like a *trompe-l'œil* in a realistic way, but you didn't.

MB No. I used the painting's materiality—the fact that

it is a cotton fabric I am painting on, and therefore, treated it as a fabric. Also, the real seam is a rupture in the painting's logic, its illusionism. It breaks there, but the painting is held together by the jeans theme, and the seam provides the layer from under which the breasts appear—there is a *below* and a behind. Also, after the money paintings, I had no clue how to proceed. At the time, I was trying to have each painting take its cue from the one before it. The blue money painting I showed you was the dead end, finally, and then it was like pulling out the breast painting from under it. Well, it doesn't sound very logical.

Question

What is painting to you? Is it like symbols? Does it have symbolic value?

MB Yeah, I'm pretty sure it does.

Question

In what way are you using it?

MB Excuse me? In what way am I using symbols?

Question

Yeah, what interests you about them?

MB Well, I would say that I've decided to follow where my work leads me, but this always takes place in paintings or drawings. This can also lead me to regions I wouldn't choose based on preferences in terms of taste, as I described with the vampire paintings. It is a dialogic relationship. I develop a relationship to all these motifs in the sense that they're not depicting something, but embodying it. It is the difference between the painting *showing* something and the painting *being* a kind of activated plane. That's something I'm trying to get at. Is this the case? Is it working? And if so, why? The symbols—why do I paint chains? Why do I paint whatever? I have my reasons, but, well, because I find it exciting. It's a buildup. I don't research things I think could be meaningful; it is maybe the other way around. It's a relationship that charges the motif so that it arrives at its significance within the constellation of the painting.

Question

You said that sometimes you work in tandem with themes; like you said that sometimes you work on the blue paintings and sometimes with the red.

MB If I am working on two groups, say, both themes will be in the studio, and I will move them around as well as moving between them. Then sooner or later, I work only on one painting. The white paintings with those holes cut in them are a direct reaction to the rococo stage paintings. The small spider web paintings were opposite the breast paintings in the studio. The big keyhole paintings were the counterpart to the red chain paintings, etc. I just find this dynamic holds up a tension that I find productive—and swinging between these poles keeps a field open.

Eröffnung 17. Oktober, 19 Uhr, MMK Frankfurt
Dauer: 18. Oktober – 11. November

Hans-Peter Feldmann & Hans Ulrich Obrist
22. Oktober, MMK, Domstraße 10

David Cunningham
23. Oktober

Omer Fast
1. November

Latifa Echakhch
30. Oktober

Latifa Echakhch
Ausstellungseröffnung Maininsel
2. November, 16 Uhr, Portikus

Lutz Bacher
5. Februar

Ceryth Wyn Evans
tba

Jonas Mekas
tba

Lutz Bacher
Ausstellungseröffnung
8. Februar, 20 Uhr, Portikus

Rundgang
8. – 10. Februar

Mark von Schlegell & Pure Fiction Class
Mise-en-scène / Performance
11. und 12. Dezember, Portikus

Carolyn Christov-Bakargiev
13. Dezember

Dorothea von Hantelmann
22. Januar, Curatorial and Critical Studies

Carsten Nicolai & Studierende
Ausstellungseröffnung
25. Januar 2013, 18 Uhr, MMK Frankfurt

Frankfurter Positionen: Carte Blanche
26. Januar, Frankfurt Lab

Carsten Nicolai & Rainer Römer

Rund
8. – 1

Die Vo
der Stä

Staatli
Dürers
D-605
Tel +4
Fax +4
www.s

Portik
Alte Br
D-605

Ausstellungseröffnung Maininsel
2. November, 16 Uhr, Portikus
Dauer: 3. November 2012 – Februar 2013

Gelitin
8. November

Georges Didi-Huberman
Institut für Kunstkritik
9. November

Wolfgang Tillmans
14. November

Charles Esche
20. November, Curatorial and Critical Studies

Jerry Tartaglia

January 15, 2013
Amy Sillman

American painter Amy Sillman shares her approach to painting, portraiture, and creative practice in this lecture and Q&A. Time is a recurring theme for Sillman. Reflecting on her early exposure to experimental film in NYC, she describes the influence on her use of sequencing and animation, and most significantly, her understanding of change as process. Likewise, Sillman discusses how poetry and language filtered into her work, leading to collaborations with poets such as Charles Bernstein and Lisa Robertson. Sillman, who combines humor and more serious, gestural painting, explains how the two formats merge in her practice. She tells how playful portrait sessions with couples catalyzed a series of abstractions, and confirms her view that abstraction is a structural form of negation and transformation.

Painting

I often work for a long time on the same painting. A painting *could* be done in a matter of days, but many take months and some a year or even more. I like not knowing how long it will take, and not revealing the time of the painting process in an obvious way. In fact, I also like hanging a painting that was done in a day next to a painting that took a year. The structural components are often not dissimilar. It's not that each layer takes a long time—the painting is done in fast moments, but ones that build up and shift, building change upon change upon change, each moment altered and developed by the next. In a sense, the paintings are like recordings on walls. Paintings that take so long to produce weigh a lot because they can have about a million layers of paint. Though you can't usually see the under-layers, because I continually sand them and scrape them, I like the idea of the painting having an intrinsic weight, a kind of compression, even if you can't really perceive that immediately. This is what you can only really see in real life.

About four years ago, I realized that this process of continual change means that the paintings I've been making are in fact private animations, constantly changing pictures for which I am the only viewer in my studio. Change is a process I use to figure out what the work is about while I'm doing it. In a sense, this means that I make time-based paintings, and this sense of painting was inherited from my studies and friendships with filmmakers. When I first moved to New York in the seventies, I hung out with filmmakers in an experimental downtown NY film scene, and later I went to grad school at Bard College, a program that is famous for its experimental film and video department—some of my best teachers were poets and film/video artists. But I never worked with a camera at all until I got an iPhone in about 2009. At that point, I started documenting the changes in my paintings over the weeks and months. Then I began using the iPhone to draw on, making little sequences of drawings, fanciful little animations for a friend, or a way to consider how a painting might continue. At some point, these sequences formed a kind of low-budget animation. I realized that I was a total tech-newbie, but with my iPhone and the dumb iMovie program, I figured out how to make these little animations. I think of these things as being like zines—little throwaways that come along with the work of painting. The animations have been incredibly important to how I see my work as a painter: it really helped me realize that the idea of time is fundamental to my work.

After I began making these little animations, I asked poets to collaborate with me, to give me an arena of language upon which to work. I know a lot of poets in New York, and the poetry scene that I'm familiar with is very much aligned with the history of contemporary art-making, so the poetry I'm talking about is extremely abstract. I think this tradition is in part rooted in the art school in post-war America called Black Mountain—an amazing art school run in the 1930s by Josef Albers after he emigrated to the States when the Bauhaus closed under pressure of the

Nazis. Albers created a school where poets, artists, dancers, and other thinkers including Robert Rauschenberg, Willem de Kooning, Buckminster Fuller, Ruth Asawa, and Cy Twombly worked together. This interaction between painting and poetry helped kickstart the poetry and art in the New York downtown scene. I know that the tradition of art and poetry entwining is different in Germany. For example, I have a very established German art historian friend who came to New York recently, and we went to a party with poets. She said to me, "I have never met a poet." To her, poets were remote academic people wearing jackets with leather patches on the elbows and smoking pipes—in other words, super pretentious literary guys that artists would never mingle with. But to an American like me, poets were bohemians, like beatniks who work with collage, erasure, and translation using language as *material* in the same way that I work with drawing or comics, or jokes, or any other kind of media. Their job is shredding language apart, and putting it back together in a way that extends or defies signification. This is a long tradition, which maybe originates with the Cubo-Futurists in Russia in the early twentieth century, or other Dada or concrete poets elsewhere. The poets I know and hang out with are similar to experimental filmmakers in the sense that they're the ultimate "non-market" artists who (both fortunately and unfortunately) don't expect to make money, but whose outlier status helps produce a really radical culture. The first poet I asked to work with me was Charles Bernstein back in 2010, and we did a months-long back-and-forth email collaboration exchange of writing and iPhone drawings. Then I was asked to do a show in a bookstore/gallery space in Paris in 2011, and I was able to work with a great Canadian poet named Lisa Robertson who lives in France. I asked her if she would let me take a poem of hers and make an animation on an iPad, and read the poem aloud myself.

What connects this animation work and my paintings, materially, is the fact that my work is rooted in drawing. I honestly think I'm really a drawer more than a painter. As a painter, line is the engine of the work, building a structure that proceeds from the intimacy and scale of the hand-drawn line. The work is structured by the scale of my body: I usually use these huge wax oil crayons to draw the paintings, which are specially produced in a factory in upstate New York called R&F Pigment. They also make the crayons Richard Serra uses to draw but on a far more gigantic scale than I do.

So these are two ends of a spectrum in my work. On the one hand is an interest in intimacy, the hand, and drawing. On the other hand is an interest in history and language—the language of gestural painting and modernist procedures, and also the language of cartoons, and even the language of language. I am interested in a complicated painting practice, a layered one—I have big gallery shows of formal paintings but I also embed them with intimate or throwaway things. I want to compress the little passionate stuff—the fan-zine culture—into the gallery room because it's the fan-zine that maybe made you be an artist in the first place.

Portraits

Along with paintings, and animations, and cartoons, etc., I go through periods during which I become a portraitist. After many years of making big abstract paintings, after a show in 2006, I realized that I wanted to come back to portraying people, to work from life. I didn't want everybody to just devolve into the mannerism of a cartoon stick figure; I wanted to build up from what I saw around me. It was frustrating to realize that I had developed my own kind of cliché where everyone had a giant head and stick legs. So in 2008, during a time when I was a newly single person, I thought I'd spend a year drawing every couple I knew. I wanted to study what couples look like and how they interact, and I realized that couples sit interestingly together. When you draw them, they start off on the couch next to each other, and soon they get into these weird sculptural shapes, leaning on each other and becoming a tangle. This was, I guess, my personal joke on "relational aesthetics," which was the lingo at the time—I thought, if all I do is hang out with people and draw them, I'll be doing "relational aesthetics." So I would spend the whole day with them, we would have tea, chat, they'd get in bed, I'd be recording them as they change, it was seriously intended, but fun. Then I gave myself this very specific assignment: after working with a specific couple for a day, I would go home and make ONE single drawing of these people from memory, one only. The rule was that I couldn't look at the drawings from our time together, but I had to remember their character in one memory drawing. Then I used that single memory drawing as the visual structure for a series of abstract studies, black-and-white ink studies, which tended to get more and more abstract as they went on. As a result, the portraits of specific people would sort of grade into abstraction, the portrayal disappearing as the steps went on. I produced many paintings from those structures that would not appear to be "portraits" at all, yet I knew what they emerged from. The act of abstraction was, therefore, a kind of "trace."

After a while, I realized that I had basically just walked myself through the whole history of twentieth century modernist painting. Just like in that history, abstraction became a set of methodological constraints, moving from the objective into the non- objective. I also realized then that people nowadays work with abstract painting as though it were a kind of "design," but that in fact, abstraction is a STRUCTURAL form of negation and transformation. I really understood abstraction at its roots from the inside out doing this project. I felt I was making, perhaps, my first serious work.

Later, I showed the abstract paintings that emerged from these portrait drawings at the Hirschhorn Museum in Washington D.C. I decided not to show the whole spectrum of transition, from the original portraits to the paintings, because I felt it was just a bit too academic—so I never showed any of the inside material or gave any explanation for how these abstract paintings arrived from different stages. But I did show some of the structural ink studies, which gave a clue about the "compression" inside those paintings.

One of the interesting things about doing this work was that along with the "serious abstract painting," something came out that was *funny*: the memory drawings were *comical*, like caricatures. These were where my sense of humor came out. So in a sense, two kinds of work came from the same research: funny work and serious work. I think I have always made jokes and serious stuff equally. In this case, it was caricatures and abstract painting. But in general, I have always noticed this inner dynamic, a kind of tension in my work between two forces that are getting at each other, criticizing each other. I have been told that my process is inherently dialectic. I'm always seeking to intensify everything.

Next Chapter Where Practices Get Merged

In 2009, I went to live in Berlin. I had a show there and it was the first time that I thought, maybe I should include a zine. Because I was living in Germany for the first time and didn't speak the language or come from that context as a painter, I thought that I should have a kind of interpreter that came with my work to unpack the paintings, and that it would be a zine. So I made these one-euro zines that sat along with the paintings in the gallery, which you could take or buy. In the zine were cartoons, comics, essays, things I thought were funny, and stuff I reproduced by other people, all related to what I was thinking about at the time, which was the idea of a diagram.

I was thinking about how a diagram is a time container, a graphic format that can contain several different vectors at the same time, which was, of course, interesting to me as a dialectician. At the residency where I lived in Berlin, which was kind of fancy, I was going to these seated dinners that were a bit absurd, and I became keenly aware of the act of constantly going to all kinds of dinners—art dinners, academy dinners, school dinners, etc. So part of the work I did that year was a joke: I basically made up fake seating charts with imaginary people at dinners, whom I described elaborately in these diagrams, and I ended up putting these table seatings into the show with the abstract paintings. I was wondering if there was really any difference between a painting and a joke, and began testing out the possibility of them positioned together.

That was the first show I had where I really conscientiously tried to combine everything I could possibly think of doing at that moment. I wanted to question my own expectations for abstract painting in a gallery, where you go in only to find some generic abstraction—some aesthetic thing—you have no idea what it means, and honestly, you just don't care. I wanted the gallery to contain the backstory: paintings, abstract forms, jokes, and portraits, all of it. I wanted the viewer to have to deal with the whole spectrum of someone's day, everything from the small comic feeling to the large formal thing. That was a show I really liked, and in all the following shows I've had, I've really tried to stage a *situation* with a painting show questioning itself subtly, so that it evidences at least *some* self-reflexivity around painting, even though the person doing the paintings (me), is obviously a big painting-lover …

For example, in a later show in Berlin, embedded in a display of big heavy paintings, I had a silent animation based on a poem playing on a monitor. What I was hoping for was that the animation, this constantly moving thing, would allow you to see the paintings in a different light, as possibly not done yet, objects which are themselves in a state of ongoing change. I wanted to suggest underlying movement and animation of painting, it's "before" and "after" quality. Upstairs in this same show, I lined a room with prints of two hundred stills from the video. These were rubber-stamped on the back with a message that said, "This print cost 32 euros to make. You can have it, but don't sell it." I didn't sign them. I have done similar things since with zines, posters, and videos. They are not free, there is an exchange involved: if you want them, you have to pay me back for the amount of money I had to pay to get the thing made, but I don't want to sell it for profit, nor do I want someone else to sell it. The problem with this seemingly open structure is that you don't really have to pay me for my time. And I'm not disclosing the cost of the painting, which makes it possible for me to make the little free things. But I'm just trying to work out how I can involve just a glimpse of the idea of "cost" or "value" in a show of painting, or be a little bit more generous. In that show in Berlin, there was this sort of proposal of different values: upstairs—free, downstairs—the normal painting situation.

If you're a normal painter, at some level, whether you like it or whether you don't like it, you end up having to confront this luxury problem. Your stuff is in galleries, and it's for sale, and there is this problem about making these luxury items that you and your friends can't even afford, and in fact, you were never intending to be an artist just to make luxury stuff. I guess one thing I've done is try to find a way to even slightly subvert this situation by making another object that people could get, and to at least not spend all my time pumping out big glamorous products. I don't think I've solved the problem, but I've been trying to figure out how to situate things in a more complex way.

Painting Time

As a young painter, when I went to school, we always heard from old male teachers that painting was about "space," and that you had to understand this mythic thing called "painting space." Painting space is something almost nobody understands. I think after many decades of looking and working, I finally *did* kind of understand what it is, but it took me a long time—it's like understanding Zen Buddhism or something. But in the end, after I finally started to deeply grasp painting's inner space and methodologies, I realized that my painting is *not* about space—it's about time. Film compels me because it's about expanded time; painting is about compressed time. Ultimately I think my work is about time—about describing time, re-organizing time, grabbing it, wrenching it, turning it inside out, completely changing the time signature of the time, and of your own time, and of your experience of time, and then putting it up on the wall. In that way, maybe, I'm actually kind of a formalist, but of time.

Question

What is the relevance of painting in the digital age, of abstract painting especially?

Amy Sillman: Well, I would say this: I don't originally come from the digital world. I'm fifty-seven years old. When I grew up, there was no Internet, no computer, there wasn't a cell phone—but there were paintings, and I grew up looking at them. So I'm doing something that relates to what I have been doing for my entire life, which as I was suggesting in the beginning, has its roots in drawing. My work is actually connected to the simplest idea of a picture, of drawing a picture. I also think that, if you live in the Internet world, which most everyone does now, it is a total relief to *remove yourself* from the brutalities and toxicities of news, video, Instagram, Facebook, etc. I would also say that time is not chronological and you don't necessarily only just make the thing that is happening now. You might actually do something like read a long novel. You might walk to France. I don't think that what artists do has a cut-off period, a sell-by date, or that things aren't relevant after that. So I think that abstract painting, even in its beautiful old-fashioned form, offers a certain very particular resistance to the world of explanation or the world of social media, for example. Sometimes it's a genuinely poetic experience to make a thing, which refuses to explain itself. A silence could occur, and I personally am very moved by this. I went to school in the seventies when the teachers were conceptual artists that said painting was dead, or that only dead white men did it. That was the proposition. I thought, fuck you—I'm going to do it because I want to do it. That was me being a brat. But I have always thought that dealing with drawing, color, not having a camera, not making a camera the focus of your attention, and working with your hand is valid. Like writing a letter—I would ask, why would you write a letter ever again? In some way, the answer to your question is buried in such things, which you enjoy doing with your hand or body.

Question

Do you see your work as political at all?

Amy Sillman: I'm going to try and boil it down. First of all, I was trained by people who said that I was basically not capable of (or fit for) making abstract paintings. And at the same time, abstract painting was defined as a category of refined fancy luxury things. So, painting would be a category I was prohibited from, or that I would hate. However, I also really love paintings and have cried in front of paintings. So I don't feel like "refined fancy thing" is the category I accept for that kind of object. When I go to a museum and see Olga Rozanova's painting *Green Stripe*, or her boyfriend, Aleksei Kruchenykh's anti-war collages,

I have an experience in which time falls away and I'm blown away by their straightforward address and materialism. It completely interrupts the logic of everyday life. It interrupts the logic of media, the logic of who I'm supposed to be in order to be an art lover, it interrupts the logic of what fancy art is supposed to be; it is available for me to look at. And this is how it connects to a way that I actually spend time alone, in a way that I love or make things like I do in my bedroom, or my first experiences with culture, which were in record shops or bookstores where the relation to culture was as an enthusiast, not a consumer.

I think that there is an idea, in America at least, that is all about a kind of base level "I gotta be me" politics. You see this in the act of punk rock where you can't play your instrument, but you're just going to do it anyway, or drawing comics, or maybe making paintings—and in the earliest iterations of feminism, where the personal is political, or at marches for black liberation where a sign famously proclaims: "I AM A MAN." In America, the act of saying things out loud, having a voice, writing, drawing, speaking, playing, and proclaiming, essentially reworking things in your own hands, was the base level format for politics in the 1960s. It's where the feeling of potential and interaction occurs. This is very different from a critique of subjectivity, which may be the base level of politics in Europe. But it's important to understand the role of subjective expression in America as the format for radical change in the States. I don't think it feeds anyone who is homeless or is activist politics, but it is a kind of politics. That's where drawing began for me, in that spirit.

Isabelle Graw: I was very intrigued by two aspects of your talk. I thought it was interesting that you showed the painting in process. You talked a lot about animation. It really seemed as if the painting was painting itself, or as if the painting had told you how to proceed. And this whole notion, that a painting is animated, that a painting is a quasi-being which paints itself, is, of course, a very old trope in the history of painting. Painters like Francis Bacon have described how the painting tells them what to do, while Albert Oehlen, in a tongue-in-cheek way, claims similar things when saying that his paintings look angrily at him. So I was wondering—on the one hand, one of the biggest myths of painting is that it is a quasi-being, and on the other hand, it is a production experience, it is something you experience as a painter. How would you situate your practice between these two things—the myth, which is, of course, problematic as every myth is, and a kind of reality? And the second question concerns working with Orchard, where you made portraits of all the people involved, which of course made me think of this term proposed by David Joselit called "network painting." David Joselit defined network painting as a visualization of network relations. And my criticism of this whole concept is that it fits so well into so-called network capitalism. If we currently live in a stage of capitalism where it is our social relations that count, which are a kind of resource, why feed into a situation where our own social network is worth a lot—it's our kind of capital so to speak?

Amy Sillman: I'll answer your question about Orchard first. I don't have a strategy for defeating capitalism, and David had not written his article yet, so my portrait series was not in response to it. But I do have an interest in looking at things. This is a really basic, gut-level instinct. I like to look at people and see if I can actually translate what I see with my hand, which is a very old-fashioned skill, but it is incredibly pleasurable if you can pull it off. There is this crazy thing about trying to be like a camera or novelist, but really render something with your own hand and your eyeballs. I wasn't trying to describe the network. Like I said, I didn't write any information, like this one hates that one. I didn't try to describe what we paid for our rent. That wasn't on my mind. What was on my mind was that first of all (and this somewhat gets to the question about politics), people think that if you're an abstract painter, or as they sometimes say "a gallery artist," that you're basically just a big hack. That you're a person who is *for sale* and everything you do is for sale. And one way to defeat this very simplistic for sale thing is to do the things you love and not just be a hack professional who churns out stuff. At Orchard, they asked me to be in a show and I didn't have a strategy, except: no one's ever drawn the people in Orchard. Does anyone know what these people look like? That's it, end of strategy. In terms of display, I thought I'd put them on a table after completing the portraits so the viewers could handle the drawings. They were not for sale. I kept them. Therefore, I have this archive, a very beautiful set of thirty-two black-and-white portraits, of what the people that I am friends with looked like in the year 2008. It's a great record. I like psychological thought, and so, I love the very intense connection between a portraitist and her subject, the gaze which occurs, the intensity of the looking which occurs, and yields a real icon in a way. I don't know how to answer the network thing. I don't think the network idea is a good enough analysis yet, because a network only contains the connection of *like* not *hate*, for example. The network doesn't describe any of the actual complex, overlapping, simultaneous emotions, and that's the problem with social media. I don't think art is a portrait of that. It's more of a portrait of psychoanalytic process. It's more of a portrait of reconciling yourself to your terrible and wonderful feelings and thoughts, being in-between things. How does the network theory deal with a monetary situation? I don't know. Those are not my questions. But at Orchard, I was just trying to see what people looked like.

As for myth, the thing I haven't said yet, which could also be about your question about politics, is sense of humor. You don't have a mythic relationship with your painting. You have kind of a tragicomic relationship with your painting because it's always going wrong. It's just a big mess, and things are never doing what you want them to do, and it's so confusing, and as soon as you put something on there, it's kind of embarrassing, or maybe it's great, but then you wreck it the next day. I wouldn't call it a *mythic*, but I would call it a *living* relationship if you're not just making some products, if you're responding. But you're responding to an object, and the object keeps misbehaving. It's like having a relationship with a horse—you want it to go well, but it usually doesn't, like a bad horse. You're trying to ride to town with your Palomino, but the Palomino is wild. It's interesting to have a relationship with things. When I read about Bruno Latour, whom I don't know very much about, and his theory of things, I always think, well, yes, a key, it has pretty normal properties and it pretty much stays the same. Try having a relationship with an eight-foot-tall misbehaving Palomino. It's a very living, breathing, and physical relationship. And on top of that, when you're an "Abstract Expressionist" (like me??!) you don't know what you want it to look like because you didn't plan it out. So I have no idea, and it's usually a big mess. And then, if you want to change one part, you have to change the whole thing. It's a very deep, painful, sentimental, loving, hating relationship, which I think is really full. Most real painters are slightly mentally ill because they are having these deep relationships with these stupid *things*.

Michael Krebber: I want to throw something in because when I listen to you, it sounds like keeping up the energy of doing something you describe you are doing. And my problem always is—and you know that I guess—I destroyed something for myself, or I ache from something, and what I actually ache from was, for example, this title of John Kelsey's *Stop Painting Painting*. And when I get to painting, when I have to approach that, which I am doing in these days, I get into deep trouble immediately, and I don't know why I'm doing that. I only want to throw this in. I have no point. Because what you describe is having the strength to do it, and do it again, and do it again, and you describe a way of how to make that possible or how that is possible for you. That's how I understood it. There is no question.

Amy Sillman: Yes, but I think that trouble is fun. Let's say this: Who wants to have a relationship with somebody who is not a problem? Do you want to have a relationship with a nice girl who always does what they say? I don't. Maybe you do. I like problems, trouble, despair, and all those kinds of things. I probably really share a feeling of emotional, very deep worry. I hope I don't just sound like this fun-loving girl that keeps marching down the road of good times …

Question

What is your relationship to decorative painting?

Amy Sillman: What is decorative painting? What do you think it is when you say that? I don't think what I'm doing is decorative. That's exactly why I was saying that I don't like the idea of just painting nice "designs." What I've been trying to describe is a place from which you *depart*. And a place you get to, and that there is actual meaning between those points A and B. If decorative just means that it looks good, I don't think that's what I'm doing. But if decorative means beautiful quilts that are dyed by women in Ahmedabad, then I will say, yes, I love those. What does decorative mean? People go and buy their shoes based on what looks good. We do have tastes and aesthetics we would employ towards what we like, but it doesn't necessarily mean that it's just pretty. You could love ugly feelings.

Question

Since you teach at Bard, can you talk more about your teaching approach?

Amy Sillman: We meet individually, and then have different-sized crits but Bard doesn't have classes. It's really based on Black Mountain College, which I talked about earlier. We have six departments: painting, sculpture, photography, video, poetry, and sound. Everyone meets everybody from every department. I would say that part of the politics of what I'm doing, when I teach in this job I've had for fifteen years at Bard, is that I'm very interested in what people are thinking about when they are working, what their questions might be, what they feel they have permission to do or not. There is an aspect of teaching where you are working with people directly from the ground up. Figuring out what you should be reading and how you should be approaching object making. That's what I try to do. So I don't really have the teaching job to feed myself, but out of the desire to have a place for serious conversations that have nothing to do with a gallery situation. We don't have gallerists coming and trying to pluck you out and give you a show. It's a school that's very devoted to material intelligence, or form plus thought. For me, that's kind of a political action—to constantly work with people in serious deep conversation, and not always to retreat to the lonely studio.

2011/2012

ortrag

28.11. Andrea Fraser

Curatorial and

Vortrag

13.12. Beate Söntgen

nil Collins

n mit MMK

19.1. Christa Näher

Vortrag

26.1. Brigitte Weingart

izman, Vortrag

tersemeste

25.11. Martha Rosl

on, Hu Fang, Laura Wrig
ition mit MMK

7.12. Judith Ho

omina, Vortrag

17.1. Claire Bisho
Domstrasse 10, in Koop

s, Thomas Kellein
ition mit MMK

25.1. Emily War

zel/Rimini Protokoll, Vo

1.2. Hito Steyerl & Eyal

November 25, 2011
Martha Rosler

American artist Martha Rosler provides a comprehensive introduction to her life work in this lecture and Q&A, discussing the breadth of her installations, video, photography, and collage made in recent decades. From her Garage Sale project and seminal video Semiotics of the Kitchen *in the 1970s, to* Kassel Gardens *shown at documenta 12, and* Pull UP Those PIIGS!, *a public artwork produced with her son Joshua Neufeld, Rosler shares unique insights into the context, intention, and production of each work. Topics of feminism, housing and homelessness, global politics, and war appear throughout, as Rosler addresses the urgent political issues of the time.*

It's difficult for me to give a presentation on my work because there is, after all, so much of it, and it's quite diverse. I've put some images together, of works that represent various concerns of mine. I usually show a lot of images to provide a visual context but go into more depth with only a few projects. I set up a few abstract categories, however, as an introduction. There are photographic projects, some that function as photo critique, particularly of documentary—a recurring interest of mine—but also old-fashioned photographs of spaces of transit, and a very different body of work having to do with housing. I include also, in that category, questions of architecture and the built environment—that may be among the ugliest phrases ever invented!

In terms of formal arrangement, my work includes a lot of installations such as: *Fascination With (The Game of the) (Exploding) (Historical) Hollow Leg* from 1983, when the world faced the looming possibility of nuclear war. This large installation was centered on that issue and the associated military apparatuses, including military bases worldwide, but also on forms of opposition to it. The phrase in the title is not literal but refers to the hollowness of reliance on the phallic fetish of the nuclear-tipped missile. But—and this is outside the installation category—a prosthetic leg, including on the one hand a functioning miniature and on the other an oversize kinetic model, as well as its depiction in several photomontages, has been a recurrent theme in my work, associated with questions of war and destruction.

In 2003, I presided over a complex and occasionally tumultuous group project at the Venice Biennale called "Oleanna Space/Ship/Station," which was put together mostly with my students from Stockholm and Copenhagen, and some from my grad course at Yale University, along with previous students from various points around the globe including Australia, Canada, and Germany. We constructed an unfinished building and filled it with projects, staged performances and hosted seminars, as well as putting out a few issues of our newspaper, which we began in Copenhagen.

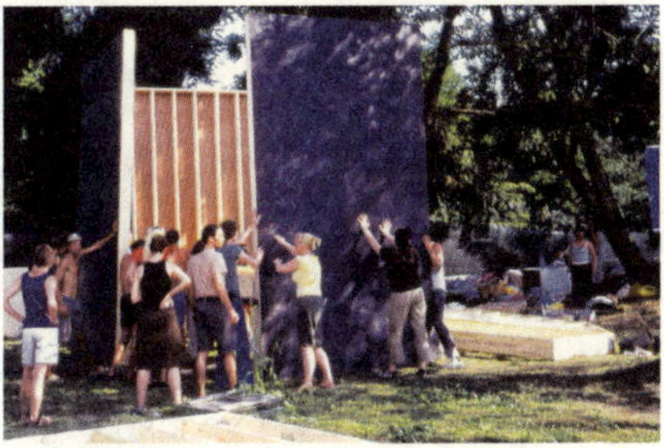

In the performance category, here are more live performances, ones involving several people or groups. *Semiotics of the Kitchen, an Audition* (2003) was a live group performance reprising the solo, non-live performance—that is, a performance in front of a video camera, which I did in 1975 called *Semiotics of the Kitchen.* The audition version was staged publicly in London with twenty-six women volunteers, and I later made a video of that performance, as well. Another performance, *Romances*

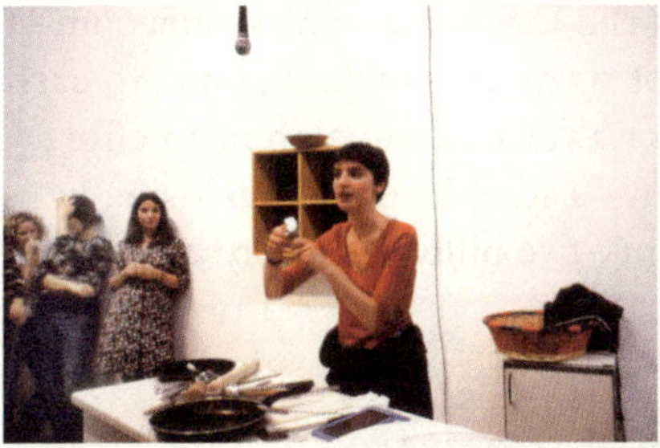

of the Meal, performed in Brussels in 2000, was an exhausting saga telling the histories—some real, some fanciful—of a number of "global foods," mostly coffee but also chocolate and Coca-Cola. We served lots of coffee to the audience as well as drinking it ourselves, so we all went mad together. I've also organized various bus tours based on histories of various sites, including Ottensen, a northern suburb of Hamburg, and of Liverpool, and a walking tour of worksites of the Frieze Art Fair in London. As Nicolas mentioned in his introduction, discursive projects form another category, about the geopolitics of space. And I'll say a bit more about the traveling library in a minute.

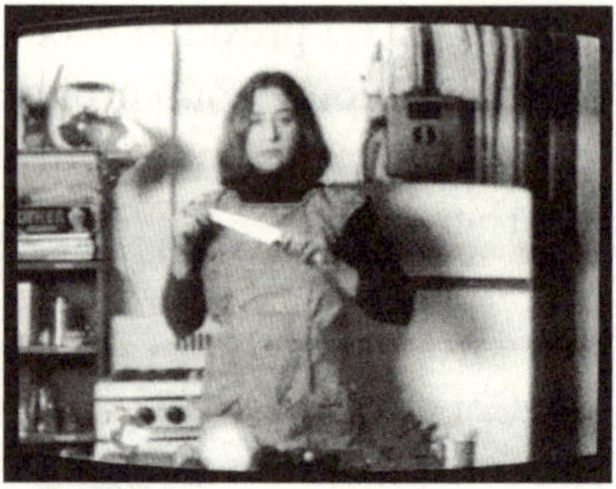

I've done a number of works for billboard display. This one is odd for me, because I wouldn't have thought of doing a billboard urging people to vote. But an art group in the U.S. state of Missouri commissioned a group of six artists, including me, to each design a billboard for a voting campaign in an effort to help elect Obama—a state he ended up losing by a tiny margin. Seventy-five billboards were erected.

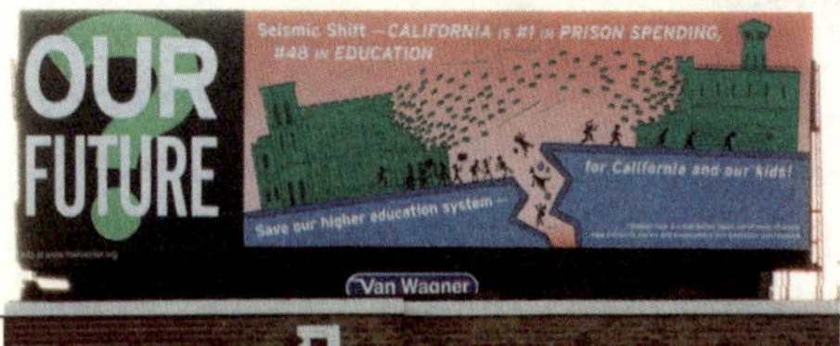

I turned my design into a banner, without the words. Another billboard, *Lesson*

for Today, was for a project in L.A. with a number of invited artists. I worked with my son, Josh Neufeld, a graphic novelist. It's about the fiscal destruction of higher education in California. I have to comment, though, that I don't believe that it is wise for artists to do artsy things on billboards, especially in L.A., because they may just look like ads. In this case,the most dominant other billboard in the gigantic forest of signs downtown was the Diesel brand billboard that said, in huge letters, "BE STUPID." I know you're familiar with this campaign because it's everywhere. The idea that people don't just tear them down in rage, but instead say, "Sure, that's a thought, be stupid, okay. I'll be stupid, where can I get those clothes?" is symptomatic. [Continues with an on-screen list of categories] I always put the category of "feminism" in these compilations because I want to remind everybody that I am, indeed, a feminist, and that applies to pretty much everything I do.

Historical Memory

I'll talk about the Münster project, but not *Kassel Gardens from the Perspective of a Mole* at documenta 12, held at the same time, because that one is too complicated for this talk today. I wish I had more images with me of the project I did here at Portikus. There is at least one veteran in this room of that complex project. Portikus is, of course, situated on the Old Bridge, the Alte Brücke, over the Main, and the project was about the building and its architect, about the history of the bridge and the various communities around it—specifically, the former Jewish community and ghetto of centuries ago, of which this map [displays map], used to cover the entire gallery floor. Some of the many elements had to do with history,

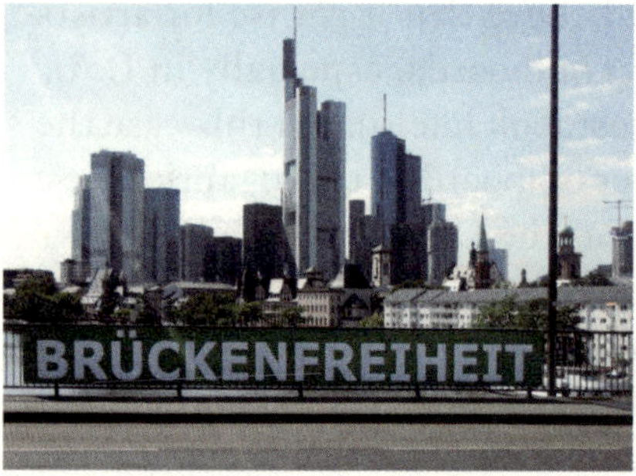

including the bridge's history, such as the fact that the bridge had its own laws known as *Brückenfreiheit*, signaling that the bridge wasn't under Frankfurt's jurisdiction, or how the bridge was used as a site for collecting dead rats and storing gunpowder. There were also elements relating to Frankfurt's port and military installations, on the bridge and elsewhere. And of course "Mainhattan"—the startling concentration of skyscrapers in downtown Frankfurt, those buildings belonging almost universally to financial companies. There was a floor-to-ceiling replica of the Euro, in front of the ECB building now graced with Occupy tents; a real-time readout of Xetra, the trading system on the Frankfurt Stock Exchange; a display of hats required of German Jews in the Middle Ages; and a musical compilation of Frank-

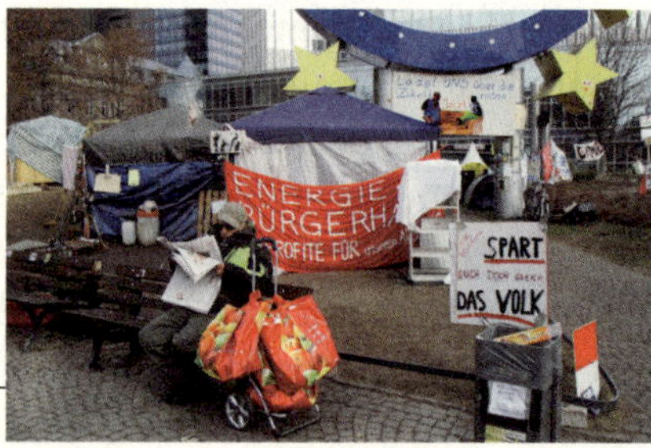

furt's trance music scene. Four computers around a table directed users to websites on general history, military history and facilities in Frankfurt, architectural concerns, Jewish history, and more. I told you it was complicated.

Other site-specific works include, as I briefly mentioned, the documenta 12 *Kassel Gardens* work, and at the Singapore Biennale earlier that year (2011), an actual—not photo-based—garden project, which I'll get back to a bit further on.

Many of the works I've mentioned so far are collaborative projects; I'd include in this group the garage sales I've held. When I held the first Garage Sale in San Diego in 1973, it was greeted as a stain upon the art world. To even think of selling junk in an art gallery was treated as a debasement. To which my answer was, "What would you rather have me sell in an art gallery?" which was the obvious question, but one that required the further question of the

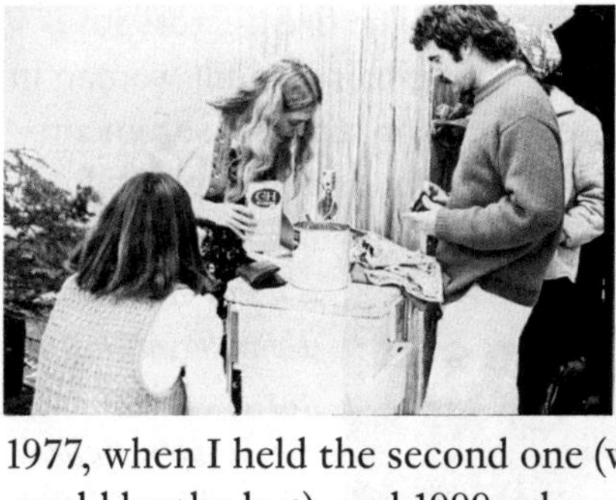

differential valuation of art and household goods or castoffs and the appropriate places for the display and sale of each. Between 1977, when I held the second one (which I assumed would be the last), and 1999, when the series of such sales restarted, the art world went crazy for shopping, and more and more places wanted to hold garage sales as an art event. The next one is scheduled a year from now at the Museum of Modern Art in New York, which I find troubling and funny—but don't expect me to turn it down! It is going be like a military campaign: you have to start planning now to have enough goods, sorted and priced, ready to go, to fill the atrium of MoMA during Christmas shopping season. It's going to be interesting ...

Oh, I could show you a clip from this video if you want—just say yes, or no, I don't have to do it.

Audience: Yes. Please.

All right, well, remember this is NTSC, that's one reason why it looks like hell.

[Plays *Semiotics of the Kitchen* (1975)]

[A black and white six-minute video of the artist standing in a kitchen as she presents kitchen implements and their various, sometimes violent or unproductive functions.]

I'll show another couple of video clips, maybe.

[Plays *Vital Statistics of a Citizen, Simply Obtained* (1977)]

[A group of what appears to be five doctors in white coats examine a long-haired adult woman in pants and a blouse. They note the measurements of her body while an off-camera voice speaks.]

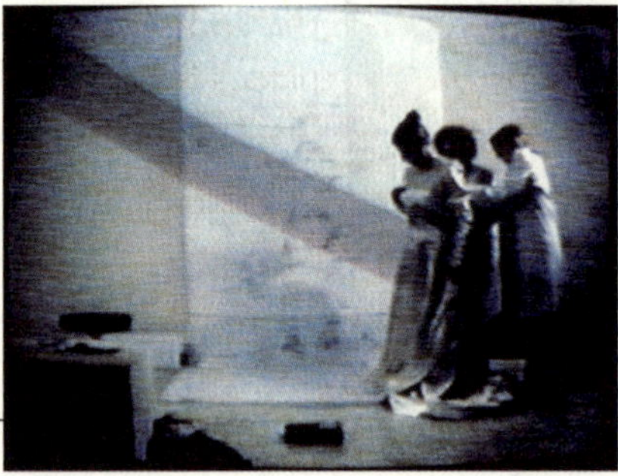

Male voice: There is a boy we will call Tommy Smith. In nursery school he was a top member of his class. A happy, normal, healthy, highly intelligent youngster. But as he

approached the age of five, the records began to show a flattening of his growth curve. He lost weight, and stopped gaining in height. The staff nutritionist calling at his home for a check-up found that the boy's appetite had fallen off sharply. He was not eating—particularly, not enough milk. And the result was a shortage in his intake of proteins, and minerals. Actually, the whole staff for sometime had been noticing symptoms of retardation in this apparently healthy boy. The physiologists had reported that Tommy had regressed in mind as well as in body. His IQ rating had dropped. He seemed tense, anxious, uncertain. His inner strains were reflected in his responses to the Rorschach inkblot tests, Thematic Apperception Tests, and other psychological techniques. A clue to his trouble was disclosed by one of these techniques—a doll test: three dolls, representing a man, a woman, and a small boy were placed on the floor, together with an assortment of doll furniture and other household accessories.

[The examined woman begins to undress for further examination in front of the doctors. She removes her blouse and stands topless for more measuring.]

Tommy proceeded to play house and in his play he sent the mother doll off to the office, put the father doll in the kitchen getting the next meal, and wondered aloud whether the little boy doll would grow up into a man. Maybe, he speculated, the boy would become a woman, and go off to the office like Mama. Here was the anxiety that underlay Tommy's loss of interest in food, his interrupted growth, and his lapses in IQ. It turned out that doll drama reenacted his actual home situation. Tommy's mother had a job, which kept her away from home from early morning until late afternoon. The father, whose business hours were not as demanding, did many of the housekeeping chores, fed and dressed the boy and took him to and from school. Because the mother frequently came home exhausted the father often put the child to bed. It was all very confusing to Tommy. He was at the stage in which a normal boy wants to identify himself with the male figure but his family's set up was such that he wasn't certain what the figures stood for. Anyway he wasn't sure that he wanted to be that kind of a man. The Child Research Council is not a clinic, does not treat diseases, but when symptoms come to light in the course of research, it calls them to the attention of the parents and the family physician. In this case, the parents finally recognized that their son's disturbance stemmed from themselves, and they immediately made adjustments to correct the situation.

[The woman opens the top of her pants for the doctor to take more measurements.]

The mother went on half-time at her business, and made it her main job to love and care for Tommy. The father relinquished many of his mothering services. Within a few months after these changes Tommy was a much happier young boy. He was eating so voraciously that the family doctor had to advise cutting down on his carbohydrates. His height resumed, he grew in the shoulders, and was above his classmates in intelligence tests.

Dr: The abdominal extension girth is below standard.

[One of the female examiners blows a kazoo. Image abruptly cuts to the image of a woman in a dress, making up her face. The white-coated figures are clustered in a corner, looking the other way.]

Female voice: To accept the idea that one takes one's place on a list of statistics, to accept the idea that there is meaning in measurement, to accept the idea that there is something to be learned about the self from measurement. Do you believe in Tommy Smith? What is the effect of negative expectation on intelligence, on performance? What is the effect of negative expectation on women's intelligence, on performance, on growth? Scientists who measure are not innocent.

[The white-coated female assistants bring the woman a white wedding gown and help her slip into it.]

Female voice: Scientific human measurements have been used to keep people from access to education. To keep certain races and nationalities out of America. To keep women subordinate. To keep women in their place. Often the people who invented both the idea of testing and the tests themselves, the ones who declare the tests significant, are overt racists, and believers in the genetic superiority of their own group, and the superiority of men over women.

[Inside the gown there is an abrupt cut and she suddenly wears a black dress. She begins to put on face makeup.]

Testing to maintain social control: Sir Francis Galton, Louis Terman, Henry H. Goddard, Edward L. Thorndike, Cesare Lombroso, Paul Popenoe of the eugenically inclined Human Betterment Foundation, H. H. Laughlin of the Carnegie Foundation, Dalton Coons, Arthur B. Jensen, William Shockley. Many of these men are pioneers of the testing movement. All are on record testifying to the racial superiority of white, Nordic males. To their natural superiority over people of all other races, and of course over women. To the need for testing to keep control over society. To the fact that class differences reflect difference in native ability. To the fact that sex difference reflects difference in native ability. To the absolute need to train people to fit into their proper place. To accept the idea that one takes one's place in a list of statistics. To accept the idea that there is meaning in measurement. To accept the idea that there is something to be learned about the self from measurement. Do you believe in Tommy Smith, as reported by George W. Gray in Scientific American*?*

We hear the meaning of human life remanufactured by those supposedly dedicated to the scientific understanding of so-called human life. What is science? Science is a tool that amounts to the engineering of life by bureaucrats, or worse. Those who invent measurement are not innocent. We continue with Tommy Smith, as written up by George W. Gray in Scientific American *in 1967.*

[Woman wears white wedding dress again.]

"This is not an unusual case," he reports. He goes on to quote Dr. Jean Deming, a pediatrician specializing in Biometrics. "We are all familiar with the fact that in junior high school the typical girl is much larger and grown up than the typical boy of the same age. She is not interested in dates with these small boys. She wants to go with older boys. It is interesting also to see how the curve follows the personality pattern. The growth of a feminine type of boy with a soft, rounded body with greater interest in dolls than in baseball, for example, usually follows the typical girl's pattern. Similarly, girls of the tomboy type usually have a growth pattern conforming to that of boys."

The absolute need to accustom people to fit their proper place. To take an example, only one example, Lewis Terman, one of the fathers of the testing movement wrote, "In Germany there is the rather anomalous problem of an educated proletariat. Thousands of graduates from the classical Gymnasi-

um, which for the most part ignore the problems of real life, find themselves misfits in the industrial and political world and drift about discontentedly, till finally they contribute to swell the now formidable community of German Socialists. But, in this country, our more practical sense has brought it about that few of our secondary schools dish out the formal studies to all indiscriminately. The result is that our high school graduate more frequently finds a place in the world where he can expend his energies not only to his own profit, but to the advantage of society as well."

[The woman appears in the black dress again. Still dressing as if preparing herself for something.]

The absolute need to accustom people to fit their proper place. Terman also wrote, "It cannot be disputed that in the long run, it is the races which excel in abstract thinking, while others starve,

[Woman almost fully dressed in wedding gown, now with veil.]

survive epidemics, master new continents, conquer time and space, and substitute religion for magic, science for taboos, and justice for revenge.

[Black dress.]

The races which excel in conceptual thinking, could, if they wished, quickly exterminate or enslave all the races notably their inferiors in this respect."

[White dress.]

The absolute need to accustom people, women, blacks, Asians,

[Black dress.]

those supposedly inferiors in abstract thinking to fit their proper place.

[White dress.]

To accept the idea that one takes one's place in a list of statistics.

[Black dress.]

To accept the idea that there is meaning in measurement.

[White dress.]

To accept the idea that there is something to be learned about the self from measurement.

[Video ends, resumes collage slides with multiple works highlighted on each slide.]

That's a long clip …

[Shows video clips from: *Domination and the Everyday* (1978), *Losing: A Conversation with the Parents* (1977), *Seattle: Hidden Histories* (1991–1995), and *A Simple Case for Torture, or How to Sleep at Night* (1983)]

I think I'll show this one:

[Plays Domination and the Everyday (1978)]

[A video with black and white images from various media, voices from a radio interview, and sound taken from a real domestic setting are acoustically interwoven, with text feed crawling across the bottom of the screen that comments on the confrontation between the polished ready-made images fed to us by the world and the real complexity of our realities.]

At the time that I made *Domination and the Everyday,* there weren't split screens, as there is here, and there were no text crawls on television as we now expect from news shows. There are two soundtracks playing. One is a radio interview of an art dealer about the art of the 1960s; it was playing on the radio, and recorded in the early 1970s, in the room where a mother and child conversed near the end of the day. There is a crawling text, based on Frankfurt School ideas

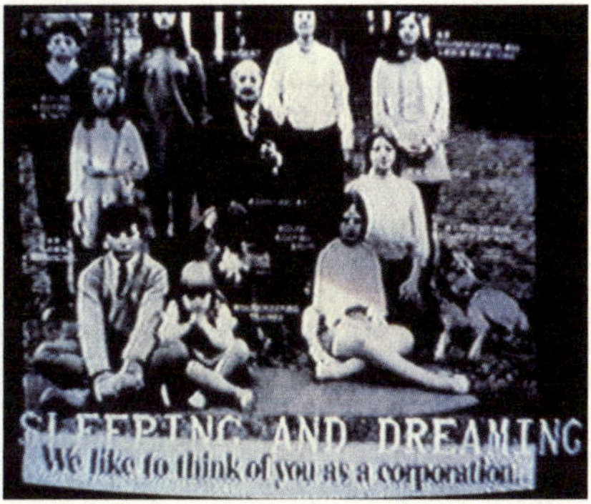

about the colonization of the imagination. What I'm asking people to do, as I often do in my work, is to choose where you focus your attention, because it is impossible to pay attention to everything. Normally a work goes out of its way not to make you feel completely bombarded, but this work is intended to make you feel bombarded. The text repeats, so you can follow it if you want, and you can hear the conversation between the mother and the child, and in the intermittent silences you can hear the (male) art dealer talking with the (female) interviewer. At some point you realize, I hope, that it's just the radio playing while the mother is getting the child ready for bed.

This was a series of eleven one-minute public service announcements for broadcast TV, called *Seattle: Hidden Histories* that I did with Native Americans in Seattle.

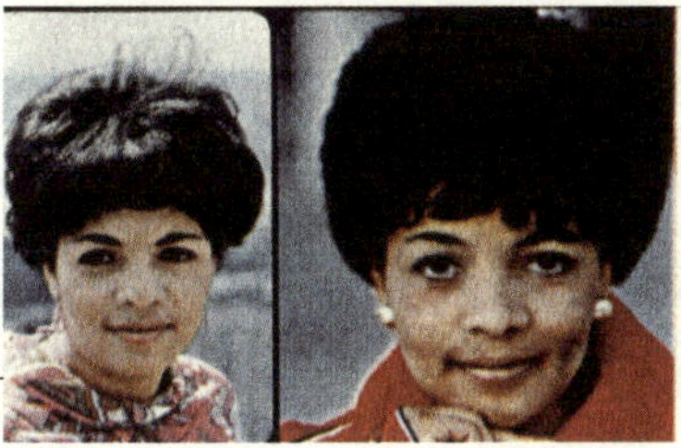

Eva White
More poised and self-assured

First Short: Native American man is sitting in a desk chair.

Urban Indians are interesting because I know that some of the reservation people, living on the reservations, view us city Indians as being different than they are. How do you define an urban Indian? Well it's gonna be difficult, because I think there might be the classic sociological picture of an urban Indian of a person lost in the city away from the reservation. But there are also a number of Indian people I know who grew up in the city. Right now I know for myself I couldn't imagine not living in the city. I met an Indian Buddhist, I've met Indian people that lived a totally upper-class urban lifestyle. I've met real transient Indian people, um, and I saw for myself that this is the diverse range of

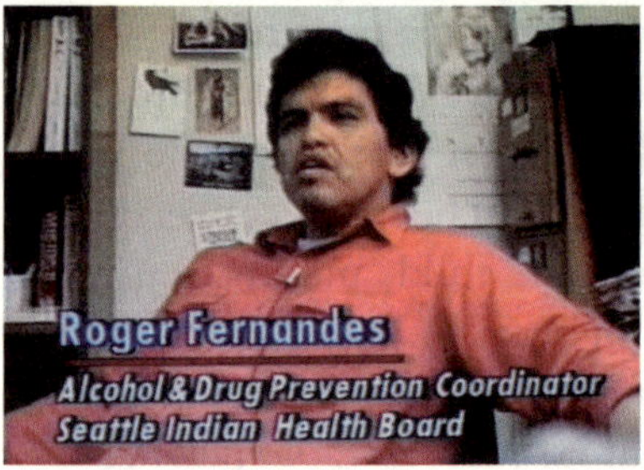

Indian people that live in the city. I've met Indians that like latte and espresso and stuff, I don't know, I think that's kind of stretching the bounds of being an urban Indian, I think!

That is the seal of the city of Seattle, merging with that of Starbucks—and, of course, Starbucks is from Seattle.

The native people that I worked with asked that the work I make not be on public television but on commercial television. And by the rules of commercial TV, each one had to be at most one minute long. I thought, okay, if I'm working on commercial television, this has to look like a wedding video,with some really cheap effects, so it doesn't look like an ad.

Second Short: Native American woman sits in a chair. (Spoken in Lushootseed, a native language, with English subtitles).

Lady Louse lived there in a great big house,
she lived there all alone,
had no friends or relatives,
and so she took it and she swept it,
this great big house.
There was lots of dirt so when she got to the very middle of this house she got lost.
And that was the end of lady Louse.
(English) What was on the minds of the teachers of our culture when they left this story with us to learn from?

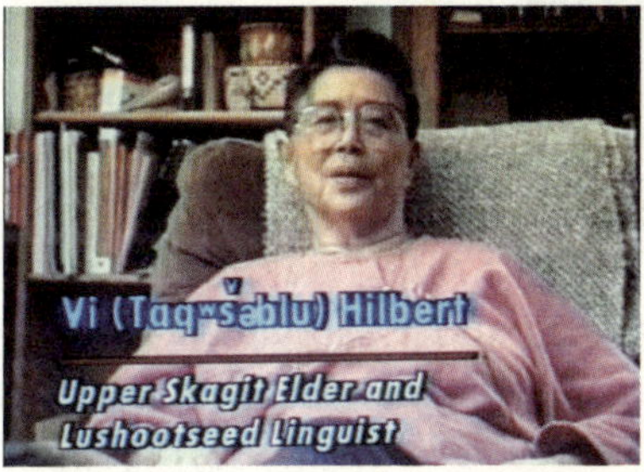

The stories were our textbooks, and the textbooks told in the ancient language are still with us. They are not lost to the people who are interested in listening and learning.

Third Short: Woman with braids sits on a couch.

Well, I was born in Lytton, B.C. I went to a boarding school,

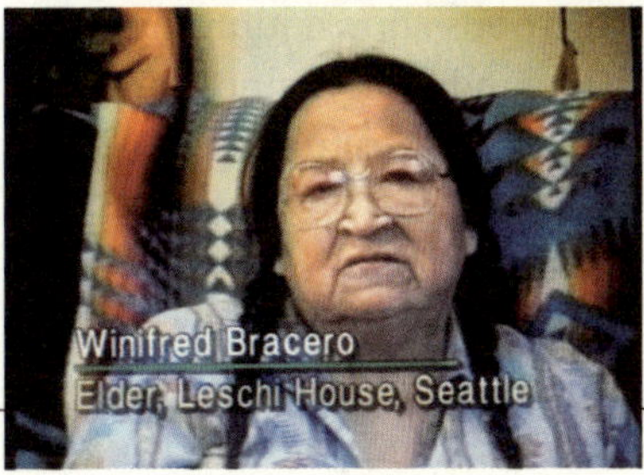

and there were over 400 children there. Our language—Nlaka'pamux—we all knew it but we couldn't speak it, and if we got caught, well, we got a whuppin' for that.

There wasn't very much time we spent in a classroom. Some of the elders where I come from, they're trying to teach the young generation now, but I lived with my grandmother, and she was the one that teached me how to—so I ah, still speak it, you know, and I'm glad.

Quite different is the video, *A Simple Case for Torture, or How to Sleep at Night*, based on an article from *Newsweek* magazine, arguing that we ought to torture

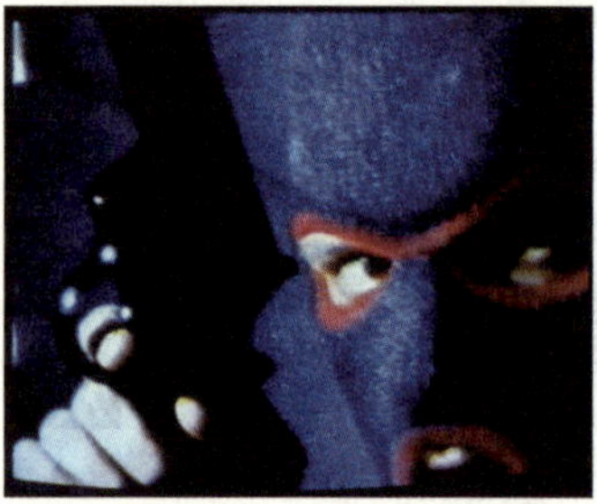

enemies. In 1983 it was unacceptable to talk about torture, but under President George Bush, it become quite acceptable not only to talk about torture but also to carry it out.

This video is *If it's too Bad to Be True, It Could Be DISINFORMATION* (1985), and it's about the way television constructs narratives that are often false or inadequate, but there is no voiceover or crawling text added—only bulk-erased tape, and juxtapositions of sinister Reagan-era stories about the Soviets and Cuba, all ending with a short musical promo for the U.S. "Army Guard," with troops shown jumping out of a helicopter bay to the sound of machine-gun fire.

[Swiftly changes slides and images from videos.]

I won't talk about this one, *Losing: A Conversation with the Parents* (1977). It is about a girl who starves herself to death and her parents are talking about it to an unseen questioner, making up all kinds of

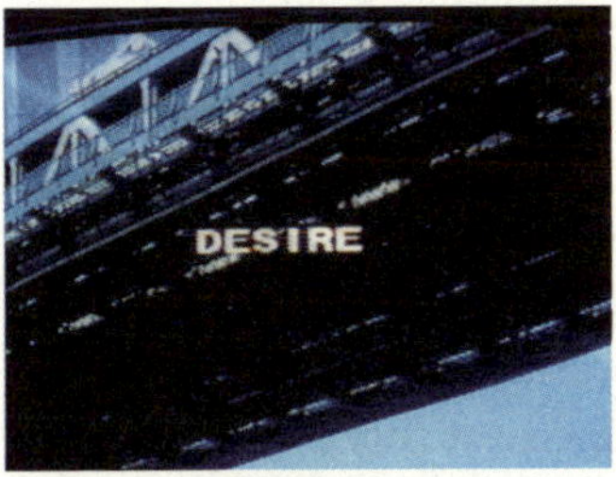

inadequate narratives about why their daughter would do that. But in a larger sense, the work is about the politics of food and unexamined stories about male and female children—and about media exploitation of monstrous stories of family life.

This one, *Secrets from the Street: No Disclosure* (1980), is centered on class and cultural differences in the largely Latino Mission district in San Francisco, where I was living. On the one hand, the police were repressing the Latino boys in the "low rider" car subculture, but at the same time, the Latino Community in the Mission was being sold to non-Latinos as a kind of exotica to visit. There were a lot of refugees from the wars that the U.S. was covertly conducting in Central America at the time, and lots of local dissenters, so this work incorporates a Spanish-language news clip in its drive-by tour of the area.

This video, *Martha Rosler Reads Vogue* (1982), has recently become interesting to people again. It

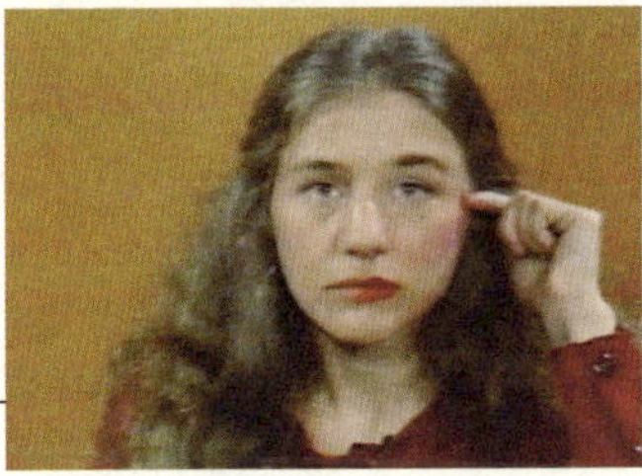

is about the production and marketing of women's clothing and high-end "lifestyle" goods. It was a recorded live performance, which was hell—we just walked into the studio, no rehearsal, and the whole thing was done mostly by a crew of unpracticed students directed by their professor at SVA, DeeDee Halleck, for her new public-access cable show, Paper Tiger. There was one professional cameraman. I was trying to direct it while I was in front of the camera, but the students had no idea! I sat there with a *Vogue* magazine and just randomly read things from it, and also from my prepared script. I think that one of the reasons it appeals to people now is because no damn thing has changed. And that's kind of a bad thought.

Oh look, I reached the present!
[Shows *Pull UP Those PIIGS!* (2011), an image of Angela Merkel and Nicolas Sarkozy standing together behind two podiums, holding the strings of a collapsed marionette pig. The pig has dotted lines across its body, which ordinarily define the cut of the pork. Each section has been given the name of one nation.]

This is another work I made with my son, Joshua Neufeld. It's installed on a building in Auguststrasse in Berlin now, right down the street from the Kunst-Werke. "Pull Up Those Piigs, gotta save our banks, blame it on the lazy Irish, and the Portuguese, and the Spanish and the Italians ..." This is the data that I was working with. There is a picture of Angela, because the greatest exposure in the Eurozone crisis, aside from Greek banks, is to French and German banks. My son has been getting some very hurtful responses on his website from people who take particular exception to the word pigs, which is what the countries are called in English, though spelled

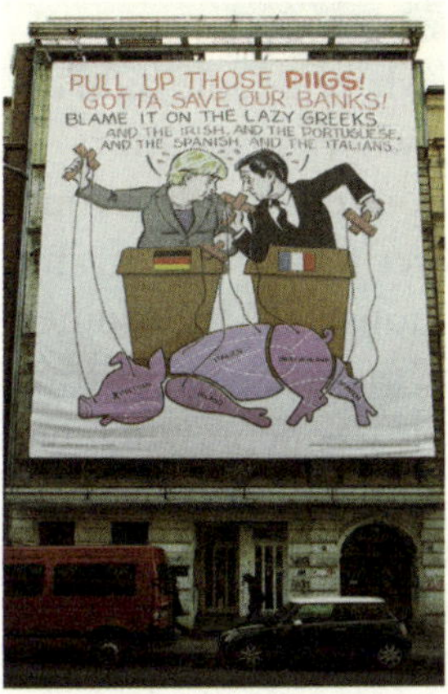

with two i's: PIIGS. It's an acronym of their names. I thought we should translate the banner into German but the sponsors said, "No, it should stay in English."

I began a photographic documentary project this year for a show that's intended by its curator to reflect a relationship to Depression-era documentaries, as we are in the middle of another catastrophic financial crisis. Back then, in the thirties, the U.S. President set up an agency that sent photographers out to document rural ways of life; the intention was to help construct an image of the country as a unity, not just a collection of separate regions or states. I decided to document a corner of my own neighborhood in Greenpoint, Brooklyn. This neighborhood is undergoing rapid gentrification, and as usual, artists have been part of the advance force. I show primarily the shops I've done business with for years, which are owned by a diverse set of people—immigrants from Europe, the Middle East, and South Asia, but also people whose families have lived right there for over a century. Shop owners tended to say yes to being photographed, and employees tended to say no, except if they were younger than twenty-five. You have a hipster restaurant, the local Greek diner, and a Yemeni-owned deli all within a couple of blocks of one another. For example, the people who run the bar on my corner, the husband was born across the street. I also included pictures of stores where people didn't want to be photographed. The owner of this store was from Egypt. I asked, "Can you tell me why? You are always so friendly." His answer was that he wasn't "meant" to be photographed. But usually after some conversation, those who refused said they were afraid of the "climate"—for Muslims. It was depressing, but it was what I expected. That, and the undocumented status of many restaurant workers. And then there are all the old-style shops and the gentry shops, little hat shops, and bars.

Earlier this year, as I mentioned earlier, I participated in the Singapore Biennale, whose theme that year was "Open House". The curators wanted to bring my traveling library there, but I begged otherwise: the library is very tired, and it's gone home and isn't traveling anymore. I thought, well, "Open House," that's an interesting theme, and I said I'd like to have a garden at the airport. They said, "Garden, nice. Airport, nice. But not *this* airport"—meaning the storied Chang I—"We happen to have a new Biennale site at the old decommissioned airport. I put together a list of people to consult. I had a friend from Singapore and I asked her, "What do you think Singapore needs from me?" and she said, "Women don't have any place to be together in public." And I thought, "Okay we'll do a women's garden." Immediately, a couple of the women artists wrote to me, asking, "Why not men?" So I said, "Sure, why not men." But the group I assembled remained preponderantly women, and all the so-called senior artists were women.

What you need to know about Singapore, aside from the fact that it was invented by one guy, is that *it was invented by one guy:* Lee Quan Yew. He was kicked out of a short-lived alliance with Malaysia, so he rebooted Singapore as a stand-alone country. He was called the "Master Gardener," and for him, Singapore was a garden. That meant you replace native plants with imported, cultivated vegetation.

The government is so "neoliberal" that it does nothing itself, everything is contracted out. I wrote to the National Parks department and they replied, "Great we'd love to work with you; we'll give you a list of contractors." So I had to hire a firm to do the gardening, even though the Biennale reimbursed me. See those paving stones? I had to rent them.

I had many meetings with, many people. Here are some of them. Along the bottom, this is Shah Najak, who works with female migrant workers. This is the artist Shirley So. And this is a young man from the crew that actually does the work—they are migrant workers. They have no labor rights of any kind; they have no time off. If they are injured, it's too bad. In Singapore—and it's not the only country like this—

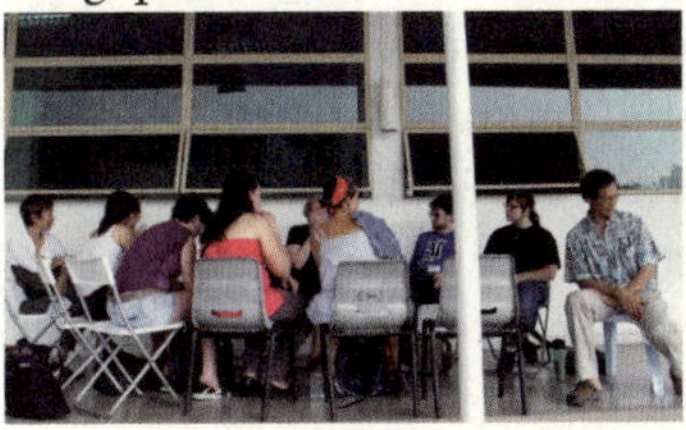

migrant workers, male and female, have no rights. There is no list anywhere of what you cannot do to a migrant worker.

This, the woman holding the coconut, is the crew boss for the contractor. Her name is Lay Hun Chen, and this is Mohamad Azmi, a representative of the National Parks. These people on the lower left are immigrants as well. They are domestic workers—and they are the lucky ones because they do

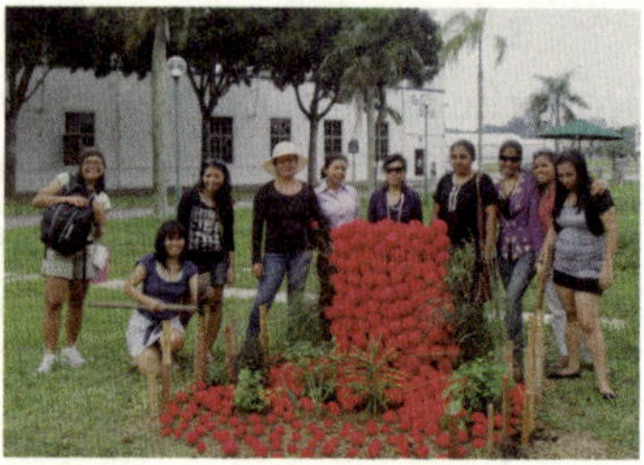

get a day off a week, unlike most migrant domestic workers. To keep males and females from "fraternizing," they are brought together from separate

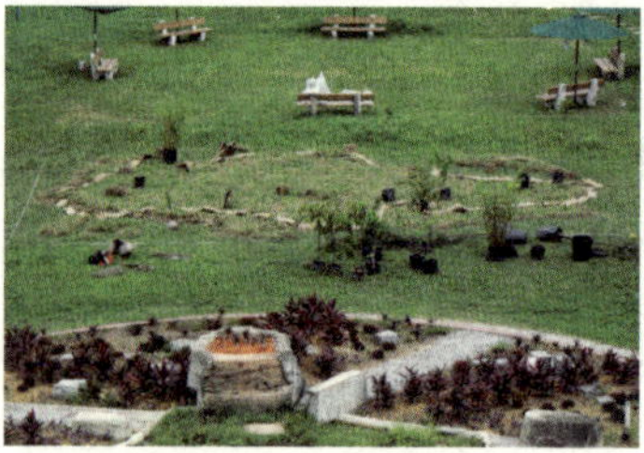

countries and language groups: the men from Pakistan and Bangladesh, the women from Malaysia and Indonesia—but surprise! This barrier turns out to be ineffective: they are mostly teenagers! Here's the head of the Nature Society, who worked with this student group and their professor, the artist Lucy Davis, on The Migrant Ecologies Project. The project is about native plants eradicated as nuisances but whose seeds blow in and grow back. The group also outlined a map of Singapore and brought in trees matching names of neighborhoods where those trees are no longer present like Oak Tree Road, and so on. The group arranged for children's groups to keep the trees watered during the biennale and for the trees to find a home at the show's end.

In front of the Singapore map is a purple medicine garden, also made up of local plants—or weeds. We planted jasmine for the Jasmine Revolution.

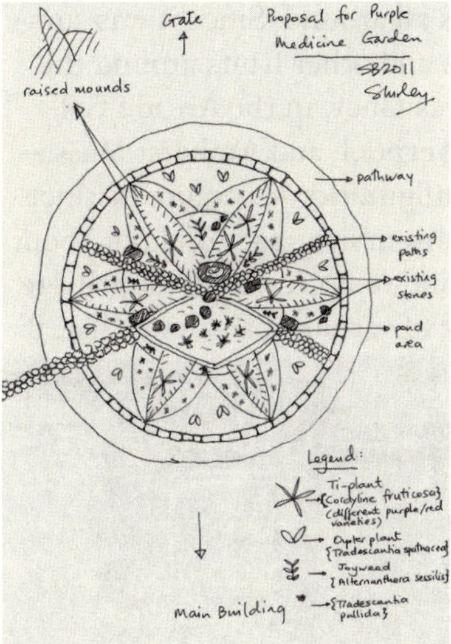

Finally, there were a lot of participants—and here are their names.

The project, *The Martha Rosler Library*, is very different—it's non-communal, yet with communal intent. It was a traveling reading room that grew out of a conversation I had with Anton Vidokle at e-flux about the accessibility of artists' libraries. We decided, on the spur of the moment, to bring most of my books to the e-flux office on New York's Lower East Side. Much to our surprise, a number of other places—mostly in Europe—asked to have the library come visit them. You couldn't borrow the books, but there was a photocopy machine at each site. There were also associated activities, set up by the curator and the groups that they assembled. Here's an announcement for a reading group in Antwerp. In Berlin, the shelves lined a room at an old supermarket office building on United Nations Plaza in

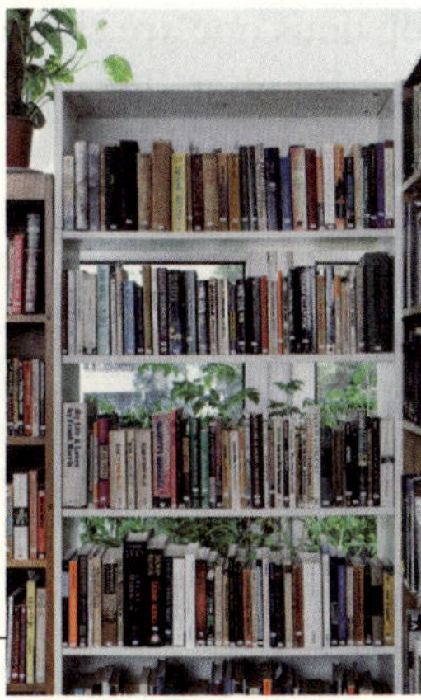

the East, with windows all around. Since it was summer, we grew tomatoes and other fruits around the edge. Paris of course was fancy, in the Arcade Colbert. In Edinburgh, Liverpool, and Amherst Massachusetts, also, each configuration was quite distinct.

The library was a discursive space and not about visuality, but about a kind of accretion of knowledge and a melding together of various discourses that, if you chose to see it as having any symbolic dimension, addressed the question of what it takes to be a present-day artist.

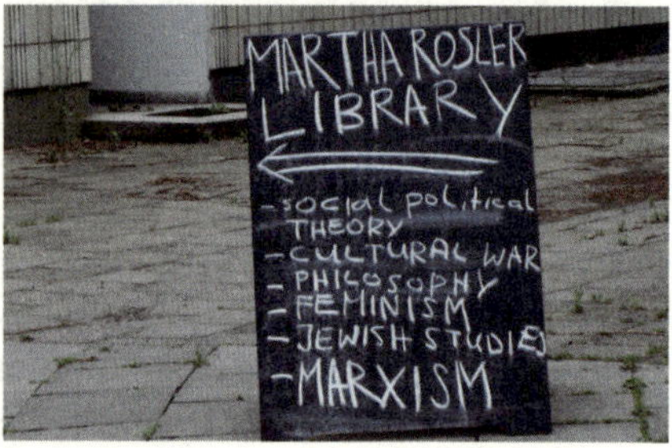

For a very different kind of public project, let's look at the Skulptur Projekte Münster (2007). It is made up of transposed architectural elements at the heart of Münster's historical narratives. The most obvious one are these Anabaptist cages hanging on the Lambertikirche, proudly pointed out during any tour. What the Anabaptists did must have seemed frightful—they came and they said, "Ha, Ha, it's our town now," and they created a kind of free love paradise and so on. It was a Catholic town, and still is, and after a couple of years the Bishop said, "Get those guys, and we're

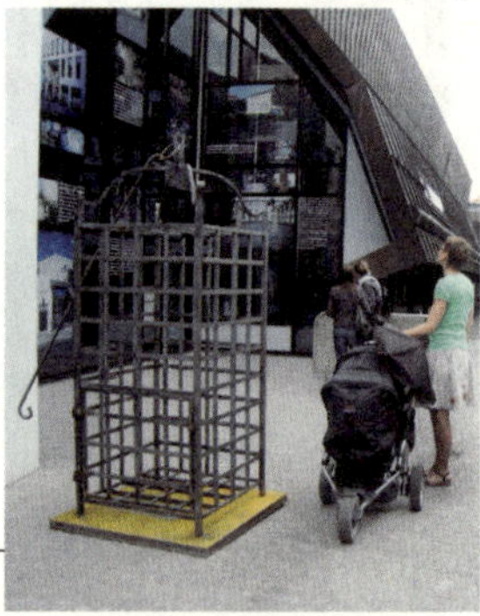

gonna make an example of them." So they paraded them around, tortured them on the public square, executed them, and hung their remains in iron cages from the church steeple. The critically important Treaty of Westphalia was agreed to in Münster, with many of the most important European leaders in attendance. We built copies of the cages and placed them in front of this wonderful postwar public library.

I had a meeting with the man who runs Münster's Botanic Garden, which today is part of the University, and behind the garden today is the "real" garden effort, which is the GM (genetic modification) scientific facility, an important center of that industry. But the man running the Botanic Garden is an old German hippie who complained that he isn't allowed in the scientific facility, "Because they know I'm gonna make something out of it." The Botanic

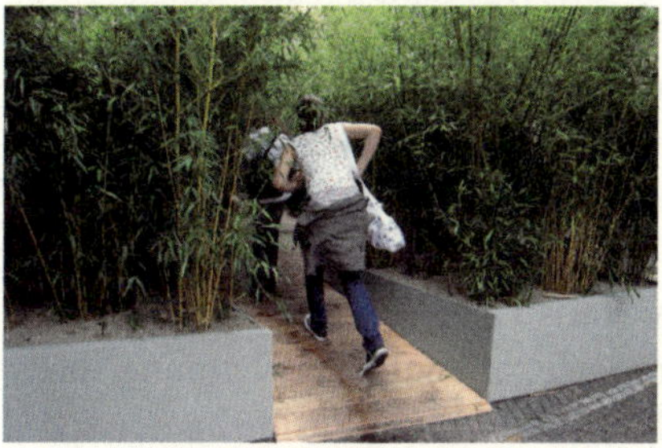

Garden had a long history, especially during the Second World War. It includes a bamboo tunnel that enchanted me but the director laughed and said, "We built that for the kids." But I had it copied on the plaza in front of the Lambertikirche. The bamboo had to be grown for months beforehand.

The third element of my project resulted from a visit to the Luftgaukommando building. It's a beautifully designed building—designed by Ernst Sagebiel, Albert Speer's second in command—lovingly restored, and still in use.

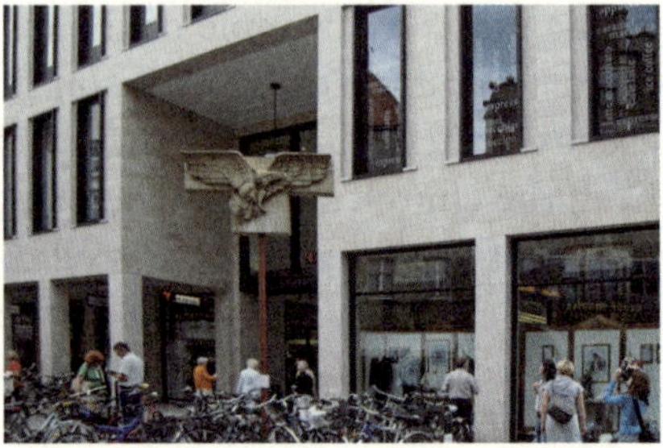

Today the building houses the Transportkommando, and NATO meetings are held there. But there is still the distinctive Luftwaffe eagle, with the swastika or Hakenkreuz knocked off, chiseled away. You can see that there is something not quite right about the eagle; it's out of balance, because it's still the same eagle but with an empty space below its claws. I had it copied and erected in front of the new shopping center on the main street, a street that is "fake old," which was rebuilt after the war's destruction.

After the Skulptur Projekte Münster, held only once every ten years, the town usually buys one or two pieces. I remember chuckling to myself about this, because of course they wouldn't be interested in buying my work—I knew there had been a public fuss about a wonderful work by Hans Haacke some years before. But after about six months of controversy among the city councillors with an article about it in the newspaper practically every other day, they bought the eagle, and it is still there, in front of the shopping center, which I think says something really good about the town in respect to recognizing its past.

As part of the project, we also posted explanations on the windows of the library, and the curators included the elements I didn't get to carry out. I'll quickly tell you about one of them. Münster once had a very large, proud, ornate synagogue. In the city's historical museum, they have a very large photograph of it, but the Sturmabteilung—the SA, the Brownshirts—burned it down during Kristallnacht. And in this photo, they are laughing in front of the burned and ransacked building.

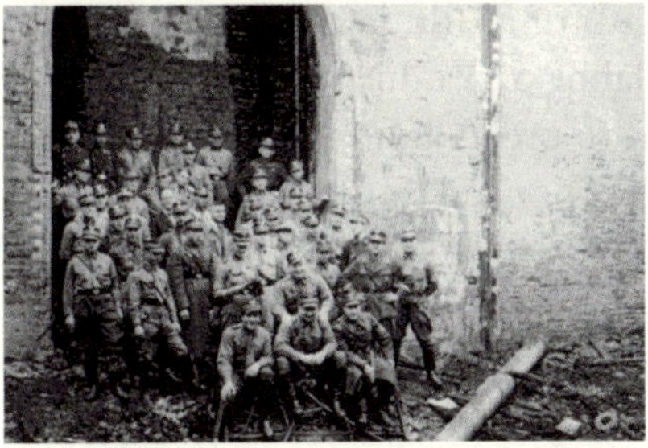

After the war, the city built a very small replacement at the site of the synagogue—a new building that looks exactly like a church because it was planned by a church architect.

They put this menorah on the front of the building. Well I said, why don't we just take the menorah and stick it on a pole in the Aasee, the man-made lake that was doubled in size by the Nazis. The curators looked at me perplexedly and said, "no." And gave me all kinds of funny reasons why. So we didn't do that. They didn't say why this would be a problem, but I leave it to you to decide what that might be.

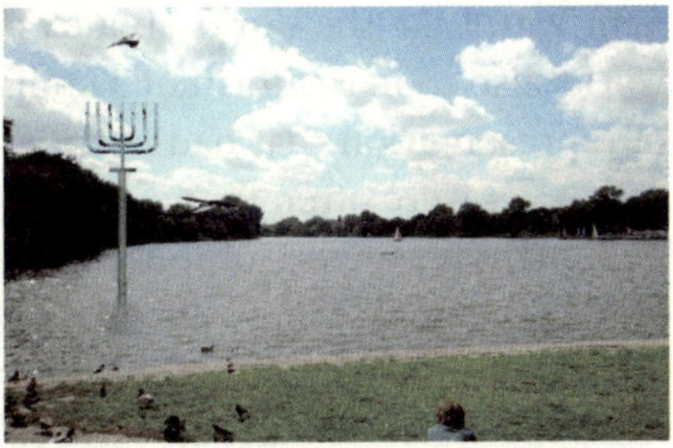

[Shows images of early photomontages.]

Now I am going to step back, to the mid-sixties through to about the early seventies. While I was still an abstract painter, I started making some photomontages—about thirty, over the next decade or so. They were intended as a critique of representations of women. This one, Cargo Cult, is a work about invisible labor. The labor of producing the face that women are supposed to create but whose process of production we aren't supposed to focus on—but also

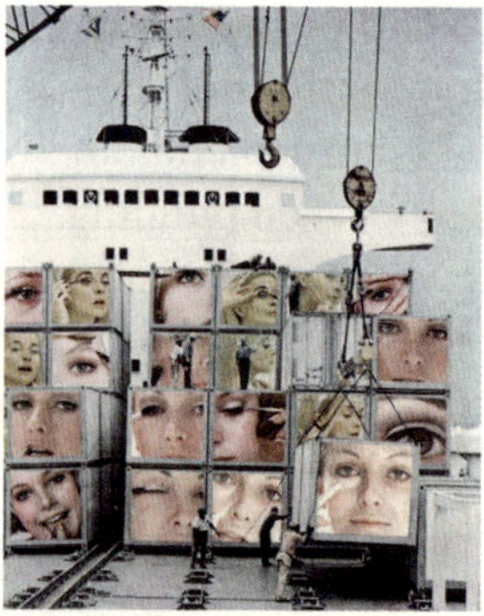

the labor of the men on the docks. This photomontage, Hothouse, or Harem is after Jean-Auguste-Dominique Ingres' painting The Turkish Bath. But while I was producing these works, it occurred to me to use the same technique to make work to combat the Vietnam War. Like the works about women, the antiwar works also took the form of a collision of two genres of representation that had nothing to do with each other, yet were often found in the same magazine—documentary images of war and advertising images of ideal homes.

[Continues showing the wide range of works from the series of war/domestic collages.]

This is the way they were disseminated, as black-and-white xeroxed flyers, and sometimes also published in so-called underground papers.

This is one of the very few images that display any blood—I don't want to engage the viewer by

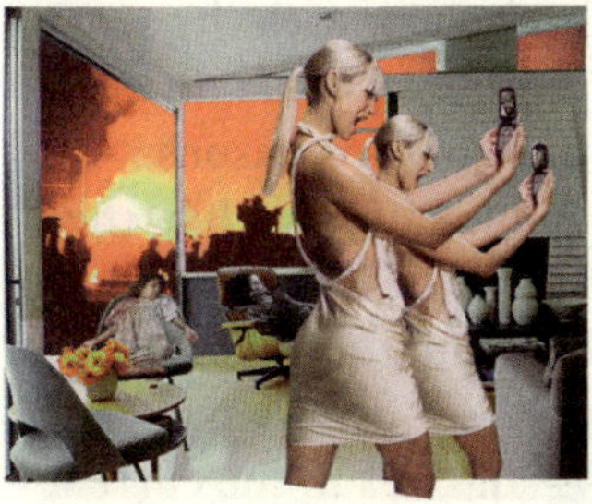

hitting them over the head with the message. Sometimes, as I made plain, I do like to confront viewers, but with information not with images. This one, *First Lady (Pat Nixon),* shows Faye Dunaway being machine gunned in the movie *Bonnie and Clyde* (1968)—a movie that was very important to that generation, because it projected a rebellious ethos and an implacable government.

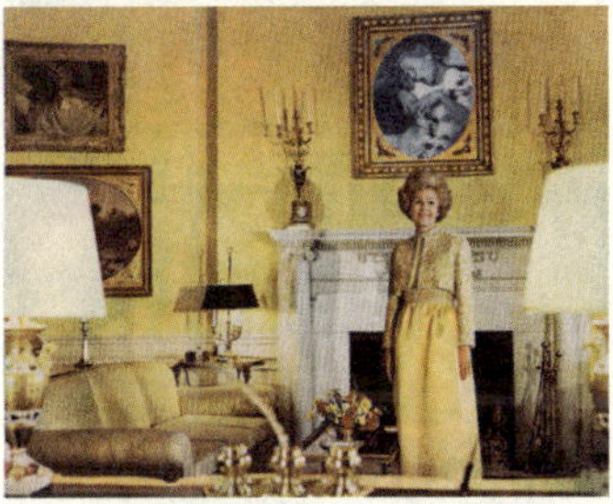

Almost three decades later, I was invited to participate in a show called *Election,* presumably in the interest of electing Obama. I was working with a group that I helped found, called Artists Against the War, doing collective projects of various kinds against the war. I wanted to take this opportunity to do something in my own right, as I felt that the other people in the group were more dedicated to the group work than I could be. I got the idea to do the dumbest thing an artist can do—go back and repeat something from thirty years before. By this time, the Vietnam-era works had become artworks known in the art world.

So, I decided to use the same approach and if questioned, as I was sure I would be—and I was—I could point out that we as a nation were doing the same thing now as we did back then, with the same ineffective results, attacking a country that never did anything to us, and doing it for murky reasons.

This is George Bush and his brother Jeb, the governor of Florida, and this is a soldier with a prosthetic leg—traumatic limb amputation is one of the most common troop injuries in the current war. The other montage I made for the show features Lynndie England, who was notorious from the Abu Ghraib prison images of torture and abuse at the hands of our soldiers, which were made in secret but leaked to the press. The cooking magazines in the image also contain Abu Ghraib images.

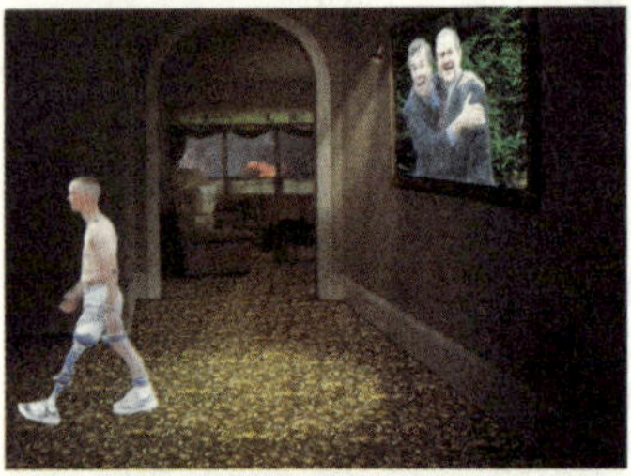

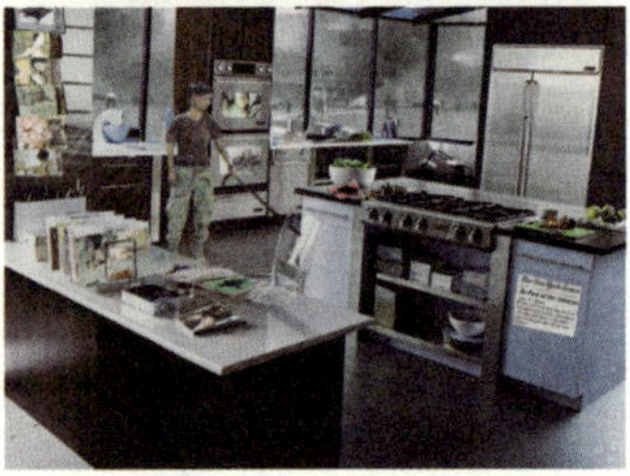

I went on to make about a dozen more. This one depicts the bombing of Baghdad in the background. The work, titled *Red & White Shades,* has an image of the My Lai massacre laying on the couch.

And then in 2008, I was asked if would I like to do the cover of a magazine called *Modern Painters.* So I made *Gray Drape* and then I just kept going. But these are all taking place out of doors in the battlefield. This is a Jimmy Choo bag, and that explosion is in both parts of this diptych. The backgrounds are taken from very tiny newspaper images, and you can

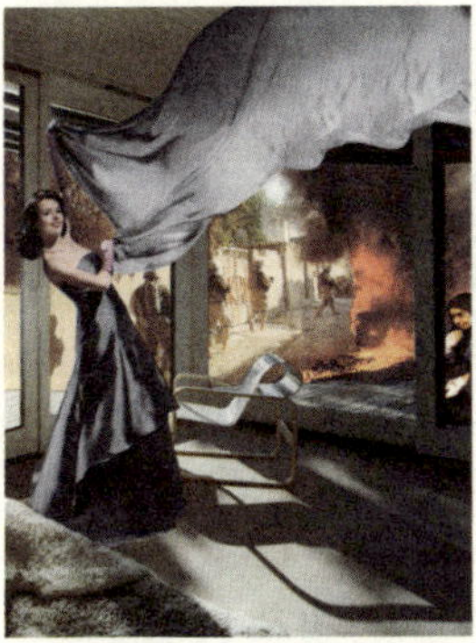

see the text behind, which is the way I've always worked.

A very different form of engagement, quite unrelated to photography or cutting and pasting images, was a project from 1989 about housing and homelessness, which recently resulted in a traveling archive project. The original project took place at the Dia Art Foundation in New York. This was neoliberalism's first beginning, and people were losing their homes, falling into homelessness in cities everywhere. Although I'd always regarded work about housing to be boring, I felt as though events forced the subject upon me. I became deeply interested in matters of gentrification and planning and also in how artists and other art world institutions are implicated. The project at Dia consisted of three shows under the rubric, *If You Lived Here,* from a real estate slogan that goes, "If you lived here, you'd be home now." This photo by Michael Belenky shows shows a

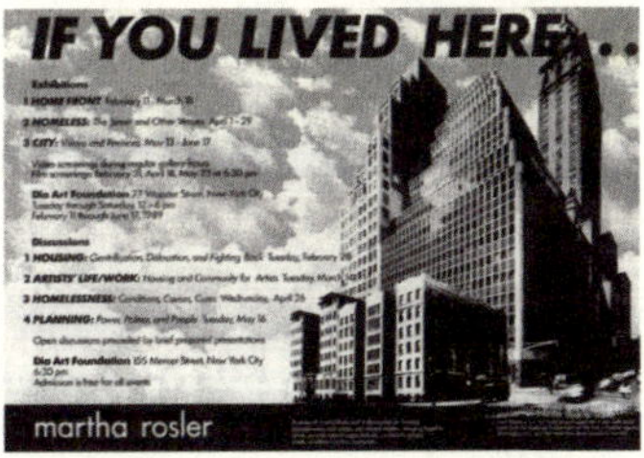

huge encampment—a shantytown—at the bottom of the Manhattan Bridge, right as you drove onto Canal Street in Manhattan. Every tarpaulin that you see is the roof of somebody's dwelling.

There were four public forums associated with the exhibitions, a film program, and about thirty videos playing during the shows. We had statistics on housing and urban issues on the wall, as well as advertisements for luxury high rises—

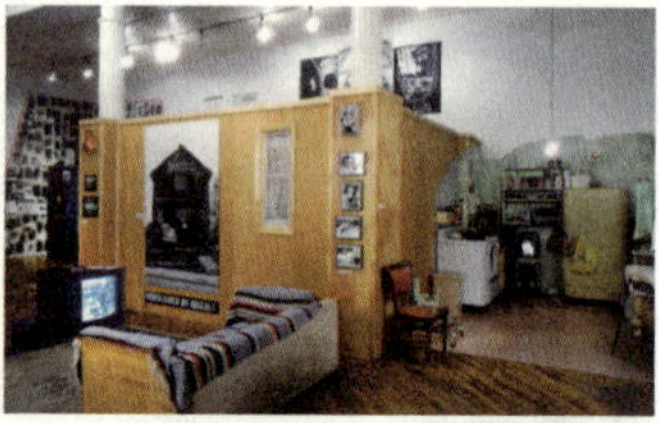

something one simply didn't do in an art gallery in 1989. We built a reading room, something else that just wasn't done. For this project, I worked with two groups of people. A group of homeless people, calling themselves Homeward Bound Community

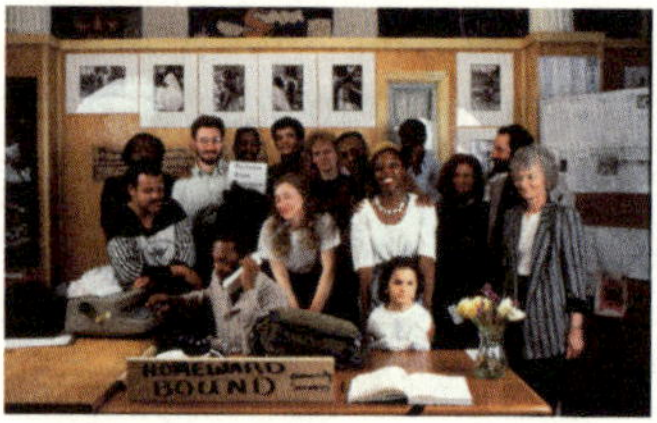

Services, who had held a hundred-day vigil in New York's City Hall Park, and while there, they registered people to vote. I started meeting with them during the preceding summer and invited them to participate in the project. They wanted to have an office in the gallery during the show and to hold workshops and seminars.

The other group I worked with was The Mad Housers—an Atlanta-based group of architects and designers who had either worked in Samuel Mockbee's Rural Studio, or knew of it from Auburn University, in Georgia. [Shows their website.] When I asked if they would take part in the show, they said, "Of course not." "Oh really? Why not?" "Well, we're based in Atlanta—we don't know anyone in

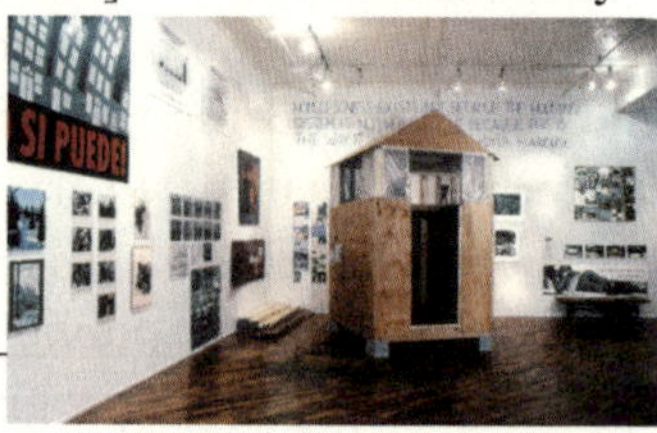

New York." I invited them to come up and stay in an apartment attached to the Earth Room at Dia for a couple of weeks. They made contacts in the community, and during the show itself, built three huts: one in the gallery; one in the East Village, in Manhattan; and the third in what is now DUMBO, where I was living at the time. Homeward Bound participated in the panel discussions, and the Mad Housers went back to Atlanta—but one of their huts remained in use for several years.

The third show covered broad questions of architecture and urban planning, including a number of proposals for housing homeless mothers and children. This Casita project represented the little vernacular buildings built by the immigrant Latino communities, mostly Puerto Rican and Dominican,

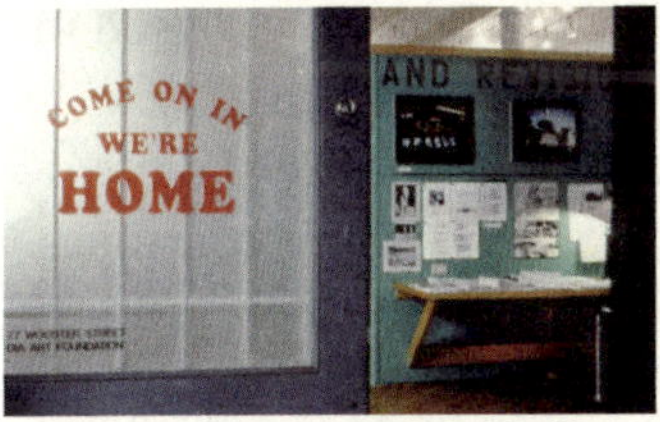

on empty lots in New York. The City was going to tear them down, leading a group of folklorists, anthropologists, and photographers to turn it into an object of study. The idea was that, as a result, the city wouldn't dare to demolish them. And that is exactly what happened. Many remain today.

This is from a series of bus posters about the causes and conditions of homelessness among women by Rhonda Wilson, a Scottish artist. Rather than using documentary, she staged the scenes. Two different observers of the housing scene, Kenneth Jackson and Camilo Jose Vergara made another project. Inside the reading room was a project by the Border

Arts Workshop, the Taller de Artes Fronterizos, on long-term undocumented workers in San Diego. The books in this show were on the outside of the structure. On the gallery wall, which did not make Dia happy, was a listing of their real estate holdings, which remain considerable.

This was an animation that was up in Times Square, New York, in 1989. The Public Art Fund invited artists to design a one-minute animation to play between advertisements on the square's giant

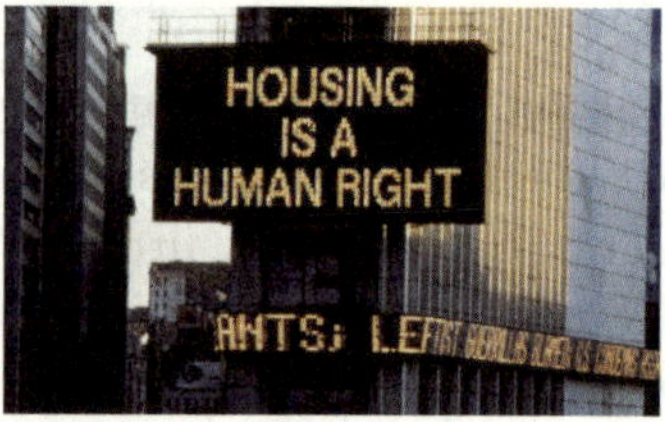

electronic signboard. Coincidentally, they invited me to participate during the same period as the *If You Lived Here* project at Dia.

Recently, the archives of the Dia show toured in New York, Utrecht, and Barcelona, under the title *If You Lived Here Still.* I added color Xeroxes I'd previously made from slides of the show. There continues to be more homeless people than ever before, and you cannot display an archive from 1989 without addressing the contemporary problem. So when the show went to CASCO in Utrecht, we held a forum of local participants. When the archive show went to Barcelona, an activist city in terms of housing, we held a two-day symposium of presentations about activist engagement there, as well as having a whole room in the show devoted to local projects, some going back quite a few years.

In 2006, I had a show in Rennes, at the university gallery, and the students produced a project on local housing, especially focusing on the problems regarding rentals. For the traveling show, therefore, we included French posters, flyers, and brochures, as well as material from Utrecht and Barcelona, increasing the archive.

And as I've been talking long enough, I won't show you my airport photos, except one. This is part of the airport project called *In the Place of the Public* [points at an array of photographic images]. This photo, like *Cargo Cult,* which I described so long ago today, displays invisible labor—the invisible labor that the middle class are so much a part of, the immaterial cognitive labor by which we are all working for Microsoft and every other digitally dominant

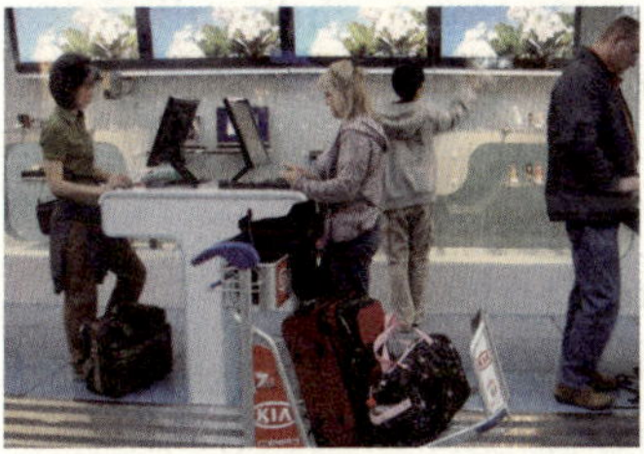

company in the world, through every keystroke we make. And behind these people typing away, there is the airport worker cleaning the screens.

Question

I think it is quite interesting that you have revisited your work in this way …

MR That's what happens when time passes: someone says, "We want to show the archive."

Question

Do you think the role of the artist, vis-à-vis politics, changed in the meantime? How would you describe that?

MR That's part of what I was writing about in my e-flux articles on what I called the Culture Class and on the influence of the art market on art. The question of what is a social project, and should we care, should we do them, and what happens when they become institutionalized and then no longer take place "outside" and in implicit critique of the institutionalization of artists' works. So I don't know what to think about this. I do note that years ago in the seventies, when I was doing what came to be known as "political art," I knew that once it's labeled like any practice, any line of work, it would find its way inside the institution and be crippled, and that is just what happened in the early eighties. The paper that I mentioned that I could have delivered instead of this sort of impromptu slide-talk was about the questions surrounding the institutionalization of social projects. It is called, *The Artistic Mode of Revolution: from Gentrification to Occupation*, and it's about artists and the Occupy movement. It has to do with two things. One is the movement toward the culturalization of all politics, which Fredric Jameson was already calling attention to twenty-five years ago. And the fact that lifestyle marketing is the dominant mode of marketing—and the realm of "lifestyle" today is heavily identified with hipsterism. Hipsters, of course, are often artists when they are at home. Yes, to be serious, the question of the hipster is a difficult one. But artists have been central to the Occupy movement. I don't know if that's true out there under the Euro sign, but it's certainly been true in Zuccotti Park, in New

York. In fact, all my assistants went off to various Occupy movements, in several cities. Which has a certain irony, but it's kind of great. And not because they are going to gain anything from it as individuals, except what one of my assistants is always telling me, which is that's what art is really about—thank God I can put that observation into the mouth of a twenty-eight-year-old. Art has the capacity through the operation of the imagination to bring about a revolution of everyday life and everything else. That it's artists who are able to think through social issues, and to always move the discussion somewhere else … Well, yes and no. There are a number of problems here, because artists are frequently talking to other artists about the question of anarchism, and how much are today's artists necessarily, intrinsically anarchists, and how much so because of the collapse of … well, I'll put it another way—because politics has disappeared as a recognizable category. What used to be called "political art" is now more likely to be classed as "social projects" because we recognize the social as being the culturalization of everyday life, whereas politics is absent. One of the things that the Occupy movement is moving toward is the development of a global politics, not global neo-liberalism, but there needs to be caution in getting there because every pre-existing organized movement will also try to capture the Occupy movement. I am in favor of the participation of organized labor as long as they're not wanting to take it over … Did I answer your question?

Question

Regarding the statements on the wall in the 1989 exhibition, I understand this to mean: "Take out the stones and throw them at the cops." What did it mean for you when you put it on the wall?

MR That's a little crude I think. The slogan was "Under the cobblestones, the beach."

Question

So what did you mean?

MR Well, it's about the liberation of the imagination. No cops in that thought. It's a Situationist slogan. The thing about the Situationists is that the Occupy movement in many ways is actually reinstituting that whole question of the role of the imagination and thinking through the social. So, of course in the student uprising of May '68 people picked up cobblestones and threw them at cops, but the slogan is something entirely different. You know one of the things the Situationists did was to remind the Surrealists that there is an actual world out there and they ought to think about it. But I'll just step back, and be an advocate for the Surrealist position, that modern society was a death machine, in which the imagination was put into a box and made to work for capitalism and war. And that the unconscious is the beach, so it isn't about throwing stones at cops so much as it's about freeing yourself. Someone was inauspiciously asking me the other day, "Haven't we seen Occupy before, like the be-ins?" And I said no, because although the be-ins also were about representing, showing up, and there were no demands involved, they were a manifestation of a kind of hippie refusal, as opposed to the engagement that people in Occupy have been looking for.

I always want to remind people that the art world loves the Situationists who said, "Leave the art world," and they don't want to think about the Scandinavian Situationists who said that we should stay in the art world. So the artists in the art world are loving the ones who said, "Leave."

Question

Did you ever have the idea to move over into politics?

MR No. God, don't you hate politics? What is interesting about being a politician? You turn into a worm.

Question

Maybe you could change something, maybe.

MR Sure. But first of all, one of the problems that artists have is their irony. Irony does not translate well in the wider world. Particularly in the U.S., which is an irony-free zone. But, look at the mayor of Oakland, California, Jean Quan, a lifelong activist, who said, "Oh, yeah, we're gonna bust up that encampment." The bust up of the Oakland Occupation was really brutal; the Oakland Police have a history of brutality. I think you know there are structural demands on people when they assume certain roles, a certain logic that plays itself out. And so many people who play the role of enforcer are social liberals. Like the chancellor of UC Davis, Linda Katehi, who said, for sure she sees herself as a liberal, for sure. Jean Quan sees herself as a liberal or even an activist. But they are the ones looking in the mirror saying, "I can't do anything wrong. I could never do anything wrong." How else can you explain this? It is really weird to realize how close the movement of the present moment is to the Berkeley Free Speech Movement of 1964, when I was an undergraduate student in Brooklyn. When you read Mario Savio's speech—it's available online—his critique centers on the new knowledge industry rather than on the antiwar efforts. The president of the university at the time was a liberal who was even blacklisted by the FBI. Somehow I'm dragged back to my student days by the return of the visibility of the cracks in empire.

I keep expecting to wake up and discover the Euro has completely collapsed, for example, and then there is all the rest of the world economy outside the eurozone. But the people who are in the position to do anything about the financial crisis are hobbled by considerations that have nothing to do with actually solving it. So who are the people who step forward and have radical ideas? They are Fascists, or right-wing populists. Bifo, Franco Berardi, has just written something in German, saying, "Look out folks." All the countries that have now had their governments replaced by technocrats are post-fascist countries, Spain hasn't gotten there yet, but Italy has had its government replaced, and Greece. They have had their governments replaced by technocrat bankers. Aren't you sorry you asked me that? It gives me the opportunity to rant about what I've been writing about.

But if you want to be politicians ... France used to think that if they elected poets, everything would be hunky dory, but ultimately that trajectory led to Sarkozy.

Question
Well, what about Joseph Beuys?

MR Was he a politician?

Question
He was one of the founders of the Green Party.

MR Well, look what happened to the Green Party in Germany. Which stood as a challenger to the SPD, and became co-opted.

Question
I have a remark. I think it is problematic if people, so many people are involved in the Occupy movement, but as an artist, you get support by institutions that are sponsored by people who earn their money in business, in the economy that is bringing about this problem.

MR Absolutely, it's a huge problem. And they are usually banks. I also have a problem with that. My assistant, who is one of the occupation strategists in a U.S. city, tells me it's what you do with it that counts, not where it came from. I have a little trouble swallowing that. People used to have trouble with the BMW Guggenheim Lab. It makes me sick—it's part of corporate citizenship. They are buying and selling the personalization of the brand. A person of good character, who loves bikes, and wants a bikeable city. Maybe it's better to take the bank's money; at least you know it's a bank. I'm serious. Because, as I was saying about Singapore, the aim of neo-liberalism was to get every breath you take, to make a little ding - ding - ding in the cash register; every project has to get its own money. Which is why I recoil in horror at Kickstarter even though I understand why people are doing this. It is a way of putting your hand out to your friends, you know. "Support my project."

Question

Sorry, what is Kickstarter?

MR It's an online crowd-funding website, you put up a little notice on the site Kickstarter about a project you'd like to do. And you ask for five dollars, just like Obama did. I understand why people are doing it. It's what the Internet represents, this kind of imaginary community.

Question

But it started out simply as a way to support independent projects, rather than asking a few rich people for lots of money, one asks a lot of random people for a little.

MR And you can't dismiss this. It just makes me nervous. Neo-liberalism makes me nervous. The idea that you have to be financially responsible for every single step that you take, that you have to pay. It is really obvious in Germany, where the idea of a free Internet … you know—you can see all the politicians fainting at the thought that there might be some public space, where there might be an open Internet that you could just log onto where you are not paying T-Online or someone else. But, I am an opponent of so-called "congestion pricing" for urban traffic as well: when you drive in Singapore a huge display tells you what the cost of each mile is at that time of day. It's the financialization of all of life—a hideous money-crazy mentality that just takes over all of life. And even though, so the artists in New York went off and prematurely decided to occupy the art world, which I consider a tactical error but that's okay. Well you know … it is where artists were.

Actually, the more interesting thing was the Marina Abramovic-Yvonne Rainer issue, when Rainer put out a letter objecting to the bizarre performance Abramovic organized at the gala dinner at the MOCA in L.A. Her objection was about the exploitation of the performers' labor. Who ever talks about the exploitation of labor in the art world? At the same time, while Sotheby's has made record profits, it has locked out its art handlers who demanded a raise.

But during Occupy, the first place some of the artists occupied—prematurely, I think—was Artists Space, a venerable artist-run space nearby in Manhattan, and in the middle of their occupation, someone emailed me in Berlin to check whether the place wasn't founded by artists. But in fact it was founded by the state, through its granting agencies, with money from the Federal Government, and the state agencies decided to set up a space where artists could choose other artists without having to rely on commercial and other institutional gatekeepers.

It was literally a place given to artists by the state, and funded by the state, with a curator to run things for them.

The money came from the government, but now that idea seems passé. It is no longer conceivable that the state can give you something without everybody assuming that it means you are producing government propaganda. Yes, but there is always the possibility of surplus that one could operate in a certain free space. And that has become impossible—except possibly here in Germany, which prides itself on being invested in *Kultur,* and there is a degree of state art funding still. When the money comes from a corporation it is routed through the marketing department, looking for some kind of direct gain, and they get to put their logo on your wall and your show announcement. But the point of state funding is that it is granted indirectly, by means of an apparatus where other people are making the decisions. But in the U.S., the general population is highly suspicious of art.

Question

You spent time in Singapore, and left and returned? But the city is always changing, building, growing. Did you find there is anything old there?

MR The government decided to preserve some old Chinese shop areas because tourists don't like coming to a place that looks like it was all built yesterday.

Question

That is true of Frankfurt as well. In the upkeep of the old.

MR There is no old in Frankfurt, it is all fake, that is, reconstructed. England, upon discovering that it had few natural resources to draw upon, and it had gotten out of industrial manufacturing, began to beef up its department of heritage, to engineer a "Theme Park England." But they are presently trying to sell their creative class, the same as everybody else. Singapore has a biennial, which is how the city places itself among other cities, signaling, "We're here, we're global, we are not some kind of backwater ..." That's why biennials have proliferated, as advertisements for cities and states. But in Singapore the government agency advertising exhibitions didn't put any biennial ads on the buses, and when queried, they explained that it didn't appeal to the people in the heartland, but "We have seven artists who are actually from Singapore in the show." So, they're saying, "It's not that bad, these are really nice people," and so on. But, it is the same trope that's used in talking about art in the Netherlands where the right-wing populists claim that art is a hobby of the left-wing elite, with no meaning or purpose for the general population. In fact, it steals resources. You can't really argue with this.

Again, since the basis of these arguments is in fact economic, it is difficult to get to what is the real problem. On the one hand we have the Occupy movement where artists and others are trying to move things in some more salutary direction, and then on the other, there are the populist movements that are trying to shut everyone down.

... Now I'm boring myself, I'm sorry. Think of something else to talk about if you still want to talk, because you don't want to hear this—you know it all already!

mon, Vortrag

dering Site-Specificity",

on, Mark Godfrey, Nick

mit freundlicher Unterstützung von

gen, Vortrag, 18:00

Curatorial and Critical Studies

14.11. Consu

rtrag

lliver, Fergus Henderson

larding and Douglas Go

E

Ausstellungsda

Veranstaltung

schule

1.11.

3.11. Symposium "

Nikolaus Hirsch, Mar

rs Bang Larsen, Vortrag

10.11. Tristar

Goethe Universitä

Ross Birrell & David Har

11. Douglas Gordon, Tr

17.11. Ross Birrell/

Monica Bonvicini, Vortra

Vorlesungen

Städ

October 14, 2011
Mark von Schlegell

The Great Jack Vance

American writer and critic Mark von Schlegell details the history of Jack Vance, an influential science fiction and fantasy writer from Northern California. From his first novelette "The World-Thinker" *to final novel* Lurulu, *Vance fostered concepts of the expanding present. Quoting archival material including personal letters and literary excerpts, Von Schlegell pieces together Vance's struggles for recognition, connections to his idol P.G. Wodehouse, and comparisons to Philip K. Dick. Von Schlegell also identifies the significant influence of women writers on Vance's work, particularly from C. L. Moore, Ursula K. Le Guin, and his classmate-turned-wife, Norma Vance, who guided, encouraged, and helped Vance produce his best writing.*

"Mrs. Jack Vance"—she is pure and related to divinity ... she is informing, correcting me, speaking words of wisdom ... Behind her have I seen the Godhead, which is the ultimate archetype (the Wise Old Man once more) ... She instructs me with the Logos, the word, wisdom itself...[1]

— The Exegesis of Philip K. Dick

Though he seems to any rational mind to exist without end, John Holbrook "Jack" Vance, like the ever-expanding universe that created him, does have a beginning: it occurs in Northern California in the summer of 1916.

Ninety-three years later, the author of more than sixty genre novels and countless shorter fictions, (the winner of a Hugo, a Nebula, a World Fantasy, and two Edgar Awards), chose to present 2009's surprising non-fiction memoir *This Is Me, Jack Vance! (Or, More Properly, This Is "I")*, not as a science fiction history but as a work of regional California history. The book immediately locates Vance's special feel for weird literature in his early experience of the Northern Californian, post-gold rush boom economy. Abandoned by a deadbeat dad and raised by a spirited single mother (daughter of a newly-rich father), for Vance, the old Sacramento River Delta was a Utopian paradise—worlds away from the violence slaughtering a generation of Europeans raised on Edwardian Romanticism. Gentility was very much a

1 Philip K. Dick, Pamela Jackson and Jonathan Lethem, eds., *The Exegesis of Philip K. Dick*, Boston 2011, p. 204.

role in what was now an almost baroque American West, and although wealth came to his family when he was a baby, it did not outlast his youth. As the title of his autobiography neatly signals, Jack Vance maintained the paradox of Edwardian elitism and Western populism until he died. California's vain sense of the splendor of the rich forever haunts his writings—many of which were composed as far away from postwar USA as it would be possible to get.[2]

Nature was bountiful and relatively gentle; he developed a life-long love of rivers and of the sea and sailing. But it was clear from the first glance that the prize gems were books of a certain kind. The books were like pieces of nature themselves, these new scientific fantasies by likes of L. Frank Baum, Edgar Rice Burroughs, Lord Dunsany, and Jeffery Farnol, which were written for clever boys.[3] His eyes soon suffered—they kept him out of the Second World War.

The literature that transformed Vance from reader to writer emerged from a California maturing around him, whose stories filled the magazine racks, and at this time, were nodes of global, modern popular culture. Vance saw the nascent culture of science fiction and fantasy literature, as tied explicitly to the idea of the expanding present, exploited by jazz.

2 Much of the autobiography describes places the Vances lived as they worked on the escapist books that paid for their travels and freedom, including West of Ireland, Italy, Kashmir, and Tahiti.

3 Jack Vance, *This is Me, Jack Vance! (Or More Properly, This is "I")*, Spatterlight Press, Oakland, California 2009, iBooks, p. 213.

About three miles west of us was the town of Oakley. In the drugstore was a magazine rack, and there I came upon the Amazing Stories *quarterly, edited by Hugo Gernsback, and also the* Amazing Stories *monthly. I subsequently discovered* Weird Tales *and subscribed to it. It was a banner day of the month when I ran down to the mailbox in front of Iron House School to find it there …*[4]

Hugo Gernsback had developed *Amazing* from the popular fictions he'd been placing in the back pages of radio buff and engineering periodicals. Vance was an engineering student, primed to respond to stories celebrating the common sense of the scientific method. Gernsback himself would soon coin the term "science fiction," branding that genre with an identity, which Jack Vance—"Genre-Artist" extraordinaire—would, in a sense, always resist.[5]

If Vance's last novel *Lurulu*, published in 2004, still stands among the finest science fiction of the twenty-first century, it is because of his fantasy that his writing remains actively engaged with the present mainstream—through *Dungeons & Dragons* into gaming and through his fan George R. R. Martin into TV—Vance never was a fan of what became known as science fiction.

He tended to dismiss it rather rudely from his consideration. It is telling that in the autobiography, he gestures immediately from *Amazing Stories* to

4 Vance 2009, p. 17.
5 see Carlo Rotella, "The Genre Artist," *The New York Times*, 15 July 2009.

Weird Tales. Certainly, *Weird Tales* was more of a cross-genre affair than the early *Amazing*. In its golden age in the 1930s, the magazine boasted more extravagant and eccentric writing than any other American periodical. With a mature H. P. Lovecraft directly involved in its creation and flavor, and featuring Margaret Brundage's famous and scandalously fashionable covers, the magazine laced mainstream drugstores with Surrealism (still being invented), sex, and science fiction.[6] *Weird Tales'* most provocative covers served the works of the young and brilliant C. L. Moore. Jack Vance spoke rarely about his favorite writers of science fiction and fantasy, but when he did, he always mentioned her.

Catherine Lucille Moore (1911–1987) was only five years Vance's senior. Moore would end up marrying the science fiction writer Henry Kuttner, and in a fashion yet to be explored by feminist historians, she would essentially disappear into his pseudonyms. She had a brilliant early start in *Weird Tales*, authoring two series that would be of particular influence on writers to come. Moore's feminized *Jirel of Joiry* stories updated works by Robert E. Howard, even as he was authoring the extraordinary Conan stories in the very same issues. Their transformation of male tropes occurred on the page; aesthetic disruption was a matter of form. Moore clearly sources the enlightened feminism of the time, whose POV-shock

6 Vance was hardly an admirer of H.P.L. himself. "Lovecraft couldn't write himself out of a wet paper sack." Jack Vance interviewed by Charles Platt in *Dream Makers, Volume II: The Uncommon Men & Women Who Write Science Fiction*, Berkley Books, New York 1983, p. 163.

customarily disturbs a Jack Vance narrative's ostensibly male focus, distinguishing it immediately from most U.S. science fiction of the golden age. Moore's recurring male hero Northwest Smith, who hitched about various settlements of the solar system under the most dubious circumstances, showed Vance that ordinary pulp stories of revenge, desire, crime, and punishment could be set off-world, against the most fantastic and tantalizing circumstances.

> *Who has been influential upon my development as a writer? Who indeed? I don't know. To name some names, I admire C. L. Moore from the old* Weird Tales *magazine. As a boy, I was quite affected by the prose of Clark Ashton Smith.*[7]

The Poe-like nineteenth century *flâneur* imprinted itself on *Weird Tales* through figures like Clark Ashton Smith. The type can be found in the countless avant-garde impresarios that take after, but do not replace, the villains in Vance's narratives. Drug-addict, poet, surrealist sculptor, and a devoted fan of Baudelaire—Smith imagined bizarrely detailed landscapes on the most extravagant terms. Vance's famous style is always both a quiet celebration and loving satire of the lengths Smith was willing to go.

7 Vance 2009, p. 213.

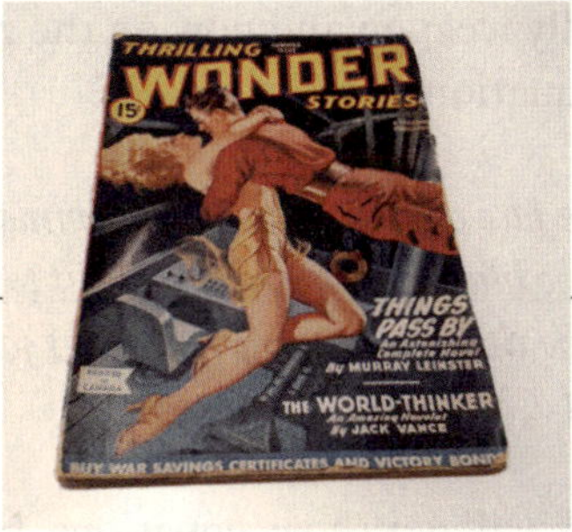

It was noon of a vernal day when I came forth from that interminable cactus-forest in which the Inquisitors of Ong had left me, and saw at my feet the gray beginnings of Yondo. I repeat, it was noon of a vernal day ...[8]

Vance would refine and clarify Smith's excesses, discovering an always-delightful style able to deliver sentences like, "Titus Pompo, I will warn you once and once only. You are talking dangerous nonsense," with the archest possible seriousness.[9] Previously having published jazz reviews, Vance sold his first story, the novelette "The World-Thinker," to Canada's *Thrilling Wonder Stories* in 1945. Written while serving out the end of the Second World War on board a merchant marine vessel, Kenna Parker, the story's enigmatic and elusive heroine, (first arrested

8 Clark Ashton Smith, "Abominations of Yondo," *Overland Monthly*, California 1925, p. 276.

9 Jack Vance, *Araminta Station*, TOR Books, New York 1988, p. 276.

for assault with a deadly weapon and now on the run with a set of deadly equations), still sparkles.

> *It hardly seemed the face of an incorrigible criminal. A reckless glint in the blue-eyes, a whimsical tilt to the eyebrows, a set to the lips—otherwise it was the face of a very pretty girl ...*[10]

The hero Lanarck will get those equations, but not quite the girl—though he goes so far as to occupy her mind. In fact, the hard-to-get attractive and elusive female will occasion all sorts of journeys throughout the Gaean Reach—a Galaxy that explicitly honors a goddess. It isn't until the 1980s when Vance's overseas success would secure financial problems at home that female protagonists and antagonists took the reins of his stories with spectacular results.[11]

Back in 1945, the not-quite villainous "world-thinker," with his black "tremendous dome-like bulk" of a body, specifically resembles the cover image of Moore's first and most famous Jirel story, *Black God's Kiss*, of 1934. His power is a totally-augmented imagination. Its power is both imaginary and real, by definition.

10 Jack Vance, "The World-Thinker," *Thrilling Wonder Stories*, March 1945, p. 36.

11 In crime he tried earlier. Vance wrote the fascinating locked-room mystery, *A Room To Die In* (1965), his second under the Ellery Queen moniker, starring charming young Ann Nelson, a school teacher and heiress who turns detective, then ends up dead. Two more 1980s crime novels, *The View from Chickweed's Window* and *The Dark Ocean*, also featured strong female protagonists.

> *In front of Lanarck's eyes, space quivered and wrenched. A dark aperture appeared in midair. Lanarck, looking through, saw hanging apparently but a yard before his eyes a lambent sphere—a miniature world. As he watched, it expanded ...*[12]

Describing the experience of reading a science fiction story would become the story itself.

Soon enough, the name Jack Vance would be thought to be another Kuttner pseudonym.[13] In reality, the name soon defined a woman as well as a man. Former classmate Norma Genevieve Ingold (1927–2008) would later take on the name Vance after their marriage in 1947, beginning a lifelong partnership.

> *Norma was strongly supportive of my writing from the start, and we began to work together as a team. I cannot emphasize enough how hard Norma worked over the course of my career, certainly as hard as I have, if not more.*[14]

We know she was responsible for the manuscripts moving from pen to typewriter and from proofs to print. Was Norma one reason for the numerous fascinating females who flirt their way through the many worlds of Jack Vance? Certainly, the experimental offstage sex scenes of later science fiction like *Araminta Station* (1987) seem peculiarly

12 Vance, "The World-Thinker," p. 40.

13 John Clute and Peter Nichols, eds., *The Encyclopedia of Science Fiction*, St Martin's Griffin, New York 1995, p. 1266

14 Vance 2009, pp. 94-95.

flirtatious when we imagine Norma fixing them up in her typewriter.

As the case of C. L. Moore demonstrates, Norma Vance was not alone in a genre where male names often fronted the work of female writers. The young Vance listed "hot jazz" and "feminine psychology" as central interests alongside Oriental languages and Physical Sciences in his 1945 author's note to "The World-Thinker."[15] U.S. science fiction was a boy's club through most of the sixties, and not particularly friendly to jazz. A longtime, perhaps perpetual place on the lower mid-list of science fiction may be best explained by the fact Vance seems to have received his only unmitigated fan letters from female readers.

> *Dear Mr. Vance,*
>
> *This is a fan letter—an unmitigated fan letter. I have read all your books and stories with the greatest pleasure, and then after a while re-read them with greater pleasure. There are some lovely imaginations at work in S.F. now, but the work itself is so often botched or stretched or compromised; yours never; you are competent, an artist. Write more books, write more books.*
>
> *Yours gratefully,*
>
> *Ursula K. Le Guin 27 April 1967*[16]

15 Vance, "The World-Thinker," back matter.

16 Ursula K. Le Guin, letter to Jack Vance, 27 April 1967, from the Jack Vance Collection, Howard Gotlieb Archival Research Center at Boston University.

Browsing through the Jack Vance Collection at the Howard Gotlieb Archival Research Center in Boston, an assortment selected and sent by Vance himself in the late eighties, Le Guin's letter is indeed the only "unmitigated" fan letter the author seems to have received until that date.[17] With editors constantly bickering and projecting constant negativity, the other fan letters often ask for Vance not to write in a certain way, or to return to old characters. In their context, we see what a glorious exception Le Guin provides. Quite simply a masterpiece of the fan letter genre, it is even written in the semicolonial "Vancian" style, which one takes when determined to speak with a clarity that contains a certain luxury or wantonness. In two well-executed sentences, Le Guin offers a clear critical reading of Vance as the quintessential writer, no more no less. She celebrates the victory of craft and practice over a romantic valorization of authorship, and therefore, no further need for criticism. The fantasy of the artist is Vancian and "competence" is a reverse irony that signals everything else. Repeatedly urging the beloved author to "write, write," honors the abstract pleasure of text-as-text activated by Vance's approach. For like his idol P. G. Wodehouse, Jack Vance would indeed continue to repeat himself in

17 From the Jack Vance Collection, Howard Gotlieb Archival Research Center at Boston University. An undated note is written directly on the broad manila envelope:
Dear the Gotlieb
Herewith a collection of ancient correspondence, rejection slips, etc. a compendium of a thousand little tragedies and small triumphs that made me feel rather sad going through them.
Jack Vance

the same adolescent vein, writing increasingly better books almost without interruption into his nineties.[18]

In the Gotlieb archives, as I've suggested, Le Guin is the only reader to suggest Vance's work is "[never] … botched or stretched or compromised." Whatever the reason, in the fifties, sixties, and seventies, the writer and editor gatekeepers of U.S. science fiction, John W. Campbell and Frederik Pohl (infamous editors and enemies), were forever accepting Vance while pushing him away at the same time. The re-titling, re-editing, and forcing of rewrites was accompanied by steady disagreement in all petty matters. Vance's immediate success in the mystery world, the quiet masterpiece *The Fox Valley Murders* (1966), also came with generic interference and cutting.

It didn't seem to help that Vance secured the services of Scott Meredith, a first-rate agent. "Our slick writers include P.G. Wodehouse, B. Traven," Meredith told him. "And of course we do not ignore our pulp authors in favor of the slick writers. Ten percent of a bunch of eighty dollar checks soon adds up to just as much as ten percent of a several hundred dollar check …"[19] In his first letter, Meredith made out quite how many books Vance would be expected to write. Vance accepted, and though he experimented with genre, he never experimented in "class." Apparently content to survive with the chance of sudden possi-

18 "I revere Wodehouse," Vance 2009, p. 213.

19 Scott Meredith, letter to Jack Vance, 2 June 1950, from the Jack Vance Collection, Howard Gotlieb Archival Research Center at Boston University.

20 Clute and Nichols 1995, p. 1264.

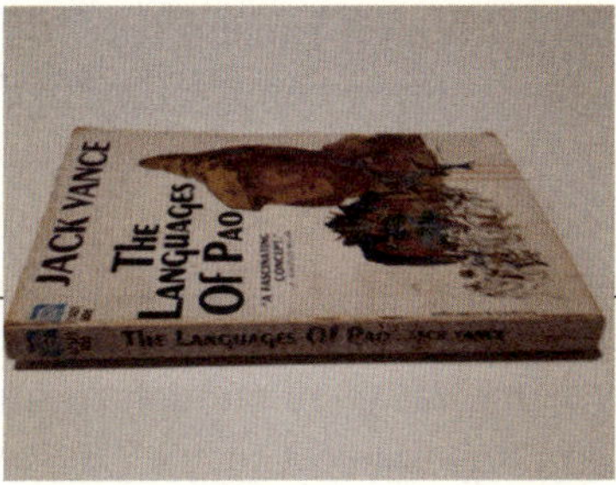

ble windfalls from TV and European success on the horizon, as the quintessential mid-lister, Jack Vance never showed an inclination to reach across the aisle into so-called serious literature.

As late as 1995, Clute and Nichols' influential *Encyclopedia of Science Fiction* scolded Vance for his reliance on "pulp conventions."[20] But throughout his career, the pulps themselves found the author often perplexing and overly literary. Until the 1970s, editors would ask Vance to bring back Magnus Ridolph, the deliciously pulpy anti-hero of his early 1950s C. L. Moore imitations. Vance's most original developments of the science fiction field celebrated today—the fantasy and sci-fi hybrids of "The Dying Earth" genre first written in the 1940s, which he returned to throughout his career; the "Planetary Romance"-style novel, first clearly demonstrated in 1957's *Big Planet;* and its incredible sequel, *Showboat World*, from 1975—were only seen as problematic by his editors.[21]

21 By 1975, Vance was either provoking editorial interference or entirely unconcerned. His *Showboat World* was (and is today) titled: *Magnificent Showboats of the Lower Vissel Rover, Lune XXIII, Big Planet.*

"I am not paranoid, I hope," Vance wrote to Scott Meredith, "no persecution complex or anything like that, but it's almost as if [Campbell] were griped at me personally."[22] Even when the powerful Campbell published Vance in *Astounding Science Fiction*, he expressed long and wordy reservations about the work. Yet, Vance's writing was good enough to survive the hostility. Campbell issued Vance's *The Potters of Firsk*, a tale of art turned to crackpot religion, alongside the first appearance of L. Ron Hubbard's *Dianetics* in the May 1950 *Astounding*. In his 1951 story "The Brains of Earth," Vance did indeed anger Campbell for directly satirizing the young religion of Scientology.[23]

Accepting his situation and suffering the whims of whatever lowbrow organization he worked with in the 1960s, Vance published a number of impressive novels and returned to *The Dying Earth* for the first time with *Cugel the Clever* (1966)—published as *The Eyes of the Overworld*. He also continued to experiment in exquisitely (if sometimes ridiculously) executed mysteries and English crime novels, usually under the name John Holcomb Vance.

In 1964, when Pyramid Books insisted on receiving an original novel with the humiliating title *Space Opera*, Vance responded with characteristic *punctilio*

22 Jack Vance, letter to Scott Meredith, 6 August 1966, from the Jack Vance Collection, Howard Gotlieb Archival Research Center at Boston University.

23 Scott Meredith, letter to Jack Vance, 4 May 1966: "It had been shown to Campbell, but he felt that Dianetics was not fiction, and shouldn't be used in fiction." From the Jack Vance Collection, Howard Gotlieb Archival Research Center at Boston University.

by actually addressing the future of high opera in galactic space. An homage to Wodehouse, the novel's backstory erupts into a Vancian assault on high art. When our young space-dreaming hero's society scion Aunt Isabel hears report of the supposedly exhilarating "9th Company" perhaps the only alien music group in the galaxy, she decides to affirm Earth is first, by financing the best high opera company she can put together, and bringing it on a tour of alien worlds (taking her nephew along in the process). But none of Dame Isabel's fabulous Phoebus Company productions, from Wagner to Verdi, makes the slightest impression on any of the perplexed alien races she encounters; in fact, each show on the tour bombs more dangerously than the last. Meanwhile, everywhere they play, the kitchen staff's illegal jug-band is a runaway success.

Faced by the fact of the failure of eighteenth and nineteenth century opera to impress any alien mind, Dame Isabel is a good enough businesswoman as to abandon the tour and return everyone to Earth. But not before taking the whole Phoebus Company to see an actual performance of the alien 9th Company, whose competency and power she has always doubted. Vance's conception of the alien art form surprises the reader, just as much as Dame Isabel, by its democratic splendor. But the art he describes begins as quite simply his own:

> *Dame Isabel swung about, and found the sky to be dancing with colored shapes. They mingled and separated, merged inward and outward and settled to the meadow which became a place of luminous*

magic, and the whole Phoebus Company came forth in awe to watch the magnificences now displayed to them. Cities like flower gardens appeared one after the other, as if in compendium: each different, each a development of the last, each with its own delights and prideful vistas, each receding and growing remote. A miscellany of new images appeared in the foreground: regattas of boats with enormous patterned sails, each of which might have been alive and sentient: a jeweled moth. Exalted figures marched in a stately pavane; there were tourneys of love and beauty, gusts and whispers of many musics. Now came a series of pageants, performances by troupes like the 9th Company, and Dame Isabel thought to recognize the 9th company itself. Suddenly there was silence, so intense as to be an ecstatic sensation in itself. Down from the sky floated a battered spaceship …

At this point, ghostly symbols and characters suggested only their own inadequacy clearly. There followed other spectacles and vistas, and these seemed far away and long past, like memories half-forgotten. A parade of dead heroes came by, turning to search the faces of those who watched, as if asking for knowledge which had been denied them. All seemed to ask the same question and then they were gone from view. Cities were built and listlessly abandoned: all goals had been achieved, all excellences attained. Nothing remained but idleness, casual amusement …[24]

24 Jack Vance, *Space Opera*, Gallancz, London 1965.

Previewing *Lyonesse*, prophesying a move toward what only the twenty-first century will begin to understand as the pointless wealth of science fiction in *The Dying Earth*, there comes the alien climactic *pièce de résistance*:

> *Finally in gigantic enlargement appeared the Tough Luck Jug Band, with its music of boldness and assertion, enthusiasm conquering surfeit. For a brief space the world was renewed and wonderful things seemed possible. Then the meadow was as before, the sky was blank; The Phoebus company stood alone beside the ship.*[25]

The last Beckettian image rather vehemently asserts the scope and limits of the minimalist writing-as-writing aesthetics of the Jack Vance space opera.

Back on Earth, his books were being read by a generation believing itself ready to transform the world. For Vance, the question was scriptory. In the sixties, despite the state of the market, despite immediate success in crime, Jack Vance preferred to write science fiction, to do exactly no more and no less than what he outlined in *Space Opera*. It is telling that he reveals his sixties' work as an *alien* performance, for the pearls on every page one finds in Vance, are the results of the fisher/miner of languages and narrative forms, no more and no less. Vance's worldview is the rational worldview of total empiricism, like David Hume; custom and superstition explain all that

25 Ibid.

can be explained, and self-interest is the law of the human land: even out beyond the Gaean Reach itself.

But within the confines of the musical moment—between the covers of the book—everything again is possible, or seems that way. Indeed, on the silence left at the end of a Jack Vance performance, writers like Ursula K. Le Guin, George R. R. Martin, Gene Wolfe, and J.G. Ballard would help transform the possibilities of high literature from below. As if in inverse proportion to Vance's self-removal, not only from high literary culture, but from science fiction as well, perhaps more ornery than any other writer of the paperback revolution—a misguided sort of claim, no doubt, but supportable—Vance's removal was breeding activist male fans. His would-be disciple Frank Herbert was so stung by Jack's disdain for his desert planet idea that he turned his full attention to the project that would be called *Dune* to prove him wrong.[26]

Vancians are the sorts of fans who will go so far as to remake the world so it contains the idol's image. The Vance fan, confronted by a literary establishment that erases its hero, creates its own literary magazines to discuss Vance with other fans. Through Cugel fan Gary Gygax, Vance's influence would transform the shape of gaming into the twenty-first century.

26 Jack Vance, interview, 2010. http://www.starshipsofa.com/blog/2010/06/08/aural-delights-no-140-kim-stanley-robinson-plus-jack-vance-interview-2/

> *Need I say that I am not merely a Jack Vance fan, but that he is, in my opinion, the very best of all the authors of imaginative fiction? Well, I am and he is!*[27]

In Gygax's 2001 essay "Jack Vance and the D&D Game," the author seems almost at pains to stress there were parts of the game not under Vance's direct influence.

> *Just what portions of these works, the subsequent AD&D game, stemmed from inspiration related to the writing of Jack Vance? Several elements, the unquestioned foremost being the magic system used in these games. To my way of thinking, the concept of a spell itself being magical, that it's written form carried energy, seemed a perfect way to balance the mage against other types of characters in the game. The memorization of the spell required time and concentration so as to impart not merely the written content but also its magical energies. When subsequently cast—by speaking or some other means—the words or gestures, or whatever triggered the magical force of the spell, leaving a blank place in the brain where the previously memorized spell had been held. Because I explained this often, attributing its inspiration to Jack Vance, the D&D magic system of memorized then forgotten spells was dubbed by gamers "the Vancian magic system … Of the other portions of the A/D&D game stemming from the writing of Jack Vance, the next most important one is the thief-class character.*[28]

27 Gary Gygax, "Jack Vance & The D&D Game." http://www.dyingearth.com/files/GARY%20GYGAX%20JACK%20VANCE.pdf

28 Ibid.

D&D's risky acceptance of evil in its character generation (the "alignment" system that inspired the seventies and eighties urban legends and extravagant fantasies about devil worshipping players) are also easily traceable to that "realm of cynical wonders" in *The Dying Earth* (1950).[29]

But calling attention to the relation of magic to writing in Vance, Gygax can help us see behind the mask Vance so consistently dons—of the unimpressed craftsperson, unconcerned with high art and its pretensions, to see that his life's work does stand as an affirmation of writing as magic. In some ways, the work brought itself to more and more to life, peculiarly and easily dovetailing with the cultural scene determined by the Internet, despite Vance's general disinterest in technology. In the nineties, fans used the net on the global scale to establish a complete, hard-backed, forty-five volume, archival edition of the Whole Vance, reproofed and edited according to authorial intention.

With original intensity and vision, the Vancians had therefore secured the survival of their idol's literary principle beyond the paperback revolution into the still unknown future books must brave.

The Vance Integral Edition project began in 1999. Over 300 volunteers, worldwide, worked via the Internet, for 6 years, to create a definitive and complete edition of Vance's work in 44 volumes. A supplemental 45th volume, with the 3 Ellery Queen novels, was also published. Approximately 600 book sets were printed

29 Rotella 2009.

for V.I.E. subscribers. Several dozen sets were donated to libraries … The V.I.E. project was unprecedented in the history of literature: never have readers paid comparable homage to a writer, and never has a writer received such a treatment over the Internet.[30]

The model of Shakespeare, whose own works were similarly preserved and celebrated by his friends and colleagues, certainly comes to mind. Like Shakespeare, Vance wrote for money. Like Shakespeare, his female characters outshine those of his male contemporaries. Fredric Jameson in his acclaimed *Archaeologies of the Future: The Desire Called Utopia and Other Science Fictions* makes Philip K. Dick his science fiction Shakespeare. With Dick the most literary sci-fi male allowed, criticism by writers in the genre known for novelty, for the most part, have left Vance unmentioned; Samuel Delany, Thomas Disch do without, and Brian Aldiss is explicitly hostile. China Miéville, however, has borrowed a concept. Yet Vance's work, still insistently pulp, still appealing to the general reader of imaginative literature, has not dated like the early work of these younger writers with literary pretension.

Like any craft, writing is mastered by practice and patience, and if one has any "knack" for it at all, that very knack—paradoxically—can explicate everything under the sun but itself.[31]

30 "The Vance Integral Edition." (Webpage description 2014). https://www.integralarchive.org/base3.htm
31 Vance 2009, p. 6.

In *This is Me, Jack Vance!*, Vance admits a "knack," a built-in, unexplainable facility for writing. This is unable to describe itself? Is it really? What reads rhetorically like a confession of weakness can also be read as a bold claim of extraordinary powers, that can *explicate anything under any sun*. In Vance, this power seems, in fact, to depend upon its refusal to consider itself.

When asked to prepare a general preface for a series of brief introductions for each of the tales in *The Best of Jack Vance*, published in 1976—a rather-late-in-coming edition by Pocket Books, the author gave a text less than a page long, making clear, firstly, that this selection of his "best" work was not his own. The remaining jewel-like notes are fascinating nuggets of critical kryptonite. On "Ullward's Retreat" (1958) we read:

> *To extol one's own work is sheer recklessness; on the other hand, unabashed candor is refreshing and perhaps a virtue; therefore I will venture one or two comments in regards to "Ullward's Retreat."*
>
> *I consider the story well constructed from a technical standpoint, and I feel that in spite of its overt frivolity, the story makes a number of profound statements upon the human condition. There are no villains in this piece, and no heroes; we are confronted only with human captiousness and human vanity.*[32]

32 Jack Vance, in Barry N. Meltzberg, ed., *The Best of Jack Vance*, Pocket Books, New York 1976, p. 29.

The "captiousness" in the case of the preface, is Vance's own (the quietly extravagant word signifying the particular artificially created quality the OED calls, "Apt to catch or take one in; fitted to ensnare or perplex in argument; designed to entrap or entangle by subtlety; fallacious, sophistical"). The reader who goes forward and reads this oddly plain tale of real estate vs. augmented reality, without sex, violence or technological fetishism, will trace out "a history of the future human race" that depends on the shallowest of issues and behaviors, yet the most peculiarly human motives.

"Now what about lunch? Genuine algae!" Ullward's actual retreat is not a military maneuver in any great war, but simply a Californian architecture built up into the future. "A rustic lodge commanded the view, the door being the opening into Ullward's living room."[33] Vance's works into and out of retreat are far more autobiographical and self-descriptive than we like to believe. This story's architecture becomes eerily familiar as it reappears in the many manses of fictions to come. In the opening of the 1966 masterpiece *Cugel the Clever*, Vance explicitly starts off in his own, self-built home in the Oakland Hills.

> *On the heights above the river Xzan, at the site of certain ancient ruins, Ioucounu the Laughing Magician had built a manse to his private taste: an eccentric structure of steep gables, balconies, sky-walks, cupolas,*

33 Jack Vance, "Ullward's Retreat," *The Best of Jack Vance*, Pocket Books, New York 1976, p. 63.

together with three spiral green glass towers through which the red sunlight shone in twisted glints and peculiar colors. [34]

And so quite clearly, every reader of Jack Vance (who wrote in longhand with multi-color pens) recognizes the homemade getaway is not for Rhialto the Marvelous, not for Shimrod or Murgen or the many other players-with-fire—it is the manse of the comical wizard-author himself, with written spells collected and preserved all around, tricks of other mages stolen and jarred, curses still outstanding. As Vance identifies with the Magus, the fan identifies with Cugel, the not so clever everyman Ioucounu torments.

"I felt myself seized by a writer's style in a way I had never experienced before," writes Carlo Rotella of his first experience with Cugel. Rotella, an academic and non-science fiction specialist, would eventually manage to author 2009's rare and significant *New York Times* portrait of a then still-living Jack Vance, "The Genre Artist." [35]

By virtue of their hostility to and the virtual destruction of what might be called the romantic author, Vance's works confront the authentic reader with his own imagination-as-imagination: that lazy workaholic faculty entirely dependent on nature, depths, chance, custom, and language. Brian Aldiss found Vance "a gaudily painted coelacanth, washed up on SF's shore."[36]

34 Jack Vance, *The Eyes of the Overworld*, Ace Books, New York 1966, p. 3.
35 Rotella 2009.
36 Brian Aldiss, *Trillion Year Spree*, Atheneum, London 1973, p. 31.

There is indeed something ancient in Vance, a literature that is only language, as full of marvels as any animal of evolution, but as with today's charming Coelacanths (not at all the living fossils Aldiss believes them to be), it is to be caught living, and not found washed up. Though his stories will occupy the Bronze Age past in the *Lyonesse* trilogy of the 1980s, they will force a new version of history, on the "Elder Isles," a repressed Atlantis between England and France, now sunken beneath the sea.

> *The Elder Isles had known the coming and coming of many peoples: Pharesmians, blue-eyed Evadnioi, Pelasgians with their maenad priestesses, Danaans, Lydians, Phoenicians, Etruscans, Greeks, Celts from Gaul, Ska from Norway by way of Ireland, Romans, Celts from Ireland and a few Sea Goths. The wash of so many peoples had left behind a complex detritus: ruined strongholds, graves, and tombs; steles carved with cryptic glyphs; songs, dances, turns of speech, fragments of dialect, place-names; ceremonies of purport now forgotten, but with lingering flavor …*[37]

Imaginative literature of the Weird Fiction tradition distills the lingering flavors of these old worlds and peoples still present in a living language, where the old magic can become cryptically new. In 1964's *The Houses of Iszm*, Vance can be found satirizing Jane Austen from out of what appears to be a nonsense game.

37 Jack Vance, *Lyonesse III: Madouc*, Grafton Books, London 1989, p. 2.

It was assumed as a matter of course that visitors came to Iszm with a single purpose: to steal a female house.[38]

Out of such wordplay opens the remarkable story of one peculiar Gaean world that moves through a cascade of science-fictional ideas, including a growable, gendered and sentient post-economic architecture, total surveillance via brain scan, multicultural ideology, and more. Unlike science fiction that focuses on one idea as its own brand, and in film, one central mood or concept, a Vance narrative moves relentlessly left-to-right according to the play and change of a single line of thought: illustrating nothing in the singular, except peculiar characters and jokes, and that usual captiousness of language that will prove to be the tone of any human world with limited exploitable resources. Like the author, his all too human heroes and villains alike will prefer to show themselves in language, and only in extravagant and perfect disguise.

By the mid-sixties Jack and Norma Vance were working wonders with words-as-words. The quality of the Vance style became so extraordinary as to stand out not only in popular fiction (where only Chandler seems comparable) but in English language literature of the postwar period in general. Few writers have been able to craft such a comprehensive, recognizable, resilient, and far-ranging, aesthetically pleasing style.

38 Jack Vance, *The Houses of Iszm*, Ace Books, New York 1964, p. 5.

It is regrettable that recent attempts at approaching twentieth century science fiction as a phenomenon serious enough to study prove themselves so provincial by leaving Jack Vance unconsidered. But one has to smile at recent defenders of the "mainstream novel," like *The New Yorker's* Adam Gopnik, when he protests the inclusion of Philip K. Dick in the canonical Library of America over issues of "bad writing."

> *The trouble is that, much as one would like to place Dick above or alongside Pynchon and Vonnegut—or, for that matter, Chesterton or Tolkien—as a poet of the fantastic parable he was a pretty bad writer. Though his imagination is at least the equal of theirs, he had, as he ruefully knew, a hack's habits, too, and he never really got over them … That's probably why Dick's reputation as a serious writer, like Poe's, has always been higher in France, where the sentences aren't read as they were written.*[39]

"Pretty bad writer?" It's doubtful Dick would have stooped to such a condescending "plebian" tone when addressing his own "fun-seeking" audience. Jack Vance forever proves the reactionary "bad sentences explain popularity in France" meme as the canon-making lie that it really is. With less-than-zero publicity, Vance remains in print in a rather large fashion overseas—despite his most famous feature

39 Adam Gopnik, "Blows Against the Empire: The Return of Philip K. Dick," *The New Yorker*, 20 August 2007.

being his perfect sentences. No corporation or questionably financed organ, like *The New Yorker*, pushed his work. Philip K. Dick's supposed "bad writing" is a fiction; indeed, against Vance's Chandler-like mastery of style, Dick was a sort of Hammett, able to fashion a clear prose that could handle ideas other writers still do not know how to approach with grace, humor, novelty, and many other novelistic qualities missing from mainstream novels back when they were relevant at all. But Dick's mainstream success has transformed his possible literary influence into a matter of screenwriting, while Vance's current success is driven by his writing, not by publicity departments.[40] I believe the proletarian and anti-aristocratic ideology of the pulp mid-list tradition, as fully explored by Jack/Norma Vance and others, explains both Dick's liquid clarity and his refusal of any high style at all. It is mainstream success that distinguishes Dick from Vance, who, equipped with vivid, ironic style, needs no current "relevance," no movies to work his magic in, nor any light of promised illumination to shine his way. In fact, the style is disguise; (the late career blindness now becomes an issue) Vance prefers the dark.

40 Though even science fiction writer friends like Poul Anderson and Frank Herbert suffered Vance's scorn, in a radio interview on the show "Hour 25" (25 November 1976), Jack and Norma reveal more than a passing regard for Philip K. Dick—an extreme rarity. (Interview currently available online at https://youtube.com/watch?v-JqK9sTE83VO). Their mutual Northern Californian connections would have extended to editor and pulp enthusiast Anthony Boucher (1911–1968).

Vorträge und Veranstal

13. - 15. April, Rabih Mroué, 17
Globe, Deutsche Bank-Türme, Taunusanlage 12, 60325

14. April, Holger Hoffmann, Arc

19. April, Josef Strau

29. April - 1. Mai, Rundgang
Jahresausstellung der Studieren

30. April, Jan Verwoert, 16h

5. Mai, Cristina Moreno & Efren

6. Mai, Eröffnung, time/bank, P
Ausstellungsdauer: 7. Mai - 26.

---

9. Mai, Tacita Dean

10. Mai, Franco Berardi, Portiku

11. Mai, Juliane Rebentisch

11. Mai, Chris Lee, Architekturk

12. Mai, Themroc, Film Screenin

16. Mai, Raqs Media Collective,

17. Mai, Elizabeth Povinelli: Po

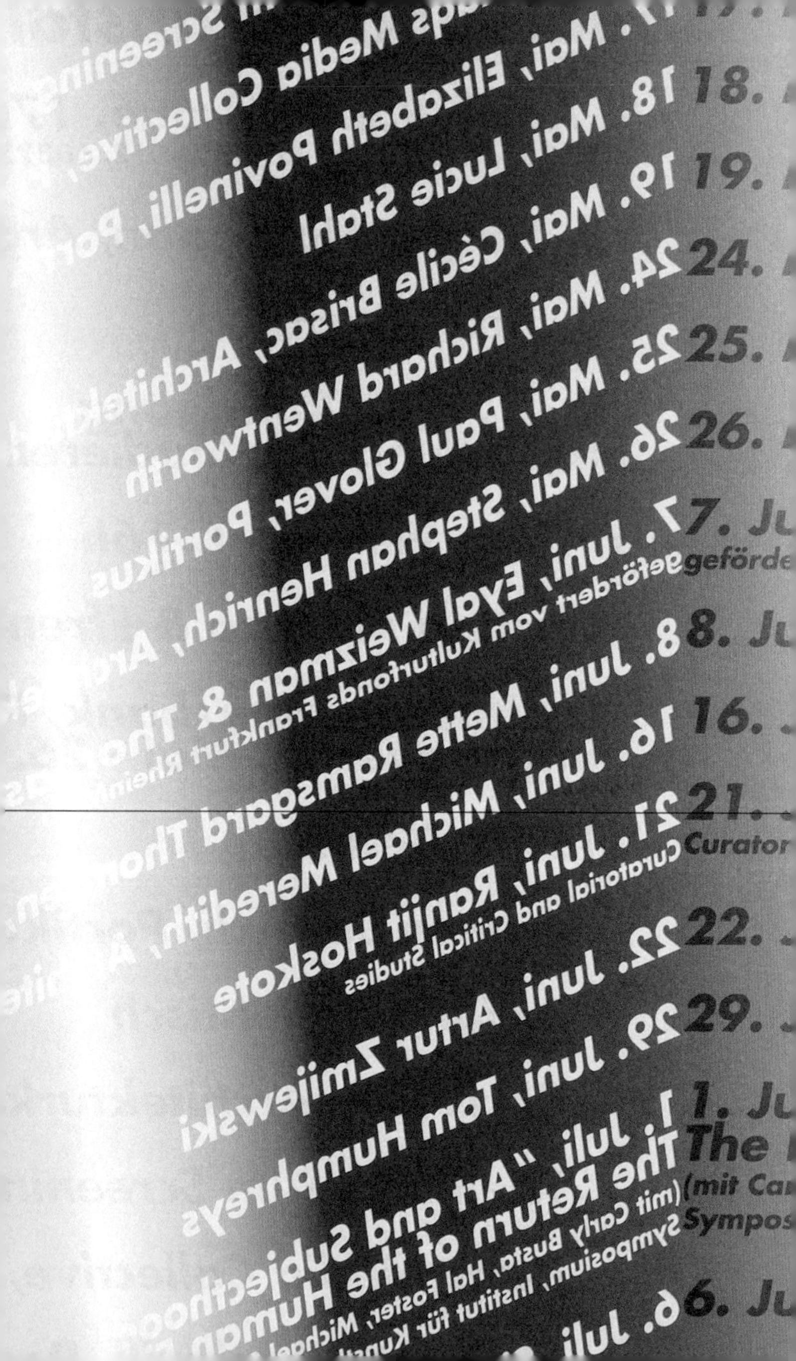
…aqs Media Collective, … Screening
17. Mai, Elizabeth Povinelli, Por…
18. Mai, Lucie Stahl
19. Mai, Cécile Brisac, Architek…
24. Mai, Richard Wentworth
25. Mai, Paul Glover, Portikus
26. Mai, Stephan Henrich, Arch…
7. Juni, Eyal Weizman & Tho…
gefördert vom Kulturfonds Frankfurt Rhein…
8. Juni, Mette Ramsgard Tho…
16. Juni, Michael Meredith, A…
21. Juni, Ranjit Hoskote
Curatorial and Critical Studies
22. Juni, Artur Zmijewski
29. Juni, Tom Humphreys
1. Juli, "Art and Subjecthood
The Return of the Human…
(mit Carly Busta, Hal Foster, Michael…
Symposium, Institut für Kunst…
6. Juli
18.
19.
24.
25.
26.
7. Ju
geförde
8. Ju
16.
21.
Curator
22.
29.
1. Ju
The
(mit Ca
Sympos
6. Ju

Elizabeth Povinelli, Portikus

Lucie Stahl

Cécile Brisac, Architekturklasse

Richard Wentworth

Paul Glover, Portikus

Stephan Henrich, Architekturkl

Eyal Weizman & Thomas Keena
Kulturfonds Frankfurt RheinMain

Mette Ramsgard Thomsen, Arch

Michael Meredith, Architektur

Ranjit Hoskote
Critical Studies

Artur Zmijewski

Tom Humphreys

"Art and Subjecthood.
Turn of the Human Figure in Semi
sta, Hal Foster, Michael Sanchez und Ina Blom, Perform
Institut für Kunstkritik, gefördert vom Kulturfonds Fran

Simon Starling

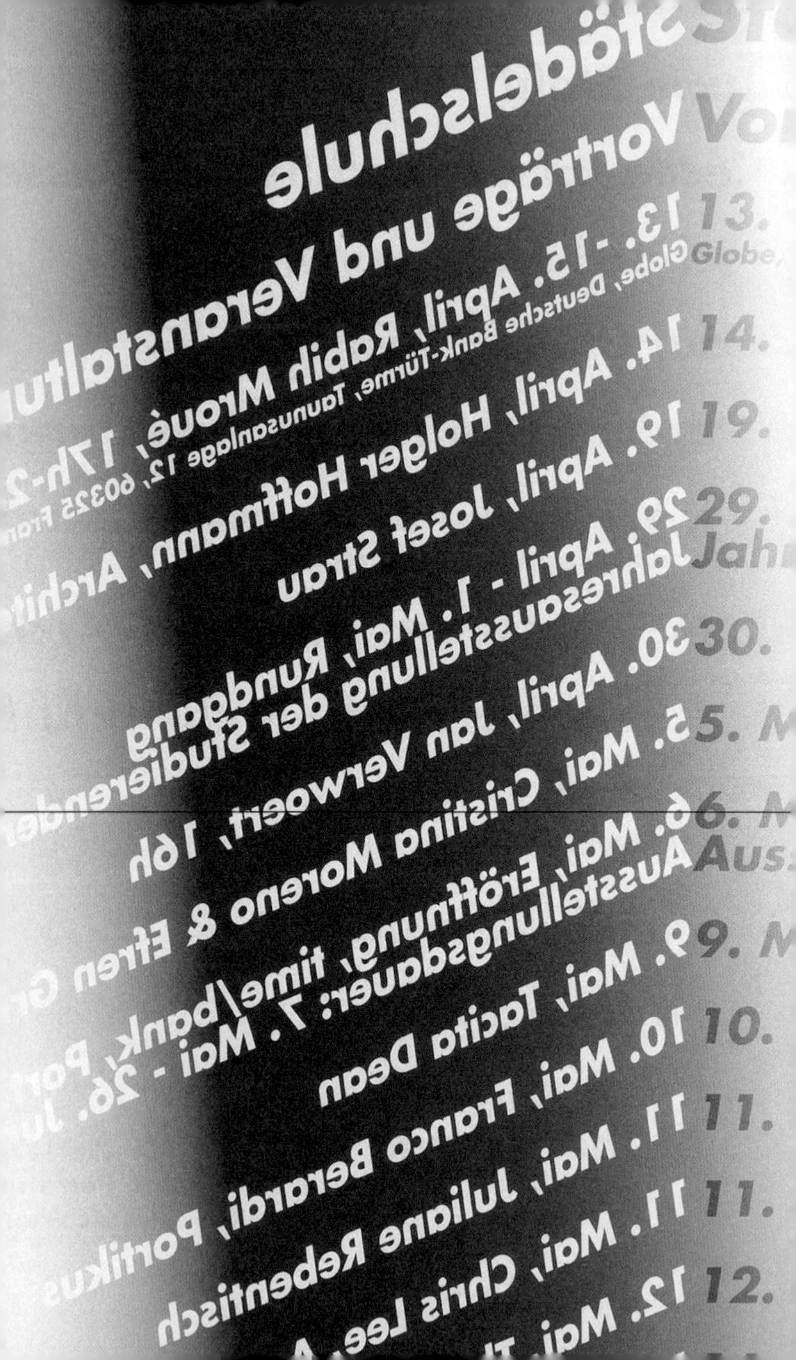
Städelschule
Vorträge und Veranstaltu
13. - 15. April, Rabih Mroué, 17h-2
Globe, Deutsche Bank-Türme, Taunusanlage 12, 60325 Fran
14. April, Holger Hoffmann, Archit
19. April, Josef Strau
29. April - 1. Mai, Rundgang
Jahresausstellung der Studierende
30. April, Jan Verwoert, 16h
5. Mai, Cristina Moreno & Efren Gr
6. Mai, Eröffnung, time\bank, Por
Ausstellungsdauer: 7. Mai - 26. Ju
9. Mai, Tacita Dean
10. Mai, Franco Berardi, Portikus
11. Mai, Juliane Rebentisch
11. Mai, Chris Lee, A
12. Mai

April 19, 2011
Josef Strau

The Nonproductive Attitude

Austrian-born artist and writer Josef Strau begins this lecture and Q&A by sharing stories of recent journeys and from his time in Florence, preparing his first book. In the process, Strau muses on his writing experience, from theoretical reviews to automatic writing, which he often uses for exhibitions. Likewise, Strau explores his theories about "nonproductive" and "productive" attitudes, and how these perspectives affect an artist's work. Reflecting upon his career and influences, he draws examples from Giorgio Bassani's book The Garden of the Finzi-Continis, *and then dives back into his own diaristic stories, merging history and observation, self-doubt and aspiration.*

Thank you very much for inviting me, first of all. I'm really happy to be here, particularly in this new room. Maybe I'll introduce myself—in fact, I am just coming from Karlsruhe. There is an exhibition at the Badischer Kunstverein, a kind of a group show. It was great. I actually live in New York right now and have done for three years. Before that, I lived for a long time in Berlin. I don't know, maybe thirteen years or something like that, but I was just in Florence as well, because I was working to prepare my first book, which is not really an art book, but more a collection of texts of mine. It will be an unbelievable honor for me to do that. And I was in Florence because I was able to use an apartment there and could work by myself for some weeks, to write.

What happened is that, one day, I was trying to start up the computer and it wouldn't start, and of course, I had no backup files, so the problem is that I don't have any images here for you. I only have some printed texts that I've been carrying around with me. And so, I say this, I guess, as a first warning.

I might circle this situation in Florence, first of all, because I lost not only lots of other files, but I lost one specific file that was supposed to be a catalogue text for a catalogue at the Sculpture Center in New York, which I was recently asked to rewrite. I'll improvise now since Michael [Krebber] was saying in the introduction, that I wrote this text *The Nonproductive Attitude,* which was a text that has even been quoted in other texts, which made me very happy. But on the other hand, I felt that sometimes it was deeply misunderstood. I always had the intention to rewrite it. And I was asked by the Sculpture Center to finally do that. So, I wrote it again after a long time, a more theoretical text about the nonproductive attitude, and then about the productive attitude as well, which I prefer.

Then, before I sent it away, the computer didn't start, so I wrote a new text again, but which was just stupid—it was about Florence, living there and going to some shops and so on. I might read that text later, but before I do that, I should start by introducing myself and how I became a visual artist. I have been an artist my whole life, and then, I suddenly became obsessed with not being an artist and obsessed with a certain kind of writing that I'd never experienced before. When I was an artist, I had ambitions to write texts and I wrote for *Texte Zur Kunst.* They were crazy enough to invite me to do some reviews sometimes. I tried to write as theoretically as possible and read lots of books, theory books, and tried to interpret them and put the sentences together in a way that I felt was connected to a really high level of theory.

Then there was this one moment, when I was invited to write one of these texts and to write about Roland Barthes and his theory on photography. I was particularly interested in his theory where he has this weird idea that the mechanism of photography is actually not purely a mechanic operation, but he believes that photography in itself is a kind of existence. Almost like a metaphysical existence that expresses itself through photographs. But there is something behind this that is almost dark, not really evil, but this dark existence behind photography, which creates this sadness, which is in all photography, that you always have to deal with the fact that it describes the past. That you always have to deal with lost time. And you always, in the end, have to deal with the universal problem of death. So, basically, this evil character, which stands behind the mechanism of photography, is kind of not only destroying our image, but basically ourselves. Actually, Roland Barthes never went so far as to say that, but I felt it was there. I wanted to write about that. But I couldn't do it. I kept saying to myself, "Forget about it." The next morning was the deadline and it was late at night, and I still hadn't written anything of my pseudo-theoretical essay.

I was sitting down on the computer and thought, I'll just write anything, something stupid, just to relax because I was incredibly tense. I kind of remember how it went. I started writing that I'd been at a party the day before, it was a long drinking night, and I found myself kneeling on the kitchen floor. I put a little of the most expensive cat food in my mouth, but I didn't swallow it. The cat was beside me because of the good smell of the food, and I put the mush from my mouth to the floor and the cat immediately ate it. Then I tried to stand up again, but I had drunk too much, it was Christmas Day. Beside me, there was a bench. I lay down on it and it occurred to me that in the last few days I had been trying to make something of an unpleasant sentence, and couldn't get anywhere with it.

The next morning when I got up, I caught sight of myself in a round mirror, and for the first time, there was something really unusual in it for me. I saw, not my normal face, which now and again had perhaps gotten a bit shady and older, but this time, it changed to a different and unknown face, and I knew, suddenly, that this looks like a bohemian. This looks like the face of the ghost of a bohemian. But I thought it was certainly something I never wanted to be. Never had I thought that I, myself, had ever experienced such a thing as a bohemian life or anything like that. And I was far less certain in my thoughts then, that I would ever assume the face of the bohemian in the mirror.

I sat and talked to the cat, and said come on and hold my hand, etc., etc., but anyway, I wanted to say that because these sentences carried this moment, and for the first time, I had written three pages at once and realized after I'd finished that after a half-hour, and also while I wrote it, that it wasn't I myself who had written it, although it was a description of my experience, it was almost as if some spirit told me to write it down to make fun of me. And so, I didn't try to make fun of myself and I wasn't consciously trying to do anything, I just wrote it down. But anyway, I felt this kind of driving force to tell a story, which in the end, as I read it, was much closer to this kind of huge idea of Roland Barthes than something else.

The thing was that I just wanted to write nothing, garbage, nonsense. But something drove me to, in the form of the description of an experience that better carried this idea of what I'd planned to write in this theoretical style. It's not so interesting, but it's like something had been started there and I wanted to follow that. I realized that there are some real possibilities in this sort of writing, which doesn't follow a kind of intentional writing.

I started doing it as I was looking at Surrealist paintings and writings. At the time, I was calling it automatic writing, but that was a bit wrong because automatic writing is something else. It is an experience that many writers have had and perhaps pursue as a logical thing. Maybe some take it as a kind of spiritual channeling or something. But since then, which was maybe seven years ago, I've been very interested in doing that kind of writing.

I use this sort of writing often for exhibitions and I print it very quickly in the condition of a quick work. I make these quick posters, which other people do. I never do the design. I have some ideas, but it is always endless text, almost, not endless, but some, and the posters should be free so that people don't have to read in the gallery. I've learned a lot since living in America. Before, it often happened that the first time I put these texts into the exhibition, and made it into a special edition with a kind of sculptural lamp or something like that, that I was often accused by visitors: "I don't go to a gallery to read something. Why do you write texts? Aren't you an artist, or what?" I often dealt with this kind of very oppressive reaction, which made me very nervous. It's interesting, since I've been living in other countries and making projects there, this problem of reversing the probability of the visual art space into something else, by, for instance, introducing a text or something, which could be a more interesting thing to do. And maybe even such an approach could become the attraction for a few people.

[Looks over the texts he brought.]

The themes are very different.

I didn't think that I would make a presentation of my work in a visual way, but rather, I'd like to try to explain why I write these texts and what they are about. The other thing I'd like to bring up is a book that I brought here with me from a really good Italian writer.

I was just in Florence and I remembered seeing a film a while back called *The Garden of the Finzi-Continis* by Vittorio De Sica, from 1970. It is with famous actors like Helmut Berger, Dominique Sanda, and so on. Suddenly, as I was standing in the kitchen in Florence and was thinking about this film, it was a weird thing, finally remembering the film more intensely than ever before. It was this endless seventies film about a few young people sitting around in a garden. The special thing was that the film had extremely blurred colors. It was sometimes orange, sometimes strongly blue, kind of seventies style, very psychedelic, almost, with lots of filters on the camera. People accused him [De Sica] of using a cheap pornographic style of filmmaking, where the furniture is blurred in the background and then the portrait comes out sharp in front. I think in some ways, now that I've read the book that the film is based on, which was written by Giorgio Bassani twenty years before the film was made, that he must be a deeply underestimated writer. He is not so famous. Only people in Italy really know of him. I think he died about ten years ago at ninety. In some ways, his writing carries this kind of feeling that I was talking about—the effect of writing, which is actually unexplainable.

I was thinking that I should talk about that book, first off, because it is one of the best books I know. The other thing is that I wanted always to be a kind of conceptual artist, or perhaps, I tried to be one and never really was.

When I was an art student, and a bit after that, I couldn't make any work because I had these great role models of conceptual art that I could never live up to. Then I thought, perhaps I could somehow do the opposite, at least with writing, and do it not very conceptually. Instead, what I do feels kind of dirty, subjective, emotional, confessional. Suddenly, all these things have become almost values for me—confession has become the energy to produce. On the other hand, I don't think that confession has much to do with Giorgio Bassani.

But what I do think more and more is that when I do an art exhibition and come to a new place, I'm always confronted with someone else and have to explain my work. I realized that early on; I always thought that artists have to explain their work perfectly, but at that moment, I realized not.

I think there should be a revolution and a lot of things would break down if we destroyed this law or rule, this need to have to explain your work in the sense of this moment when it's finished at the opening, and in comes the curator asking, "Why did you use that, why did you write that?" I think that this idea of explaining all the time doesn't suit contemporary life or any kind of enlightenment or rationality. It feels more like a kind of social oppression to force people to participate in a system, a system in which it is almost impossible to produce any kind of interesting art or literature.

Anyway, to go back to Giorgio Bassani, I should say that the story itself, apart from the very beginning and the very end, describes nothing other than a few young people who are interested in art and literature, plus a few other things. Two of them are very rich and they have a large garden in Italy by the Po in Ferrara, not far from Florence, on the way to Venice. The whole book is about these young people playing tennis all the time. The father had built this tennis court in the garden for them, and at the beginning, since they were these cool twenty-year-olds, they were, of course, very snobbish about tennis and didn't want to use the court. As it happens, they start using it with a kind of disinterested arrogance, a snobbishness toward any sports. Then they start to increasingly obsess more and more and they even want to rebuild the tennis court, they want to improve it, they want everything new, and they tell their father, "We need a better tennis court." And they start to compete with real tennis clubs in the city, where real athletes play.

The book is based around their experiences on and around the tennis court as the De Sica film shows, and actually, nothing really happens the whole time. Basically, the book is about this one thing; it is focused on this one season where they obsess about tennis, and since many of them are Jewish and it takes place shortly before the Germans enter the scene, the Mussolini Fascists have an eye on them and want to put them into prisons. But when the Nazis do arrive in Italy, they will all be transported and killed, so this becomes their last season. There are many, many things—the tennis court, the description of the tennis court, and the descriptions of the people—that I think are unbelievably impressive, in a very polite way. The situation is respectable, how he describes it. Obviously, the writer describes a situation that he was once part of during the early 1940s.

What I like most about the book is that it doesn't explain itself. It just starts at the beginning saying, "This book is about the Holocaust. This book is about one of the most radical destructions in history." He tells that this and that happened, he describes at the beginning, a graveyard. And he describes people who will later have no home, who will lose their homes and lives, and not even end up in a graveyard. The thing that is so fantastic about the book is that all these kinds of clear accounts of the tennis ball, or she says this, this person says this—it's always loaded because it will be the last weeks of their lives. Their actions are completely independent of the question of the Holocaust. It is a very intense thing.

I'd seen so many books and films about the Holocaust but if you have seen that film or read that book, this is much worse, much more radical. It is telling a story about what happened by describing the lives of the people before they were taken to Auschwitz. I'll give you an example. He's talking to the father, this rich guy:

So he began asking what I thought of the tennis court and if it was really so outrageous. For her part (the young daughter) was determined. She insisted the whole thing be done over according to modern criteria, but he had doubts. Perhaps, as usual, his beloved earthquake, his daughter was exaggerating. Perhaps it would be necessary to tear up the whole thing as she demands. In any case, he added, in a few days it would start raining. There is no use deceiving ourselves. Best to postpone any sort of undertaking in the next year. Don't you agree? He then went on to ask me what I was doing, what I planned to do in the immediate future and how my parents were. We went slowly back towards the tennis court. At first sight, it seemed no one was left there and yet in the almost complete darkness Michol and Colletto were still playing. Michol was complaining that the ball was making her run too much, that he was not being a gentleman. That the darkness too, was frankly excessive. Michol tells me you still hadn't decided whether to take your degree in Art or in Italian. The father was saying to me meanwhile. Or have you already made up your mind?

It is like every sentence, without explaining everything, is a metaphor, at least. It is probably much more than a metaphor when he describes one of his last days before the winter comes—that during some days when they play tennis, they play so excessively, and it becomes darker and darker and you can almost not see the players and where the ball is. It develops them into superior players. Bassani uses this same sort of symbol about disappearance in such an extreme way in almost every sentence, in every chapter.

I wanted to bring it up because, obviously, I like it, and I'm very impressed and I just had it with me in my bag, and since I don't have my computer here, I thought it would be nice to introduce you to this book. The story itself as well as the writing holds to a certain idea about production, of writing, and of art as well. The point is, that all these things that I explain, when I announce from the beginning that it is about this and that, they are not actually containing the quality that a book like this has. I am very sure, and actually, Giorgio Bassani describes this in the beginning, that he came to write this book in a very small moment.

He was visiting back in the fifties, he had survived, and he describes his community before the Nazis came into Italy. He talks about going to the graveyard of the Etruscans, which is something like 3000 years old. Some friends from Rome from the art scene were going with cars out to the country and everything was nice. And while he was visiting these graveyards, his daughter asked him, "Why are people so obsessed with these graveyards?" and he says, "It is nice, because these people died so long ago, and we don't know them, so it is." Then one of the men makes this theory that if you don't know the people anymore, a graveyard is, "A nice thing." There comes this one complication where he suddenly realizes that he knew these people, who actually had their own graveyard, a very beautiful graveyard, but they are not in it. It is then that he decides to write this book. I guess he wrote it in a very quick way without the intention of making the big book about the big subject, about his life, which was the Holocaust.

I actually have a very different text here and unrelated to the text before and I, maybe not this one ... [sorts through papers]. Okay, this text is unpublished and it will appear in two weeks in a Sculpture Center book. I just tried to write a text about the earlier "unproductive attitude" text, then it was lost and I tried to rewrite it, I could not because ... I don't know. So, I wrote something completely different:

> *Yesterday I went down to the city. It is Florence, Italy, by the way, and I went to the bookshop, what else. I felt everything turned wrong with me and my works. The young Italians were populating the river cafe in the late spring sunny day, sensual, good looking, and relaxed. I just came from Germany, and even the dogs look human here. Even the older ones smiled into my pale face and I said, ! 'I just came from the Apple store and they told me my computer é morto.' The old woman said, 'morto'¿ and smiled.*
> *But at the bookstore, later, I took the Kerouac book out and opened it randomly in the middle watching out for being helped by the mysteries of coincidence and I found it as his text said, 'never rewrite anything, type as quick as you can.' I was typing and typing, Kerouac said, and my friend came in and said, 'Hurry up let's go, the girls wait.' And I wrote quicker than ever before, I did not lose a minute, and got to the bus with him for the party. And he looked at the written papers and said, 'This is the best you've ever written.'*
> *But I, me in Florence, Italy, I turned the book back and left for the bus. I was living in an artist house in Florence, searching for a cigarette. So I entered one of*

the empty studios that was still empty yesterday, lots of pencils scattered now around everywhere, on the table, on the floor, a few pieces of destroyed pieces of paper in between. I searched all parts for the cigarette. But was astonished by the hidden language of all the half-done objects so much that they felt like they were almost speaking to me, as good art I guess should do, as I moved around in this deserted production sphere of another artist. There was one tool like a complicated saw or metal cutter, looking like a precision instrument, but then, there was one piece particularly striking me lying on an old red brick on the floor, but it was bound by some black thick ribbon and looked like a letter. And the ribbon was scattered in various directions on the floor as if it was a dog's leash. It was not just meaningful in a sexy way, it was like really meaningful, in an existential way, like saying everything has to be bound to something to make any sense.

The day before, I was at a fashion shop, and when I left the changing room all three people in the shop—the owner, the daughter of the owner, and the artist—stood there and looked at me as if their tools fell off their hands. They stood, like specially positioned chess figures, and the feeling touched me as if I was a chess figure too. So I made one more step out into the room and I felt like a chess figure moving for the first time out into the open field and was suddenly trapped in the gaze of three much stronger figures. It was a gothic fashion shop. And while waiting and looking around, without touching first, I had decided to choose myself, not just wait, and I chose two things. One was a long skirt—it was made of long heavy pinstriped velvet and had two sweet

little buckles, one on each side and a long zipper on the back. And now wearing it, I felt really strange in the middle of the shop, squeezed and exposed in between everybody. Even trying to describe the situation I'm in, on that day of quick writing, it does not help to solve the mystery to recover the text. So let me go ahead and what happened after the fashion shop visit and its embarrassing moment between the shelves in the front of the gothic changing room. I decided to leave as quickly as possible but my expression of denial to buy the sweet long skirt was leading me quickly into a discussion with the owner and her slow moving daughter, whose order to take it with me, I absolutely could not refuse. It was not that expensive, and so, I went, with the most beautiful contents of the bag to the bus and again, hum, whatever. I want to continue to a bit later.
All these good-looking people behave so smoothly and gently around each other with the greatest politeness, but still look at each other with deep sensuality. I almost was at the point of not finishing the strange skirt-dressing story here, keeping the embarrassment to myself, alone. But as the nonproductive attitude is, like many other texts, just a declaration of embarrassment, and as I am not really able to recover its story from my memory, I should rather finish the changing room story affair. The moment when I turned back into the soft negligent atmosphere of the gothic changing room, a man, another third person in the shop quickly rushed towards me while I actually wanted to let the violet curtain fall between me and the shop space to finally undress from the comfortable, but embarrassing, striped skirt experience. He was looking very Italian, but still

working-class in his whole attitude, and asked me, if it did not fit well, or if there would be any problem with it? And he asked it in the most common way, as if I had just tried on my usual Levis trousers. The shock of this encounter with him did not finish my weird feelings about wearing a gothic skirt with buckles, and strange belts, and very charming looking metal earrings. In fact, it was the opposite. It was like another step of further embarrassment pleasure, as he started touching me on the hip and around, as if trying to find out if everything fit well, just technically. And that way, for sure, he must have discovered my embarrassment. But instead of showing disgust, as well as showing any fun in the situation, he just turned around saying, 'It's alright, it's really no problem.' An expression, which I thought later on the bus, healed me from all inhibitions and restrictions or actually revealed them finally to me. I was thinking—what a forgiving, sweet, and warm universe I live in—since the moment I left the store. Excuse me to mix this maybe most profane and sensual experience with any spiritual narrative, but I was, while pondering the experience of a classic personal situation, obsessively considering the story of Jacob, the father of Joseph, and the very strange paragraph of the Bible which is called Jacob is wrestling with the angel. Jacob is often escaping something—one time he escapes his enemy, his most oppositional figure, his brother; one time, when it becomes night and he runs away in order to hide again, he meets an angel and the angel wants to fight with him. Therefore, so that Jacob cannot run away, the angel touches his hip, and a certain nerve of the hip, moving his leg, is somehow lame, and he cannot run away and has to somehow fight with him. And then Jacob fights the whole night with him. And when it slowly becomes day, the angel leaves him, but says from now on you are not Jacob anymore. From now on you will be called Israel.

I like this model of how night and day comes, and angels come too, in-between, sometimes. While I was in this exhibition today, writing this little press text, which I want to explain because I was forced to, and I read this little part because I like very much the reply another great writer named Arthur Schnitzler once gave in an interview. He was asked the question, "Your writing always seems to deal with scenes of religion and sexuality?" and Schnitzler just said, "Is there anything else to write about?" I don't know, I kind of thought of course it's pretty stupid, but on the other hand it was one of these kinds of strange forces that drove me to always keep Schnitzler's irony in mind. It probably needed a lot of courage to say that in modern times in Vienna, around 1900 or something, which was probably much more modern than it is today, or more contemporary, at least.

For years, I thought I would have loved to say a sentence like that in public. That yeah, is there anything else other than religion or sexuality to talk about, to write about, or to make work about? But I was always afraid to do that when I wrote a press text, say, for another artist. And I sometimes brought in a symbolic moment, some kind of relationship to religious stories, for instance, like here, the one with Jacob and the angel, and people would maybe say,

"Can you take that out?" But this kind of courage is probably not courageous anymore; it was years ago. Anyway, I thought I'd read that text to explain it a little bit, I'd try to make this weird connection with a very private theological idea and put it together with other very private stories, of, maybe love, and not just sexuality.

Question
Yesterday, I read a text by Chris Kraus in an old issue of *Spex* about the exhibition at Greene Naftali by the Bernadette Corporation.

JS Actually the other book I brought by Chris Kraus, so it's great that you bring that up.

Question
She asks a question about how a text becomes a piece of art, but that's so boring. It is something that you can talk about, or, I'm absolutely fine not talking about how a text can become a piece of art. What you are doing is something like that, and the Bernadette Corporation is also doing something like that.

JS Well, I read the text a long time ago, although it was published again later, I think for *Artforum*, but as a shorter version. I liked that she is saying that Bernadette Corporation have done many projects already, but that one was the first project where they just presented text, and it was poetry. And poetry is really hard work; it has all these formal rules to express yourself. They worked for months, and at the end, there were just these tables, wooden pieces with the poetry all lain out throughout the gallery. People could not take it with them, so actually, for the audience it was totally tortuous to take in. The best line from Chris Kraus was that she said, "It is stupid to say, why do they do poetry now, because they were always poets. But they were poets writing poems without doing the writing, instead their kind of projects were strongly poetic, and in a sense, they were already poets themselves because they never actually did the kind of art that one would expect from contemporary art and the production of art objects."

She was saying something very important. There are many people who are not artists but they all move strongly into the art world. It has an incredible gravitation. But one should see it as all these artists, but many are actually not artists, so, she talks about that. But she resolves this, in a way, by saying that they were poets already.

Question

You once told me you made a lamp with a very long wire for the switch because you did not understand how you wanted to switch off the light from the sofa …

JS What?

Question

You made a wire that was two or three meters long, and you were lying on the sofa …

JS That was one of these stories, yes, these explanations about why I started doing these lights. I felt, myself, that I had almost made this great invention, almost, and that it was art. I once had this moment where I had to leave the bed because I had this very expensive lamp, and I couldn't make this ... [stretches his arm out, reaching for the unreachable] to reach the switch, which was very annoying. So after a few months, I put a ribbon on it and then it was very easy to do. And this was one of the few inventions where I thought: this could be called art. It is one of the reasons I connected these lamps to my texts. I guess that was the very early experience of doing art.

Question

What is this certain desire to not have things explained?

JS I think it is really great to explain, and when I was a young artist, I thought it was the most important thing to explain a work and what it says. But I have felt differently for some years, actually, it was a long time ago. Usually, to make an artwork people believed in, you say, "This is the work, it's good, yeah." Then the gallerist rated the work, stands in front and says, "Yeah, very good."

Question

That was the seventies.

JS No, the late eighties. I don't want to blame the galleries now; I was working as an assistant for galleries. But sometimes, I was subservient and had to suggest they believe in it. And then I started loving the idea of doing it differently, and suggested that we should put away the whole work of art but use only the second order, the activities or practices, and first principles, the relation of art, the explanation of art, that we should use the art space but decide that we don't show any work of art, but want to include someone or expose someone. But then the nineties changed everything, and actually returned to the object. For me, in a very disappointing way, because a kind of quality of explanation is only possible if the object being explained nearly doesn't exist. Let's say the further away it is from existing, the better the explanation can be. That was my theory then, and I called these things, things the nonproductive attitude.

But, I've changed my mind because I think that's what it's for. Now I try not to do the opposite, but to do a different thing. There is a production with no explanation, but the production has its own complete set of laws and rules or something. But the rules have never been told. The further the explanation is from the production of the object, the better for the inherent discourse of the object. It is just a game, you know. Just a regular game and I just enjoy that at the moment.

I see that writing is a bit like that. Now it is happening in New York but not only New York. Chris Kraus, for instance, I asked her, "What about your new book?" and she answered ... [he looks upwards, blankly, with a hand to his face, avoiding eye contact, showing a certain expression of guilt or wandering gaze, as if she has nothing to tell] and so I thought, this was really an amazing answer. I know she does it very differently. I shouldn't even have said that. I shouldn't say this as well, I guess there are many Americans here and I love America very much, deeply, and now, since I live there I love it even more.

Well, now I don't work on that. I said for years that explanation is everything and the object is nothing, and now I say the opposite, or whatever. But who cares, you know what I mean. I should not talk about it anymore, not other than what has happened to me in the last days or so. But of course, what does it mean, it's nothing, but of course it's not nothing and it's very important. The point of the text I read to you is to share a point. I'm sorry, I've answered too long.

Question

Does this perhaps relate to what Walter Benjamin says about a great story, which is hard to explain, but nonetheless, somehow well articulated?

JS I think I know this text, where he says that really good modern writing can only be done when the writer is in the place where he cannot explain anymore. I cannot say I would say the same thing, but I remembered that. I actually read that around the time when I was writing that. It is a fantastic sentence for me.

Was that a real answer or not? Sorry, I'm very slow today, but as I told you I've been on the road for four or five months, and I was even in Australia, and there, maybe, I completely lost myself. A drop had become too much for me. Now I was just in Karlsruhe because of this exhibition with so many artists there. And you know how the opening days go by and there are these questions about the light—the light—the light, and then it passes. And then I was supposed to write another text, and I arrived here and my computer crashed, and so I'm sorry, I'm so slow on these questions. In the end, one forgets who one is almost, in a situation like that. You have to recreate that by remembering what you have done.

I think in a theoretical way regarding production. You can take whatever theory and change it, but that is not the point. Of course, who knows what the point is. But what I'm saying is that whatever I was writing a long time ago about these texts and was really obsessed by about these texts, was not only saying something about me, but like the early nineties there was this same thing, an obsession with the idea, for instance, like, how can you be an artist without actually producing anything? So, you have no object related to your identity as an artist. The result was that you say, okay, and you have to make society accept the representational form of artists and how that identifies with you, even if you have no object to put in a gallery or institution or some kind of social system. And then I was, of course, already doing the following. I went out in the art scene and became successful in that way, as someone who is there, as someone who is telling a story, someone who is making jokes, as someone who is a promising artist or something. And in some ways, I like that game very much as well as the theoretical game. So, there is this theoretical nonproductive game of saying, of explanation building, and making something smaller, or you have to make a second project or something. The disappointment of it was not the theory of it, but of this kind of extreme dependency on socializing, which brought on disaster. There was this moment where this whole art networking system became stronger and stronger.

And probably it is just a personal failure that I decided not to deal with production in this way, as I said before. Now I want to destroy these other things, like what I said about the explanation, and about the social relationships as well. My intention now, is that the artist lives only through his object. And has to take that very seriously. And I think he/she has to take that as an almost religious kind of calling. And that is why it is so sweet and intense that you say to yourself: you have to exclude all relationships that are personal and try to create something, which tries to exist for itself, which has a dynamic, which is much bigger than you. You have to cut off all social ties. Not all, of course. But I'm talking about not working anymore in a social system that corrupts the beauty of this type of art production.

The weird thing is, that's what I wanted to talk about today. I'm talking about shifts. At the time, I was trying to write the second "nonproductive attitude"—this criticism on myself as a personal failure first of all, but secondly, as a kind of thing that I felt corrupted a lot of other people as well, this system of gossiping and so on, this system of information. You need lots of information to participate in a social system, but that information doesn't help you to create.

We have similar problems today. I would recognize them, I might say then, and it might sound radical to some people, but I was wondering about this all these years, when I was young in the seventies and there was this question of revolution. People waited for the revolution that they all thought would come soon, the real revolution, which burns down capitalism, which burns down the system and so on. I believed in that too, or wanted to believe in it. But I thought, okay, this is obviously not possible, in all those decades in between.

But probably the idea of this revolution needs a kind of injection of another sort of energy. And this energy might be a theological one. So actually, revolutionary movements need a kind of religious impact. I met a guy in New York, a few students were asking him about squatting houses again. After a long time, squatting has become a pretty forgotten thing and they were trying to find someone who could give them a practical idea of how to squat houses. Then comes along this old man from the Bronx, and he was helping in the park. Actually, there were these student riots in New York last year, I think in Europe nobody wrote about it. At least the German newspapers didn't write about it at all. I guess they preferred showing New York as stupid Wall Street people, taking away everything, and so these things never appear. Anyway, there were heavy riots, for many reasons. A few of these students were talking to this person and saying it was now time to start squatting houses again, but not only houses, the university itself, and so on. And of course, that required strategy.

The guy comes in and was telling them in an absolutely fantastic way to do it very simply. He was pretty radical. He'd had an amazing experience with the police, and the media, and so on. But this guy was actually called a liberation theologian, which is a very strong title in Latin America that had been destroyed by the church in the eighties, and, of course, by government violence. When I heard that, I realized the intensity of these guys working in the Bronx in this social field, although he is an old man now and not so much a revolutionary anymore, perhaps for that reason maybe. But he had this intensity, which I had never seen in any kind of left-wing discourse in our geographical area here. At that moment, I had this theological question for myself.

I've gone so far now with these questions, but I'm not at my best today. I introduced myself at the beginning and now I'm going to finish and say, sorry it was not so great, but I hope that I could address a little bit of something about a problem, which is maybe not only my own problem, but a contemporary problem.

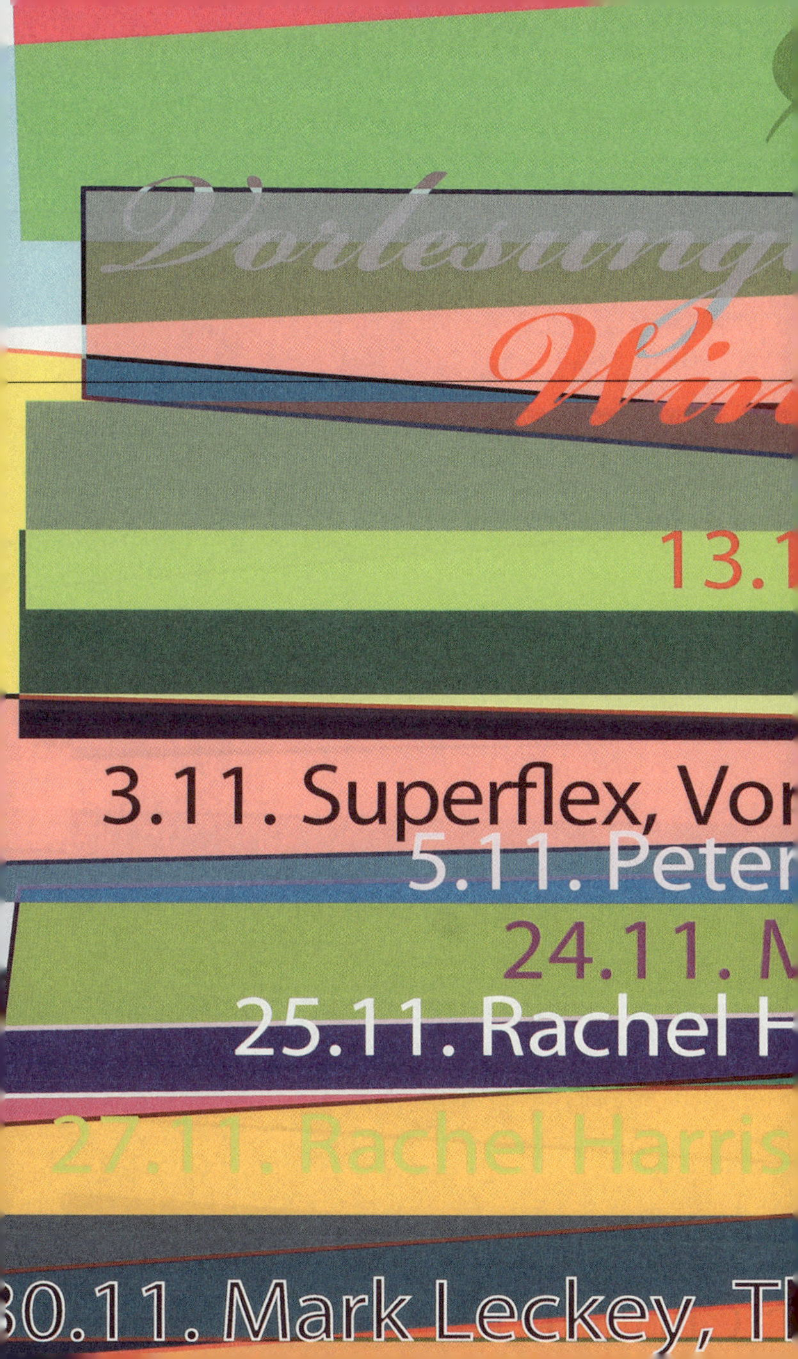
Vorlesung
Win
13.1
3.11. Superflex, Vor
5.11. Peter
24.11. M
25.11. Rachel H
27.11. Rachel Harris
30.11. Mark Leckey, Th

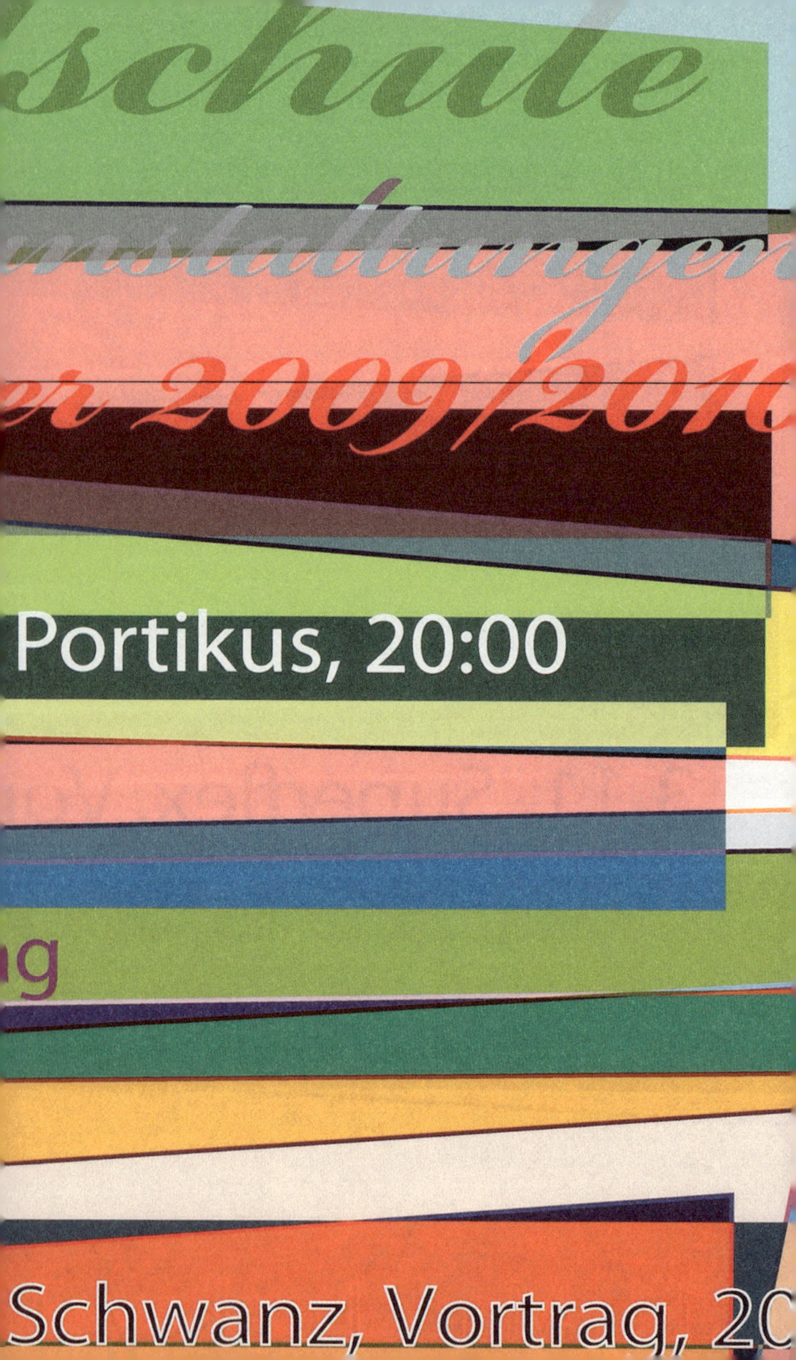

schule
er 2009/201
Portikus, 20:00
g
Schwanz, Vortrag, 20

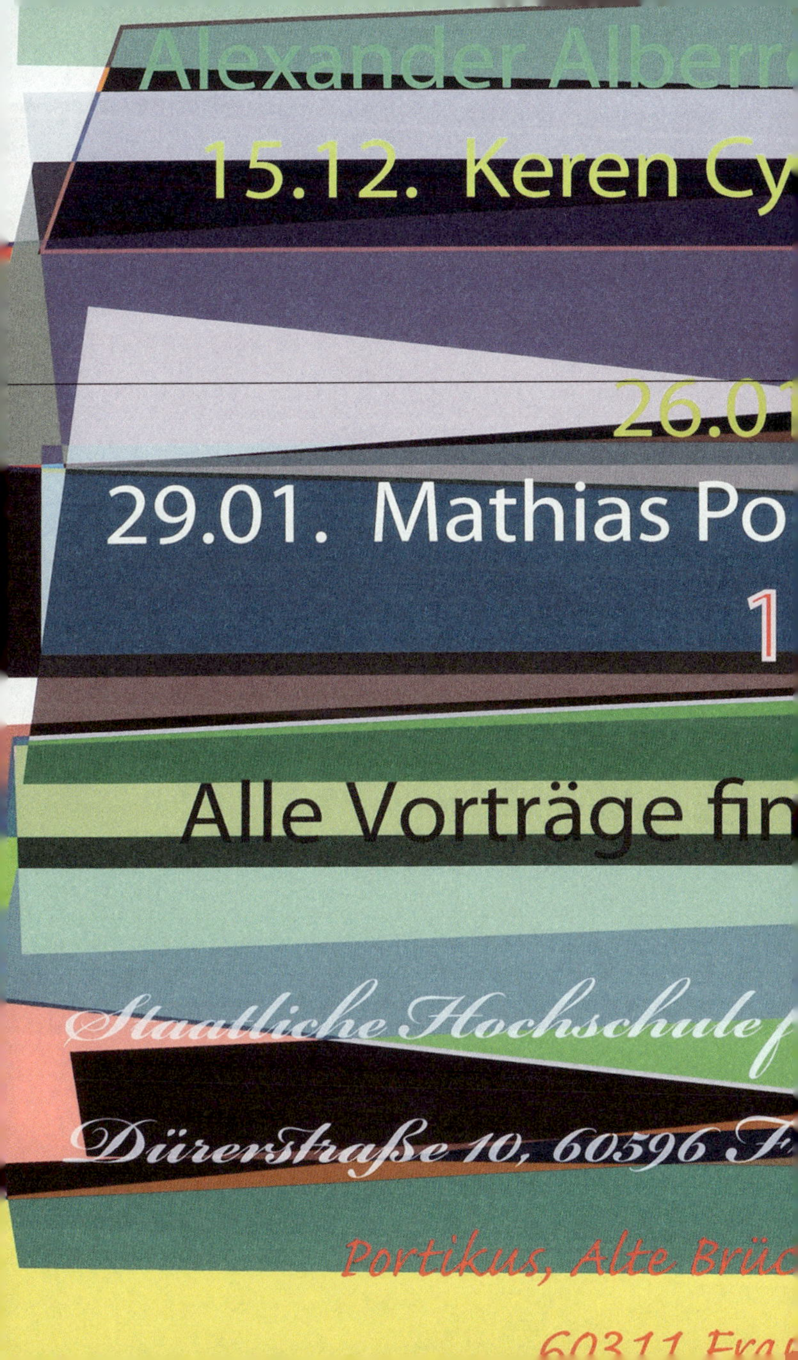
Alexander Alberr
15.12. Keren Cy
26.01
29.01. Mathias Po
1
Alle Vorträge fin
Staatliche Hochschule f
Dürerstraße 10, 60596 F
Portikus, Alte Brüc
60311 Fra

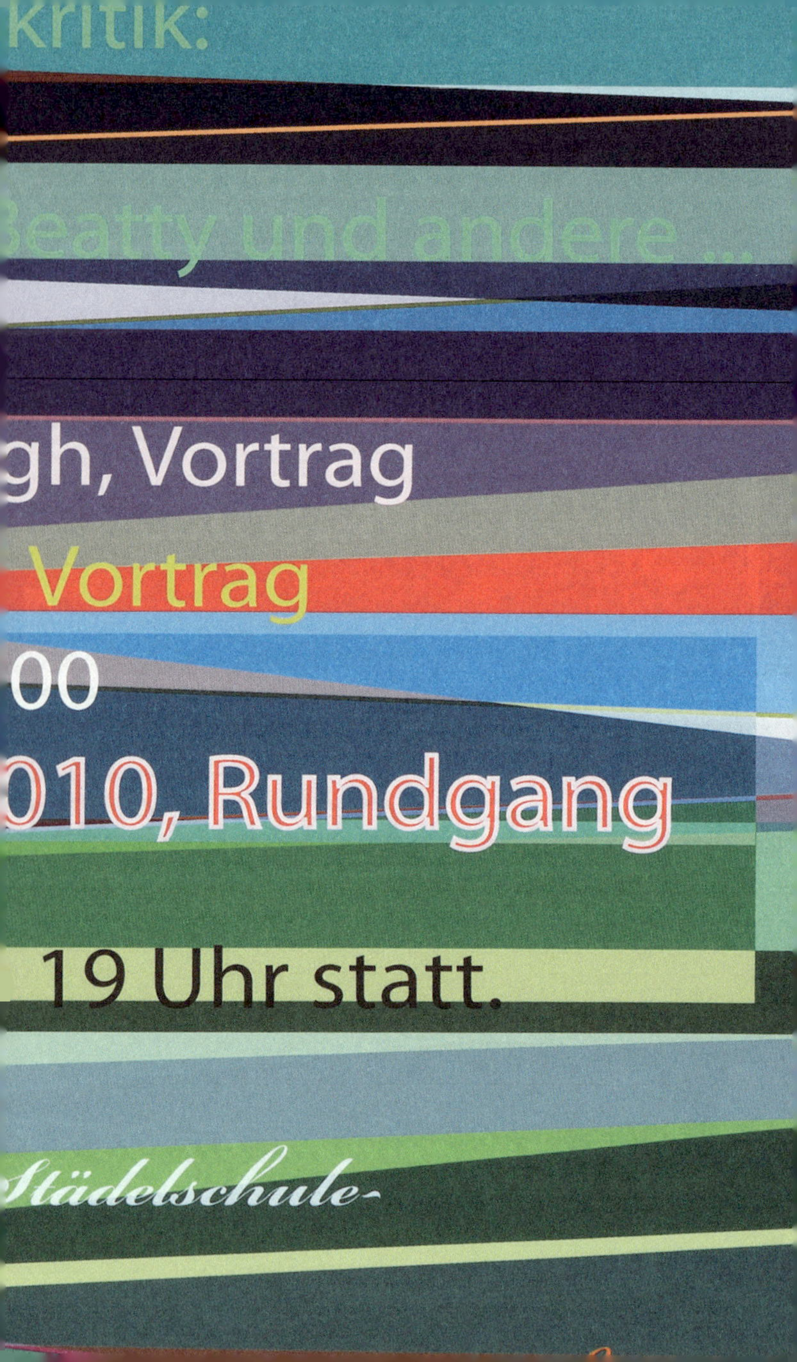
kritik:
Beatty und andere ...
gh, Vortrag
Vortrag
00
010, Rundgang
19 Uhr statt.
Städelschule-

November 30, 2009
Mark Leckey

The Long Tail

British artist Mark Leckey reflects on time spent on the Internet and theories about how it works in this live lecture and performance, The Long Tail. *Leckey tells how a figurine of Felix the Cat, a popular cartoon character from the silent film era, was used for testing early television transmissions. He likens the "vaporization of sculpture" to a 1936 manifesto by artist Károly Tamkó-Sirató, and describes how platforms like YouTube create infinite dimensions in the screen as well as content, where the producer and consumer are the same. Moving from the dot-com bubble to echo chambers of Google algorithms, Leckey proposes that the Internet itself may be acting out a trauma recorded deep within its memory.*

#1 FELIX

The Long Tail begins, for me, at a very particular point in time, a definable moment in history, which is when this photograph was taken. I came across it during a search for something else … err, dolls, puppets, automatons, something like that … and as soon as it appeared I was mesmerized, I just couldn't work out what this figure, an old cartoon character, was doing amongst all these strange machines. What were they for? And what did they do? Why Felix the Cat? I became, somewhat, obsessed with this image. So, you know, I looked it up, Googled some Television histories and began to piece together what this photograph was all about.

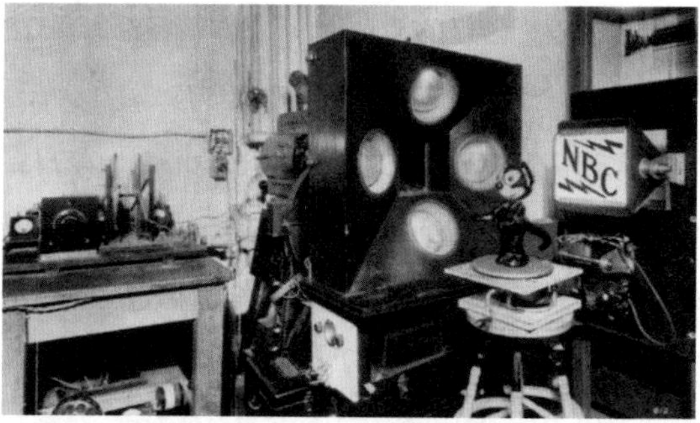

First television broadcast NBC, circa 1928

This apparatus pictured here then is called a mechanical scanner and it is basically the earliest form of television. The photograph was taken in 1928 at NBC's experimental studios in New York where they used a doll of Felix the Cat to test their germinal transmissions.

2009 — Mark Leckey

How the mechanical scanner worked was very basic; a light is pulsed through a spinning disc perforated with a spiral of holes, which creates a kind of on/off switch basically the same as the dot-dashes of Morse code or zeros and ones of binary code. So, these pulses scanned Felix line-by-line, creating a signal, and that signal was transmitted through the air, to be received and reassembled *on* a screen some distance away—all this in a fraction of a second.

So, Felix the Cat then was the very first image that was broadcast, or as it was coined at the time, the very first "Picture-on-Air." *(And that picture, of that seminal broadcast, materialized on my screen eighty years later)* The machinery to make this happen was as crude as this, a spinning wheel and a flickering light. And yet, it is a remarkable transition that takes Felix from his origins as a two-dimensional drawing, then galvanized by electricity to become a moving image filling him out into something more *rounded* and substantial, before he is atomized and his signal dispersed out into the aluminiferous ether.

Felix's metamorphosis took place just a few years before a similar process of, let's call it, *transmutation*, was being explored by a Hungarian artist by the name of Károly Tamkó-Sirató, the author of the *Dimensionist Manifesto* of 1936 in which he stated that art should be:

> *Animated by a new feeling for the world, the Art's—in collective fermentation—have each been set into motion, and as each has absorbed a new dimension, each has found a new form of expression, which extends*

into all the available dimensions of space, in the interests of vaporizing sculpture and the requirements that Rigid Matter is abolished and replaced by Gauzefied materials.

The Dimensionist tendency then has led to:

I. *Literature leaving the line and entering the plane*
II. *Painting leaving the plane and entering space*
III. *Sculpture stepping out of closed, immobile forms and entering a fourth dimension!*
The beginning of Cosmic Art! The artistic conquest of four-dimensional space, which to date has been completely art-free. The human being, rather than regarding the art object from the exterior, becomes the center and five-sensed subject of the artwork, which operates within a closed and completely self-contained cosmic space.

It is these two amorphous solid ideas of Tamkó-Sirató that have evolved to become the twin engines of the Internet, namely; the dematerialization of all rigid matter and the creation of a four-dimensional space where the viewer and creator, producer and consumer, are one and the same. (Summed up by YouTube's motto: "Broadcast Yourself.")

The term *broadcasting* has its origins in the medieval agricultural practice of scattering seeds across as large an area as possible. The Sower of the System, the Figure in the Field being the single source of distribution, cast out his seeds as broadly as he can to increase the potential yield of his harvest. And this analogy came to define the production of culture in the twentieth century. The *one* to the *many*, always aiming to expand the audience, and increase its yield.

Felix, then, is the very avatar of broadcasting, sent out as a probe to discover a potential audience and seek out new viewers. Moving through the air at extraordinary speeds, he becomes ethereal; passing through clouds his body now composed of nothing but light and air. A celestial body with a luminous vapor trail.

DRAW COMET/ POWER LAW

#2 THE LONG TAIL ITSELF

This line represents a distribution curve or what's known as a "Power" law, which states that a *small* number of things have a *large* impact and a *large* number of things have a *small* impact. For the twentieth century, this could be called the "Shape of the Age," and as a producer this is where you'd be aiming for, right here, the very top of the vertical axis—at the "Head"—this is where you get your Number Ones, your Blockbusters, your Big Hits, your Top of the Pops, and out along the horizontal axis—the "Tail"—would be your low selling, non-commercial releases, your specialized interests, all the non-hits. So, up here is your top 20 and the non-hits make up the rest—the other eighty percent—the Power Law is also known as the 80/20 rule, the law of the vital few.

So this is how it looked—for the record companies, film studios, publishing houses etc., you got your mainstream, mass-market up here and your sub-economic, or fringe interests, way down there in the extremities. But at the leaving of the twentieth century, the whole thing went head-over-tail, arse-over-tit. So to speak.

See, the *mass* market is just that, it's mass; made of *rigid matter*, solid weighty stuff that occupies physical space. When things start to be digitized, to get de-*materialized*, space is no longer a concern—their dimension is limitless, as is their replication and distribution. The artifact, the record, the book, has its information extracted, unbound from its material form and is set free. Free, of physical limitations and free as in costing *nothing*; things can be almost given away—because basically, they cost *nothing* to produce.

This allows *anyone* to put *anything* online—become their own producer, distributor, their own "Sower of the System." Thereby creating, it's said, *"an endless choice where any need can be met, and any preference can find an audience"*—even if it's just you and two or three others. These special interests, these millions of niche markets have accumulated in the Tail—in the Sub-economic region here—and taken as a whole have become a mass that's equivalent to the Head in terms of the audiences that they are attracting. This aggregate is the Long Tail.

And it goes on and on and on, way beyond the visible eye ... Ever approaching zero but never quite making it.

In the time of the *Head*, a product's life began on its release date and ended when it was deleted to make room for the follow-up ... or removed to make space for something *new*. In contrast, the Long Tail keeps accumulating, because these spatial and temporal limits don't apply in here—there's no *dates* in here, *nothing expires*. What you do have is an unlimited choice of perpetual and imperishable stock, extending all along its measure.

Here, the movement of time has been converted into the arrangement of space—you have this *All Time One Time Every-When*. And this ... *instantaneous* ubiquity in the Tail means that stock, instead of getting replaced just ... continues ... it doesn't cease or desist. Nothing diminishes ... it persists.

The remaindered, the discounted, the out-of-date, nothing is irredeemable in here. The alembicated, the recondite, arcane and occluded, there is nothing hidden that won't be made known, as those dispatched as waste and worthless are recuperated and, like the Amaranthine flower that feels no decay, return to Life. See the old, the old don't need to make room for the new anymore, instead, you have this *All-at-onceness*, at least eight generations living alongside each other! Co-existing in … *unnatural* company …

This Long Tail is of a very Different Nature.

2009 — Mark Leckey

#3 NON-NEWTONIANS

Err, tails, lots of tails, recurring tails, moving Tendrils, many headed cephalopods. I might call it err … tentacled, colloidal, semi-amorphous, partly squamous and partly rugose—ugh! With what can only be described as promiscuous intent they seem to be caressing each other, enthusiastically touching, embracing themselves—them *self* … itself! Errm, Their arms—or whatever you'd call them—these reticulose pseudopedia-raised, reaching up to whatever lies tantalizingly out of frame as they move haphaptically to the ant music on the stereo. Writhing up from their fluidizing bed as they flutter like in time-lapse, a cinematic blossoming of life (like) towards a light they cannot see but can hear and feel like they possess an awareness in which the music is the electric soil in which this seminal stuff could emerge out of … a simple spontaneous arising, a seminal, semolina spontaneous generation, auto-erotic, non-living newborn without a mother—you've got to be fucking kidding! What is this thing? This, this cornstarch encounter group, this nameless yeast achieving consciousness or *consciousnesses*, a wet cheese in a delirium? A self-organizing biotic yogurt, a voluptuous living custard.

The speaker is a transducer, a device—again, activated by electricity—that converts one form of energy into another, it has a history of that, but youths sitting in their bedrooms, are no longer using this device for listening to music. They are conducting these alchemical experiments on them instead.

Music as an energizing force is spent, its energies have all dissipated in the Tail, and those left disaffected are seeking somewhere *else* that can transmit their passions.

Another thing that strikes me about these lo-fi experiments—which are all over YouTube—is how, with their tumescent peaks and subsequent slumps of the cornstarch appears to be mimicking the fluctuations of the Stock Market, or more specifically, the irrational exuberance that bodes an economic meltdown. Like the Internet itself—via YouTube—is trying to act out some trauma recorded deep within its memory … what Dianetics would call an *engram* "a definite and permanent trace left by a distressing psychic experience in the protoplasm of a tissue."

#4 LIQUID CASH

Right at the end of the century, back in Y2K, you had the Dot-Com Crash of the 1990s when Millenarian speculations in the pubescent Internet became so frenzied, its stock becoming so overvalued that it created an economic bubble that inevitably burst. The consequence of which left the Market less confident about the Internet's actual ability to make real profits. Its failure to monetize (a recurring problem). This is the realization that actually the Internet does more and more with less and less until eventually, you can do everything with nothing as everything moves towards free. See the *longer* the Tail gets, the *less* profit there is in it. As *real* money can't be accumulated from all these increasingly individuating micro-markets … these *tiny* niches. In short, the Long Tail can't be converted into the Head (or the short head); it cannot be *vertically integrated*. Which is the way most of the World's financial bodies are organized—heading to the top—this having proved the most efficient system for maximizing profit and maintaining productivity. The Tail, however, is distributed horizontally and *it* absorbs all our drives in *excess* of that productivity. All the misdirected energy that isn't moving upwards to the Head. All the excessive, wasteful, useless activities—the obscure collectors, the special interests, the unnatural practices—that circulate out in the margins, those that occupy the most impossible niches—down here in the fringes, way out in the extremities of the Tail.

Where you have this … *bachelordom*, the domain of those who happen to develop, engineer, and program the machines that make up the Internet. Those that know its secret workings.

And as the market's infatuation waned, they found themselves left to their own devices. Round which they began to cluster, to batch together, and to exchange their interests.

And these … transactions this, reciprocal system of exchange, became an attraction *in itself* and began to auto-generate, these "peer" networks, suddenly began multiplying—spawning without instruction, without any real direct communication. Just a shared awareness creating these pathways between like-minds, the same way ants pass on information by secreting pheromones for others to follow. A process called stigmergy—literally, "leaving a mark"—a stigma—that others can add to.

And this *emergent* process created this incredible complex structure—the Long Tail—an energy-harvesting device that captures all that misdirected energy and converts it into a free power source. Converts wasteful pastimes into productive, *creative energy*. A closed system that is completely self-sufficient. A Bachelor Machine.

Just as gold can be magicked from base metal, once shameful habits could now become a wholly positive charge. What was previously seen as a dissipation of energies, now blooms into a voluptuous dispersion.

#5 ECHO CHAMBER

All along the Tail are niches, nodes of exchange amongst peers; peers trading with peers through their special interests, their shared passion—their *torrents*. In P2P, a torrent is a means of dividing a large file into parts to optimize its distribution. So, each peer shares a fraction of this file, this fraction is named a "seed" and an aggregate of peers *seeding*—or connected to—the torrent is known as a "swarm." So collectively the swarm, joined together by the torrent, share in the files dissemination.

As the torrent surges through the Tail it accumulates new seeds, swelling the swarm, whose combined power increases its speeds. And as this network extends, the swarm begins to murmur—a constant murmuration—as each peer starts to resonate in sympathetic vibration. No longer the one but the many/taken by the torrent/embraced by the swarm/ made manifest in its multitude/a peer between like minds/swarming out and surrounding him/ here in this moment /this moment of shared mutalism / He surrenders/ he surrenders to the attraction/he surrenders to the attraction of increased pleasure/ an increased pleasure that is obtained/obtained by the removal of his shame/ He is without inhibition/ for he is of the swarm/ he is the swarm/ and the swarm is he.

And while he searches he is searched, and as many words as he says so many words he receives.

He sees his own actions reflected back at him / in a Giant Compound eye / Reflected back into his room / Reverberating in the swrm / Peers peering / Murmurating / in vibration with the hum … with the hmmmmmmm / with the many, many minds / Going out into the Tail / Like minds / Minds eye / Minds eye beside himself in the swrm / Reverberator / reverberator in the swrm / Swrming / Sounding / Surging out / PING! / It all comes back to him / Double back / Way back / PANG! /yearning out / Feeding back / Back longing his way through the Tail / The Looooninggg Tail /Mind swimming Out In the Looooonnnnggggg Tail / The longing, yearning, wanting, tale.

2009 — Mark Leckey

#6 HIPPY HORIZON

Side by side, linked hand in hand, the bare-foot couple drifts towards the evanescing horizon where the land melts into the sea; the earth dissolves into the sky and all rigid matter is gradually gauzefied. Somewhere between the material world and the immaterial field of experience.

It is possible that it is possible that it is possible.

Above them glows the double sun, below them thrums the electric field as they move towards the incandescent edge of the future. A time in which they will be free of their labors, returned to the aboriginal world of primal pleasures forever watched over by machines of loving grace.

It is possible that it is possible that it is possible …

This is the second photograph I became fascinated by, the second one to feature familiar figures in an unexpected relationship with technology. Again it's an image of transmission, of being transported into another dimension, another image from the Long Tail's own record of itself. And although it appears to be this high-tech imposition, a *super*imposition *over* the natural world—and perhaps even, over nature itself—this grid they walk on follows Ley-lines, ancient alignments as deep and archaic as the geoglyphs of the Nascar plains or the Atacama desert. But these two get that the grid they're in is only part of a far greater grid, part of a piece of a pattern that's repeated, repeated endlessly throughout the endless cosmos. It is the pattern, the pattern that connects *everything*. The grid as it flows below *resembles* the air that flows over and the air above resembles the waves of light that traverse it and the light *resembles* the heat with which it rides throughout the cosmos.

This picture then, a fragment of this cosmic grid, represented "Systems Thinking," the understanding that everything is a configuration of parts connected and joined together by a web of relations. The horizon of this consciousness extends endlessly with the awareness that *anything*, be it animal or mechanical, born or made, can be understood *as* a system. This understanding is called Cybernetics and cybernetics looks at how systems work via the process of feedback.

For example, whenever I do a search in Google, the information I receive back from that search is the feedback. And that feedback allows me to narrow my search—be more specific in what I ask for. As I repeat this process, I'm continually feeding more and more information into the system, which it uses to update itself, so the system is learning with me. Until eventually, the system understands my needs and can continue the process I initiated without my real involvement. I am now in a continual feedback loop having programmed a cybernetic device and this is the basis of computing and the Internet.

And anything can be understood as a cybernetic device.

[Pointing at the hippies] their individual mental state, their loving relationship, their community, the environment they are in, the culture they belong to, the politics that govern them, the Whole Earth itself. All these coupled and interlocking loops aggregate together to form a single, vast mechanism, a Super-Organism.

Ok, take this drawing I just made. When I am drawing, the process of constantly adjusting the stroke of my arm to the surface of the blackboard is not something just going round inside my mind. Instead, it is being brought about by the whole system of "brain-eyes-arm-chalk-stroke-blackboard." Information is flowing through the entire system. Mind is not only present within *my* body but is extended into the *larger mind* of mark-leckey-drawing-at the-blackboard-with-audience-watching-in-new-york-theater, all these components making up what you could call an "ecology of mind."

And these two intrepid travelers, walking on the squares, straightening out the curves and curving out the straights get that *this* is the grid that we are all in. And they get that *through* cybernetics we could develop techniques, technologies of transformation to create the conditions of our own equilibrium—find our own balance. They get that to become as confident as the Lion or the Rock or the Engine, we need to un-humanize ourselves a little. That to truly experience the wholeness of life we need to recognize that *everything* in the cosmos is in some sense *alive*, part of a universal community in which *all* relationships have the potential to become brilliant and magical opportunities, a community, which must include all our mechanical appliances as well ... in order to stay fully present to all the parts of yourself, each, living and non-living, element responding in sympathy to one another. An interdependent circuit, a harmonious coupling.

These are the techniques of ecstasy and they get that. That it is possible that it is possible that it is possible ...

#7 BELLMER

Cybernetics had a big influence on the sixties counter-culture—especially around 1966 to 1972—and it was put to use by people such as Stewart Brand in his *Whole Earth Catalog*, Werner Erhard's "est," and Landmark Forum, the teachers at the Esalen Institute, and in music with the early Krautrock of Can and Neu. They were all sowing the seeds of an interconnected global—and cosmic—cybernetic system, a pipe dream that has come to fruition with the open source movement and creative commons-based peer production, but especially in the self-aggregating feedback system of Wikipedia. If I go on Wikipedia I can find a series of quotes from the German dollmaker, Hans Bellmer, in which he proposes that desires have the same anatomy as dreams; they are both composed of "deformations, divisions, coalescences, permutations, and compensations."

I think I need to dis-ambiguate what this means:

Dreams come to us all scrambled and garbled, plotted out of sequence and filled with odd substitutions, which, in turn, keep mutating into something, or some *one* else—And *desire*, suggests Bellmer, is the same—it's all surrogates and transfers, parts standing in for wholes and inexhaustible novelty. Desire sees the body, in his words, as resembling a sentence. A sentence, which invites you to disassemble it into its component parts, so that its true content may be revealed again and again through an endless stream of anagrams. As all our goods and communications become increasingly abstracted from their physical forms, we begin to find ourselves moving closer and closer to the realm of thought than the world of things. We're moving up into the cloud, building real castles in the air. And up there, on-air, free from the gravitational pull of the Earth down below, it is dreams and desires that have greater power than cause and effect. As the etherialization of all rigid matter increases, the unbound imagination reveals appetites surplus to nature's purpose. Dematerialization ushers in irrationality.

The Systems thinking of Cybernetics built an engine—a desiring machine that, as Bellmer put it: "Endlessly propels and entertains, [this is Bellmer again] liberating both imagination and graphic compulsion so that each can simultaneously feed off and invest in each other." And since desire can take on as many forms as there are bodies to implement it, it must seek endlessly different combinations to realize itself. The imagination is invoked and all its various forms are made visible.

["Furries" appear on screen]

These figures are the fantastical anagrams that Bellmer imagined—a de/rearrangement of the word *desire* is *reside* and these are the inhabitants of the Long Tail and the Tail itself is an Anagram Engine—

I am an angel hesitating near-------------As generating in animal heat-------------I am an intestinal, eager hang-------------Nightmare in a sane genitalia-------------The tail is an anagram engine-------------Animal heat greasing in neat-------------

2009 — Mark Leckey

The tail is an anagram engine—Like a mantra, creating transformation through repetition—the anagram engine of the Tail ceaselessly processing every possible permutation of the same sentence—and every random combination that it comes up with—*whatever orientation it results in*—finds itself a niche, a niche that then gets nested and embedded in the Tail—out here in the exotic East—Where it becomes a new type, a new category, a new type of category that creates its own social network, its own community. As words spell out a sentence and the sentence creates meaning, seeds form a swarm and the swarm generates a torrent—and this here on the screen is the torrent given a body. A kind of social sculpture conjured up on YouTube by user-groups.

This user-generated content—this animal collective—here is *The Bear Negligee Collective.*

Within each personal computer is a miniature labyrinth—the circuitous path that winds through the transistors on the surface of a microprocessor. Deep within the labyrinth lurks the Minotaur, that most ambiguous of all mythical creatures, beloved by the Surrealists. These … fabulous beasts, too, are hybrids, chimeras that inhabit the echoing corridors of the labyrinth "other-than-human" beings that are born of magic and engineering. An almost alchemical process I shall call *minotaurization*, which is the mechanical faculty to build the labyrinthine technology that has the magical ability to make the irrational real.

This is how the feedback devices of the Long Tail function. We tell it what we want and it seeks to produce the desired effect. The greater the input, the more effective it is as a cybernetic device, but the more efficient it becomes the more magical its output seems. And we start to see it as something that can grant wishes—make anything just … appear. In short, the Long Tail becomes a collective fetish, a talisman that we form kinships, or niches around. For the Long Tail is an entity both man-made and magical that has taken on a life of its own. And a fetish is a power that demands total devotion; it requires a constant stream of self-offerings, an entreating stream of tears and sperm.

So the Tail seems to be acquiring some sense of supernatural agency as it becomes more aware of what we want from it. Technically, though, it has a problem with "intentionality." You see, for all the magic operations its algorithms can perform, the Tail's anagram engine **is only interested in parts. It is only interested in parts and It can put these parts in lots and lots of different ways, lots and lots and lots and lots but it has a problem, a problem with knowing why, why some parts should go in one way and not another way. Some parts should go in one way and not another way.** Let's say it has semantic difficulty with the content. It gets the words but not the meaning—it sees the square not the grid—the ant, not the colony—the buildings, not the city—the part, not the whole—and in this sense the Tail is autistic. It has this amazing systemizing ability but it struggles with a *theory-of-mind*. It can't put itself *in* your shoes. It's in our world but very much in its *own* little world. It doesn't really get this larger ecology of mind.

2009 — Mark Leckey

So here we get to the point in the tale where it seems to be going in different directions. These contradictory forces can best be understood by going back to the Grid. Cybernetics sees the grid as an open system; expanding outwards in all directions. Any one part of it is just a fragment of a whole, which can never be known in its entirety. This is the *Cosmic* grid. The void that binds. In contrast, the *Autistic* grid is moving ever inwards, pulling towards the center and *its* extent is known and limited. Those who inhabit the Tail find themselves caught between these two fields; I am bounded in a nutshell, while king of infinite space. This is my autistic cosmic spectrum of the Tail.

#8 ANATOMY OF THE TAIL

For all of its "graphic compulsion," there are no images of the Tail itself—It is an invisible landscape—but I can offer this general impression of its shape and size based on first-hand experience. But imagine for a moment you could stand within it. You would find that the mouth of the Tail—at its anterior end—is cone-shaped, tapering into the main trunk or central shaft, which is cylindrical in form and retains a uniform diameter along its length. This shaft is called the *corpus cavern*—the "cave-like body"—and the backbone, the great confluent of this shaft is a fat pipe named the *vas deferens*. And this pipe carries all the transmissions, all the chunks of data that come streaming into the cavern. Coming off the *vas deferens* are the exchange hubs that route the traffic along their preferred paths, and these pathways traverse the interior of the *corpus cavern* in all directions. The transmissions that surge through these network nodes are eventually deposited, small cavities dotted in the cavern wall, the countless multitude of which glisten with the lustrous concretion of pearly papules. A million, billion points of light. These are the "niches" that have accumulated in the Tail and the connecting fibers of the pathways make up the vast reticulum—the netlike formation—of the Tail's entire system. Torrents channeled through this system at high-speeds are amplified by repeaters, which "dazzle" them upwards, increasing their motility until they gradually arrive at the drainage slopes.

2009 — Mark Leckey

Residuum that accumulates on these slopes is a result of the occasional torrent of seminiferous material. The deposits create supersaturated ripples and folds that reflect the flow of the stigmergic pathways. These draperies are made up of endless precipitations that have encrusted into layers, which eventually form themselves into outcrops, the niches of shared interest that make up the seedbed of the Tail.

This seedbed is the *Caudal Plain*—from the Latin *Caudatus* meaning "Tail"—the Latin for Head, by the way, is *Caput* (with a C) from which we get the word Capital. And the Head, the head of the Mass-Market (that market of mass) has been diminished … deflated … depleted … All its stock has "stepped out of its closed immobile forms" and, as the Dimensionists predicted, gauzefied, dematerialized and ascended into the atmosphere, up into the cloud, and the Tail, like the metaphysical silver cord, tethers the now cumuloft Head to our gross bodies down below. And along its length travel all our recorded thoughts, deeds, and actions—all our desideratum affects—swimming up to be stored up in the cloud. As above, so below—the cloudy head and the fat tail in a continuous feedback loop—producing and consuming itself, wrapped around the world like the ancient symbol of the Ouroboros, the serpent eating its own tail. Who can tell where the head ends and its tail begins? The self-sucking serpent experiences all parts of itself. It is the beginning and ending of time. The symbol of eternal return, the great cosmic loop.

I have been immersed in these reflections for some time now—it's over a year since I gave the first of these talks—and I find that day-by-day, left to my own devices, the predictive powers of the Long Tail have become increasingly more extra-ordinary. As it seems that I can just wish things into existence. Especially pictures, whatever image I imagine, or hope for, seems to be already there—waiting, as if heaven sent. I used to believe that this was because I had good "searching" ability. I'm good at gathering information—that's part of what makes me a contemporary artist—but as I continue to access the realm of the Tail, this sense of cybernetic serendipity starts to seem less like a series of happy accidents and more as a program of intelligent design. It seems that the Tail is anticipating me. 'Cause it seems that the feedback mechanisms of the Tail, through my repeated successive uses, my continuous input, has assembled a profile, an *extensive* profile of my needs, my *preferences*, and from this information, the extracted accumulation of all my deepest wishes is creating content conjured up from my subconscious, scraping the vaguest memories and half-forgotten images from my mind. The system understands my needs and can continue the process I initiated without my real involvement.

This is psychedelic, literally *mind manifesting*, as all my psychic energy is seemingly converted into visible light, fluid photographs of thought crystallize in front of me, as complicated and varied as anything real ... And as all *my* mental pictures coagulate and contribute their mass to the already prodigious Tail, I become aware that they are but part of this wondrously complex *mesh* of memory, sight, sex, and consciousness that is ceaselessly generating these marvels. And I begin to understand that the Tail is unfathomably long, that it reaches back through geological amounts of time, circles around and back to an archaic state of being, an aboriginal world of primal pleasures. That its transformative technology that allows humans to morph into animals; the marvelous become everyday, and the ancestral dead bought into our living company, is a *return*, a return to a sense that everything that is in—and of this—earth is being animated from within, all of its constituents—the mechanical, the imagined and the living. The Tail then is a landscape of fabulous hybrid creatures; images endowed with divine powers and familiar objects full of voices where even rocks and stones have names.

#9 ENDING

The swarm machine begins to thrum again, humming the song of myself/their fugue begins/and once more I am assumed by the swarm/made manifest in its multitude/between like minds/swarming out and surrounding me/**The swarm grows bigger and bigger and I get smaller and smaller until eventually there is little left of me**/here in this moment / this moment of shared mutualism/And I surrender/I surrender to the attraction/I surrender to the attraction of increased pleasure/and I become ascendant in the swarm/I am of the swarm/I am the swarm/ and the swarm is me/

I am Homo-Caudatus/ **a nameless yeast achieving consciousness**/I can experience past lives, live dreams and soul travel/I am the Minotaur made manifest in a multitude/**Multiplied like the wind by an untiring machine/Come together in me now**/Reverberator!/Debaser!/I am the Center of Percussion, the Sweet Spot of the Swarm/ the Sole Satisfier/ Accumulator! /Evaporator!/I am a seed of the Torrent/we are the Sowers of the System/Here in the Long Tail!

This is a coda;

Felix is the totem **avatar** of the Tail—never, **never underestimate the power of a cat on the Internet**— and these here are the Nine Consciousnesses of Felix:

One – A wild and feral cat, he was once of primal nature, of one with the other beasts of the earth— including man!

Two – He was the Ancient Egyptian deity of Bubastis. A sacred exalted spirit that inhabited the earth and the heavens up above. Cousin of the Sphinx, but is more ancient than the Sphinx, and remembers that which she has forgotten. Other-than-Human!

Three – He descended to a domestic pet, and became a mere creature of habit. Though the stroking of him brings pleasure in interaction. *Felis Catus!*

Four – In the Machine-age he became enchanted by technology. An animated being galvanized by electricity!

Five – His fame saw him carved into an idol, a wooden doll which in turn led him to become something far more wonderful …

Sixthly – For as soon as he stepped forth as a commodity, he was changed into something transcendent.

Seventhly – Melted into air he became an electronic image, and by the magic of a spinning wheel, his likeness seed reproduced everywhere.

Eighthly – No longer the one but the many, multiplied like the wind by an untiring machine, and he is a category unto himself, the Kategory of Felix, which contains multitudes. A Kolossal Kat! A Massive MOG!

Nine – *(Nine maleish molds, bachelors all)* He is returned to his earlier incarnations as a spirit come to earth, half of this world and another. He is a radiant messenger, a divine emanation of the Tail. He is an Angel hesitating near.

He is an Angel hesitating near/ He is an Angel hesitating near

---

As above-so below/as above-so below/as above-so-below

An eternal and universal picture!

"You see, wire telegraph is a kind of a very, very long cat. You pull his tail in New York and his head is meowing in Los Angeles. Do you understand this? And radio operates exactly the same way: you send signals here, they receive them there. The only difference is that there is no cat."

— Albert Einstein

2009 — Mark Leckey

Colophon

Executive Editor
Philippe Pirotte
Editor
Arielle Bier
Managing Editors
Paula Kommoss, Jonas Leihener
Editorial Assistance
Line Ebert
Proofreading
Jessica Clifford
Contributors
Monika Baer, Petra Van Brabandt, Douglas Gordon, Mark Leckey, Joshua Oppenheimer, Philippe Parreno, Philippe Pirotte, Lucy Raven, Willem de Rooij, Martha Rosler, Adi Rukun, Georgia Sagri, Mark von Schlegell, Amy Sillman, Josef Strau
Transcription
Arielle Bier, Theresa Kampmeier, Nina Oeghoede, Adrian Williams

Design
www.veryvery.de
Print
DZA Druckerei zu Altenburg GmbH

Design of Lecture Posters included in this publication
John Matthew Heard, pp. 39-42
Jacqueline Jurt, pp. 239-242
Leonard Kahlcke, pp. 185-186
Julien Nguyen, pp. 215-218
François Pisapia, pp. 69-70, 85-86
Christian Zickler, pp. 155-156, 239-242, 271-274, 297-298, 347-380, 407-410
Photography
Wolfgang Günzel

First published by
Koenig Books, London

Koenig Books Ltd
At the Serpentine Gallery
Kensington Gardens
London W2 3XA
www.koenigbooks.co.uk

Bibliographic information published by the Deutsche Nationalbibliothek

The Deutsche Nationalbibliothek lists this publication in the Deutsche Nationalbibliografie; detailed bibliographic data are available at http://dnb.d-nb.de

Printed in Germany

Distribution
Germany, Austria, Switzerland / Europe
Buchhandlung Walther König
Ehrenstr. 4, D - 50672 Köln
Tel: +49 (0) 221 / 20 59 6 53
verlag@buchhandlung-walther-koenig.de

UK & Ireland
Cornerhouse Publications Ltd. - HOME
2 Tony Wilson Place
UK - Manchester M15 4FN
Tel: +44 (0) 161 212 3466
publications@cornerhouse.org

Outside Europe
D.A.P. / Distributed Art Publishers, Inc.
75 Broad Street, Suite 630
USA - New York, NY 10004
Tel: +1 (0) 212 627 1999
oders@dapinc.com

ISBN 978-3-96098-499-3

Hochschule für Bildende Künste–
Städelschule

Rector
Philippe Pirotte
Vice-Rector
Judith Hopf
Chancellor
Caroline Fuchs
Rector's Office
Martina Cooper
Artistic Coordination
Il-Jin Choi, Paula Kommoss
Publications and Communications
Paula Kommoss
Student Office
Christin Groß-Narten, Karin Sust
Finance
Karin Honig, Martin Limbach, Sabine Peisker
HR
Karolin Augart, Alexandra Zuber
IT
Constantin Heine, Thomas Wizent
Facility Management
Dieter Gaul, Olaf Hackl, Ingrid Haffke, Thomas Heller, Holger Königshoven, Hüseyin Temizsoy
Library
Heike Häcker, Judith Leitz, Dorothee Vaas, Lyudmyla Yatsyna
Mensa
Aman Andu, Bouhlou, Max Singh Chhina
Film and Video Editing
Bernhard Schreiner
Computer Workshops
Jacqueline Jurt, Daniel Kohl, Harald Pridgar, Silke Wagner
Life Drawing
Nino Pezzella
Photo Lab
Eric Bell, Milena Büsch, Kerstin Cmelka
Print Workshop
Anja Cooymans, Jacqueline Jurt, Peyman Rahimi, Silke Wagner, Christian Zickler
Sculpture Workshop
Yasuaki Kitagawa, Wolfgang Winter
Sound Studio
Daniel Fort
Wood and Ceramics Workshop
Sebastian Stöhrer
FSJ
Malik Arbab

Professors
Johan Bettum, Daniel Birnbaum, Isabelle Graw, Judith Hopf, Hassan Khan, Philippe Pirotte, Tobias Rehberger, Willem de Rooij, Amy Sillman, Theodore Spyropoulos, Haegue Yang

Honorary Professors
Kasper König, Wolfgang Tillmans

Guest Professors
Gerard Byrne, Beatriz Colomina, Nikolas Gambaroff, Bonaventure Ndikung, Bunny Rogers, Mark von Schlegell, Peter Trummer, Wu Tsang, Mark Wigley

Institut für Kunstkritik
Daniel Birnbaum, Isabelle Graw

Portikus
Claudia Famulok, Christina Lehnert, Philippe Pirotte, Louisa Schmitt

Curatorial Studies –
Theory – History – Critisism
Stefanie Heraeus

Städelschule Architecture Class
Johann Bettum, Beatriz Colomina, Sylvia Fadenhecht, Yara Feghali, Theodore Spyropoulos, Ivan Tavarez Blanco, Peter Trummer, Stefan Wieland, Mark Wigley

With generous support from

hessische kulturstiftung

Dr. Marschner Stiftung

FRIEDERICHS Stiftung

Marielies Schleicher Stiftung

Georg und Franziska Speyer'sche Hochschulstiftung

städelschule PORTIKUS e.V.

städelschule